POSITIVELY WYRD

Harnessing the Chaos
in Your Life

TOM GRAVES

GOTHIC IMAGE
PUBLICATIONS

Gothic Image Publications
7 High Street, Glastonbury,
Somerset BA6 9DP

Cover illustration Peter Woodcock

Typeset in Stempel Garamond by
Michael Mepham, Frome Somerset
Printed and bound in Great Britain by
The Guernsey Press Company Limited

A catalogue record for this book is available
from the British Library

ISBN 0 906362 27 X

CONTENTS

CONTENTS

ACKNOWLEDGEMENTS

Although there's only one author named on the cover, this book, like so many others, is a joint venture by an unknown number of people, many of whom will never know that they were involved.

Most of this book is based on personal and original research; but like every author, I've 'lovingly lifted' from many different writers, teachers, colleagues and friends a wide variety of ideas and comments – though often placed into contexts that their originators did not plan for, or may in some cases even disagree with. Lists of names are always invidious, because there's always someone left out: but they include Richard Bach, Kenneth Batcheldor, Gregory Bateson, Richard Nelson Bolles, John Bradshaw, Bryan Branston, Cassandra Carter, Ram Dass, Werner Erhard, Maja Evans, Alan Garner, James Gleick, Felicitas Goodman, Douglas Hofstadter, Frances Howard-Gordon, Robert Johnson, Dess Kammason, Jessica Macbeth, Pat Medland, Cindy Pavlinac, Vera Peiffer, Bhagwan Shree Rajneesh, Idries Shah, Starhawk, Charles Tart, John Venables, Gerald Weinberg, Paul Whyte and Kim Williams. My thanks go to them, and to the many others whose names I've forgotten, but whose wise words I have not.

INTRODUCTION

Life is weird. It has a habit of presenting us with weird tasks, trials and tribulations – no matter how much we'd rather not face them. So for many of us, we try to resolve the issues through 'personal growth', as something we undertake in the hope that things will get better, that we'll regain some kind of control over our lives. And things do get better: though rarely in a simple, linear sequence of improvements, and sometimes not even in a way that we *would* at first understand as 'better' – the process is far more weird than that. There is indeed a deep joy and a deep sense of meaning to be found this way; but it would be unrealistic to say this without also saying that the path, always a personal one, can at times be intensely lonely and intensely disturbing. It's that confusion that makes the process hard: but it *is* part of a process that does lead us to enjoyment, to the full, of *every* aspect of our lives – a joyous involvement in life as it is.

The reality is that the path we each take *is* weird, and often doesn't seem to make sense: we get launched into new experiences, or seemingly trapped in loops time after time. And the whole process can not only be tortuous, but at times torturous, a sense of being tested again and again almost – yet never quite – beyond what we can bear. As to why it should be so, we can only answer 'Yes'. In some cases there probably *is* no 'why': it *is* – and that's all. If we're to work with what Reality Department cares to hand us, we first have to accept it for what it is: the 'why', if any, can come later.

We do always come out stronger, more able to enjoy life, and more able to face our personal issues after each of these apparent tests, as long as we face them and what they show us of ourselves: that seems to be the reason for it all, and is certainly what makes it all worthwhile. And although this process of growth at times is hard, is painful, is lonely, it's always based in *our* choices. We *always* have a choice; yet there's also always a twist. Those twists are where the weirdness lies: the effects of our choices ripple out into the world at large, and then echo back to us in a way that we can only describe as weird. A weaving and interweaving of life and lives: a sense of connection, a sense of choices, a sense of subtlety, of something we can never quite control. Within those weird twists of our lives are subtle, hidden choices: it's up to us to make use of them.

It's to this weirdness in the process of personal growth – accepting the weirdnesses of our lives, and working *with* them rather than trying to fight against them – that this book is addressed. It's also addressed to the realities of the process and its often uncomfortable twists and turns: as such, it develops a rather different view of the sequence of the changes in the process of personal growth. In particular, there's an emphasis on some intermediate stages that are often missed out in existing descriptions: the stage of 'everyone is to blame' that must be moved through, for example, before the well-known concept of 'no-one is to blame' can be reached. And there are also some guidelines on how to work with the bad times – and how not to get lost in some illusory 'good' ones.

You may find the writing style that I've used a little strange at first, but it's there for a reason: the way a book is written is a crucial part of its message. The impersonal third-person mode preferred by most psychology texts, typically referring to examples as 'case studies' or 'client experiences', may make intellectual understanding easier, but can actually block *experiential* understanding; while the second-person ("you should do this") mode popular in 'New Age' books often seems condescending and patronising. My choice here has thus been to use, where possible, a first-person or

'I/we' conversational mode, framing the text as if spoken by an imaginary narrator – a composite (whom I've named 'Chris Kelley') drawn directly from many people's personal and real-life experiences. So although this introduction is somewhat formal, the rest of the book is not. The stories the narrator tells are highly personal, and illustrate clearly the intensity of *feeling* of many of these states – so if you find yourself in the same kind of emotional spaces that this imaginary 'I' describes, you'll know you're not alone in that experience. We've all been there too: that fact alone can be a great deal of help in some of the darker times...

But since nothing changes without ourselves choosing to be involved in the change, there's also a strong emphasis on the practical: examples to put the concepts into practice will be found on almost every page. These typically consist of a personal experience that illustrates the point being made, followed by some suggestions, and questions about the resultant experience. (There are no set answers to these questions: in this field, the only valid answers for each person are their own.) All of the examples have been tested in practice, most of them independently by myself, friends and colleagues as well as many others, and often over long periods of time: they work. Whether they work for you in the same way is up to you to decide, and to experience: but you won't find out unless you try!

The four sections of the book develop a sequence of observations and changes, starting with the self, and moving outward to the world at large. Be warned, though, that the sequence is not always obvious in the usual sense: the apparent repetition that occurs throughout the book, for example, is intentional, and is not simply due to poor editing! And in particular, the early part of the book may seem to dwell on the darker emotions more than you might expect: the reason is that unless these *are* faced early on, they continue to block progress indefinitely. So the first two chapters 'set the stage', using a typical experience as a start-point, and comparing the sense of fatalistic gloom that often accompanies it, with the subtle freedom to be found from a better understanding of the original meaning of 'weird'.

The second section, consisting of roughly a third of the book, looks at the kind of pressures that get us to limit our choices – especially as we grow up – and builds some analogies and suggestions as to how to break free of our habits and conditionings. We learn to watch – and use – the way in which old issues keep looping back in oneform or another until they are resolved; we gain a peculiar – yet very real – kind of freedom by working *with* the twists and paradoxes of life, in a way that moves past the fears that drive our need for control. And we recognise that we always have choice, we always have responsibility – although at times it's neither easy to see nor to accept.

The next eight chapters – also roughly a third of the book – discuss ways to work with and consolidate this new freedom in our own lives. We do this by watching, listening and, especially, acknowledging what we *feel*; accepting ourselves for who we are, from moment to moment, whilst still maintaining some kind of overall aim. A delicate balance: we learn to trust and to let go, yet without letting go; we learn the subtle – weird – difference between doing nothing, doing something and doing 'no-thing'; we watch the ways in which our own choices echo back to us from the world around.

In the final section we start to move out into that wider world – and recognise that in some weird way it is also always a reflection of ourselves and our choices. The sense of being separate from the world, and at the effect of its forces, is to some extent an illusion: our choices are part of the weaving that makes up the world we experience, 'inside' or 'outside', 'self' or 'not-self'. Our relationships, our work and our interactions with the world at large all have the same weirdness in common: there's always a choice, there's always a twist. And the choice, and the responsibility for that choice, are always ours: it's up to us to build the world we need.

USING THIS BOOK

In keeping with the nature of its subject, this book can be read in a number of ways, not all of them obvious at first.

It can, of course, be read in the usual way, from cover to cover: as mentioned above, it does have a developing sequence of ideas, with a beginning, a middle and an end. If you're only interested in concepts, you can skip over all the 'boxes' of practical material – the text will still work without them, especially in the earlier parts of the book, which deal more with ideas. But if you only do this you'll also miss one of the key points of the book, which is to provide *practical* tools for change.

If you plan to read it from cover to cover, doing all of the practical material in sequence, take it *slowly*: experience suggests that, after the first couple of chapters, not more than a single section a day – two or three pages – is best. Change, while valuable, can also be uncomfortable, and the practical material, if it's used properly, does trigger real changes in the way we view and work in the world: if you try to rush it, or force the pace of change, you'll either miss some key points and have to go back later, or else give yourself an unnecessarily rough time. So take it *slow*: "beyond a wholesome discipline, be *gentle* on yourself"!

Another way is to skip over the main text, and use only the practical material in the boxes. That'll make sense too, though it may not be so good in terms of understanding what's going on. You can follow the sequence of examples in the book, or just dip in at random: it still works – perhaps even better than the sequential way, given the weird nature of the subject. It's up to you.

The general consensus, though, seems to be that a combination of all these methods works best. Read the first two chapters; then skim through the whole of the remainder once, quickly, stopping only to read in detail a few passages that catch your eye. That'll give you enough background for the practical material to make practical sense, whatever you do next. Then go back and read through a chapter at a time, slowly, carefully – though in whatever order you prefer. And also, as the whim takes you, dip in at random to find a passage or a practical piece: you'll usually find it has some apposite comment or suggestions to make on your current situation. Use this book to work *with* the weirdness of change, the weirdness of the world: that's how it works best.

Whichever way you choose, welcome to a different world! It's a world in which we *do* have choices – although, as we'll discover, there's always a weird twist in what happens...

1

LIVING IN THE DARK

When first we meet Chris Kelley, it's clear that our narrator has just had another encounter with one of life's weirdnesses...

It's not an easy world to live in. Right now I'm sitting on my bed, in an empty house in a back suburb of the city. It's a warm, quiet day outside; but inside my head it's anything but quiet...

I'm confused, lonely, angry, disoriented, depressed – a welter of interweaving thoughts and emotions that just will not stop. Where *am* I? What am I doing here? I've just moved to another city to be with and work with my partner – only to be told I'm not wanted now as partner in either sense. Won't talk about it; there's nothing to say, I'm told. So everything's stopped: everything we worked on together for so long. That's months of planning out of the window – quite apart from what I *feel* about it...

Who *am* I? I don't think I know any more. Chris? That's just a label I've been given – a label for a life of chaos, it seems... I don't know. I don't think I know *anything* any more...

Why *am* I here? What am I here *for*? Why does this keep happening in my life? Why do I have to keep putting myself through all this stuff?

All right. So I'm here. So now I have to start all over again. Again. Alone. Again. I've only just moved here – I hardly know anyone. No work: the local economy is a shambles, job vacancies have dwindled almost to nothing, prices and taxes are on the way up again; and now the government, in a sad attempt to distract itself from the troubles at home, has entangled us in yet another war a few thousand miles away. And I've just come back from a walk by the river, looking at the trees festooned with plastic shopping bags, and the signs warning people that it's too polluted to swim in. . .

We're 'living in the light', says a book beside me. Living in the light? Living in the dark, more like. . .

How on earth did I get myself into this mess? It's crazy. . . weird. . . More to the point, how on earth do I get myself out of it? Whatever I do, it just seems to get worse: one obstacle after another after another. Doesn't *anything* work any more? What's *wrong* with my life? What's wrong with *me*? What's wrong with everyone else? Round and round go the thoughts, chasing each others' tails. . . round and round and round. . .

"THERE'S A WHOLE IN MY BUCKET. . ."

Whatever we do, it seems, nothing works out the way we want: there's always *something* that's wrong, something that ruins it. Everything depends on everything else being right: and only when everything's perfect will anything work out. That's the way it goes, isn't it? If *only* I had the right partner. . . the right job. . . or more money, always more money. . . everything might work then. Or if *only* we had a sane government. . . if *only* the unions weren't so stupid. . . if *only* the multinationals could *see* what they're doing. . . Or if *only* I could lose some weight. . . if *only* I could do something about my hair. . . If only. . . if only. . .

A familiar feeling?

"There's a hole in my bucket, dear Liza, dear Liza. . . there's a hole in my bucket, dear Liza, a hole. . ."

And the only reply we get is "Well *fix* it dear Henry, dear Henry, dear Henry. . . Well fix it, dear Henry, dear Henry *fix it*. . ."

Very helpful. If I knew how to fix it, I wouldn't be asking. . .

What can we do about it? Where on earth do we start, with all this chaotic mess? We can try to hide from it for a while: but every time we look up, it's still there. It seems obvious that *everything* has to be fixed before *anything* can be fixed: the economy, the environment, the insane politics, the even crazier militarism – let alone our personal relationships, or lack of them. . . The old standard solutions – the authoritarian church, or authoritarian leaders – just don't seem to work any more: which is probably a good thing, in its way. But how *do* we get back to some kind of control? – to take back the control over our lives?

It's at this point that we start looking for someone to blame: usually someone else, like the unions, the government, or men, or women, or God, or the Devil – whatever. Or we blame ourselves: perhaps too often, sometimes perhaps not enough. It still doesn't do anything: we can blame all we like, yet the mess is still there, and still growing all the time. . .

But another way is to look again at the song that describes this circular trap, the one that's driving us crazy, and make a small but significant change:

"There's a whole in my bucket, dear Liza, dear Liza; there's a whole in my bucket, dear Liza, a whole. . ."

And as we learn to change the hole into a whole, watch the changes that echo in the world we see around us. . .

2

A WEIRD KIND
OF FATE

When something else goes wrong, more often than not, I'd look around for someone or something to blame. It's only natural. It can't be just some weird kind of fate: everything has its cause, we're told, so if something goes wrong for me, *someone* must be causing it, surely? So it's the government's fault, or the unions', or just 'the system'. Or my fault: everything's my fault – I'm just inadequate, incompetent, that's what they told me at school. . . When life collapses into chaos again, it's all too easy to spiral down into paranoia on the one hand, self-deprecation on the other, or more usually some subtle mixture of the two.

But wait a minute. . . Sure the unions are devious, but are they *really* responsible for my inability to shed my excess flab? Or is it *really* my fault that the man in the car in front of me throws his empty cigarette packet on the road? How? After a while it becomes clear that no one person could co-ordinate all these attacks on me, my values, my beliefs, my world. And it's at this point that I start to look a little wider. . .

IN THE HANDS OF FATE

As soon as we do look wider for some kind of understanding about what happens to us, we'll often be hit by a weird sense of powerlessness. All these things are happening – and it's all too obvious that they're not in our control. Tradition would tell us that our fate is the force behind these chaotic twists and turns – and we have no choice, it seems, but to suffer them.

But a great deal depends on our point of view: we're not quite as powerless as we seem. Rather trying to work out who's to blame for all those cruel-seeming tricks of fate, we can look instead at our own point of view about them, and how it affects what we experience. And even there, in the midst of what may seem to be a predetermined fate, we find that we do have choices – of a kind.

Imagine a path, winding through the leafy cathedral-like gloom of the forest glades. And across the path is a great swathe of nettles – a real obstacle for the traveller.

Along comes a monk, with a fierce, striding walk. At the edge of the wall of nettles, he stops. "The mark of the Devil, trying to prevent me doing God's work!", he cries. "Well, he shall not succeed!" And with his staff, he sets about destroying as many of the nettles he can reach, smashing his own wayward path through this aspect of unworthy nature that dares to defy the will of his God – cursing loudly as torn fragments of nettle still manage to sting him round the ears and hands.

Later, when the nettles have healed, along comes another monk. Deep in contemplation of the mysteries of another world, he finds that his path in this one is blocked by the wall of nettles. "Ah", says the monk, "a symbol of the pain and suffering of this world. Like my great Teacher, then, I shall purge my soul and that of other souls by taking on that suffering myself." And gritting his teeth, he carefully picks his way through the nettles, hoping to minimise the pain.

And later still, when the nettles have closed the path once more, yet another monk comes by. He's drifting along, smiling, looking around at the trees and the birds scuttering between them. Rounding a turn in the path, he finds himself facing the wall of nettles. "Nettles. . ." says the monk. "Ooh. . . another *experience!*" – and dives headlong into the densest part of the wall. Yet when he emerges on the other side, he's smiling even more broadly than before. . .

Which path would you choose through the forest? What would be your point of view about those nettles?

5

We can fight against the unfairness of our fate, and we'll find it has a sting in its tail every time. We can be resigned – 'fatalistic' – in the face of the twists and turns of fate, and 'turn the other cheek' – even though it doesn't actually ease the pain. Or we can work *with* its eccentricities, its weirdnesses – and surprise ourselves, perhaps, as we discover we come up smiling, having somehow bypassed the pain completely. It all depends on our point of view.

It sounds so easy: change your point of view, change your experience. It's not *quite* as simple as that, as we've all found out the hard way. . . But if this is our fate, so to speak, it would probably be a good idea to have a better understanding of what's going on. And to do that, it might be worthwhile to take the idea of 'fate' a little more seriously than usual. . .

Fate. Fortune. Luck. We'd usually think of them as words without much of a meaning – they describe something that's 'just coincidence', even though it might be a useful one. But in the past they meant something far more than 'mere coincidence': so much so that each was personified as a goddess. To wish someone 'luck', for example, was no trivial matter: it was a formal prayer, a wish that the gods should support their ventures. And in psychological terms, it's understood that the stories of the gods and goddesses each represent some central fact of human experience – which is not quite how we understand chance or luck or fate in the present day. . .

Maybe so; maybe not. Have you ever had the experience that 'Dame Fortune' or 'Lady Luck' seemed to be smiling on you? That you had no choice, at some point, but to 'trust to the hands of fate'? Or that the gods themselves frowned upon some adventure of yours? Why? What made you think so? What happened? And what did it feel like, to have your life apparently taken out of your control?

In the old legends, Luck ('geluk') was originally a Germanic goddess; Fortuna was her Roman equivalent. And Fate was not one goddess, but three: the 'three sisters of Fate', the Moirae of

Greek mythology. Between them – says the story – they control every aspect, every event of our lives; between them they weave a fabric of lives, the totality of Life in all its glory. One sister – her name is Clotho (from whom we get the English word 'cloth') – spins the threads of a person's life; Lachesis, 'blind chance', weaves that life into the greater fabric; and Atropos, dispassionately, cuts the thread when its part of the weft of life is done. No choice, it seems; no hope. You can't fight the Fates. . .

We dream of control; yet in the background always are those three sisters. One spins; one weaves; one cuts. . .

But there's something not quite right with this picture: a gap in the fatalistic gloom. It's clear from our own experience that we *do* have choices in our lives – choices of a sort, at least, even if they do so often turn out to be the wrong ones! Our lives are not entirely outside of our control, lost to the whims of a cruel fate; yet at the same time it's equally clear that our lives aren't *in* our control either – and also clear that the more we try to make them so, the more definitely some random chance breaks that control back down again.

Control is a myth; and fate – a life without choice – is no better. Somewhere between those two extremes is a way of life that *works*, one in which we *do* reclaim our choices: but it can take more than a hint of weirdness to reach it. . .

A SUBTLE HINT OF WEIRDNESS

The theme of a 'thread of life' recurs in legends all around the world; the story of the 'three sisters of fate' exists in many versions throughout Europe and beyond. And the old Greek myth is more than a childish fairy-tale – it's almost usable as a point of view about reality once we strip away the surface layer of metaphor.

> Think about that image of the Fates for a while – of 'blind chance' interweaving with the ordered thread of Life. Our lives as a fabric of choice and chance; control interweaving with chaos; our

infinitely rich reality. How well does that describe your everyday experience?

It's a good metaphor: but it underplays the role of the choices that *we* so obviously have in our lives. Life's not merely fate, but a fiction: a story in which we're intimately *involved*. There's always a choice; we always have choice. But there's always a twist. . . that's the part that's weird.

Another version of the myth, an aspect of the Old Norse world-story, brings a different twist to the tale – one that is, quite literally, weird. And one that we can put to use in living *with* – not merely survive – this increasingly crazy world.

Why 'weird', though? We tend to use the word to describe something strange, disturbing, odd: but historically it's a synonym for 'fate' – in fact the old Scottish idiom 'to dree one's weird' means 'to suffer one's fate'. In the legends, 'weird' is not merely something strange, but an aspect of nature itself: like light, or electricity, or wind and wave, it simply *is*. And in Nordic myth it's personified by the 'three sisters of Ur_r' – pronounced 'wyrd', or 'weird'; the Nornir, the 'three maidens from Giantland', Ur_r, Ver_andi, Skuld. They're the 'three weird sisters' in Shakespeare's 'Macbeth', who have the power to foretell the future, or affect the course of events: like the Fates, one spins, one weaves, one cuts. And their names also mean 'past', 'present', 'future' – so they bring the remorseless flow of *time* into the world.

"Wyrd", says one scholar, "is the compelling power and final destiny which no man and no thing may escape". We can't escape time: it *is*. We can't escape our fate, our wyrd: it *is*. . .

But there's always a choice, there's always a twist. . .

And that's the difference between the story of the Fates, and the far stranger sense of Wyrd. In the Greek legend, the fabric of life is a simple sheet, a cloth-like grid: the threads of life run in parallel to each other across a framework of chance and opportunity, meted out in time. In that story, there's little room for choice: each chance will never come again.

But the fabric – *the* wyrd – that the Norns weave is very

different: the cross-warp of the web can be very warped indeed! It's not a simple grid: it's full of loops and twists and tangles, yet with a subtle sense and symmetry behind it, like a Celtic knotwork in infinite dimensions. Not a fabric of lives, but a fabric of *life*: a fabric on which *we* weave the story of our lives, at one time following the predictable line of the weft, at another catching a passing chance – the cross-warp of wyrd – to jump from one line, one life-choice, to another. Lives weaving, interweaving; a fabric of *choices* that we weave among the threads of wyrd.

Each thread of this fabric is not, as with the Fates, an individual's life, but an archetype – 'tinker, tailor, soldier, sailor, rich-man, poor-man, beggar-man, thief'. The Home-Maker, the Factory-Hand, the Teacher – a simple structure for a standardised life with a predictable beginning, middle and end. We always follow along a thread: but across this fabric of loops and twists and turns are an infinite number of choice-points where we can change our own story – change to another thread, another archetype – in some weird way. Wherever there's a choice, there's always a twist; so although we can feel for a path through the fabric, nothing is ever quite predictable. Is this closer to your experience than that story of the Fates?

There's always a twist; and wherever there's always a twist, there's always a choice. It's just that some of the choices are so weird, they're hard to see. . . At any moment there may be a choice, a junction of the threads – a decision we have to make, each one with different results, leading to different journeys. And a decision to make no decision is still a decision. . . There's no evenness to it, no certainty: for long periods it seems like there's no choice at all, yet at other times the choices cluster so closely together – a choice-point that cannot be evaded – that there's even a warning, that weird sense of 'impending wyrd'.

A Möbius loop gives a good illustration of the weirdness that even a simple twist can create. Tear a strip about an inch wide

---

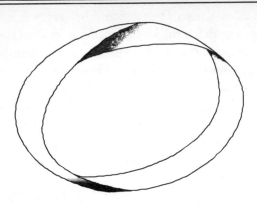

A Möbius loop – a twist of paper with only one side

from the long side of a piece of writing paper. Put the two ends together to form a loop: it still has two sides, as you'd expect – an inside and an outside. But now take it apart, give the ends a simple half-twist, then rejoin them into a loop, and you'll find that you now have a piece of paper with only one side: the inside becomes the outside, the outside merges with the inside. And there's no one point where they change: yet each time round the loop, you're on the opposite side. Weird. . .

To make this, we've bent a two-dimensional object – the piece of paper – into a third dimension, and then twisted it again. Imagine doing the same in an infinity of dimensions. . . if you can visualize *that*, you'll have some idea of the complexity of wyrd!

There's a further twist to this image: perhaps the most important of all. Imagine, if you can, that *every thread passes through every point in this fabric of life*. The threads are archetypes of a life – the logical outcome in time of a given point of view. At first sight, only one or two are visible at each point – the 'obvious' point of view, we'd call it – but every characteristic, every feeling, every attitude is right there at every point. Everywhere is similar: but nothing ever quite repeats.

This isn't easy to visualise. The nearest I've seen to an image is some computer-generated graphics of a mathematical structure in which every point, no matter how close we look, is a boundary between three different regions. This fabric of the wyrd, though, is more where every point is a boundary between an infinite number of regions: it's impossible to represent on paper.

But I have a much simpler way to imagine it, right in front of me now. Hanging from the window-frame is a Chinese streamer, a ring a few inches across, from which hang a large number of coloured threads, several feet long, drifting gently in the breeze. All the colours of the rainbow; all the colours of emotion, of belief, all the colours of the mind and heart. I can spin the ring to form the threads into a brightly coloured twist of rope. If I grasp this rope at any point, some colours will be on the surface of the bundle, while others will be below, concealed, invisible; yet all will still be there. And if I move my hand down the bundle, the same threads will tend to stay in the same relationships; but by changing my grip slightly, new colours will drift to the surface, and others will fade into the background. Whatever's at the surface, though, the whole is always there: "there's a whole in my bucket, dear Liza, dear Liza, there's a whole in my bucket, dear Liza, a whole. . ."

Where am I in all this? Which thread is *me*? The short answer is: all and none of them. The threads are archetypes, not people; characteristics, not characters. 'I' is not that which changes; 'I' is that which chooses. So 'I' am not the threads in this image: I'm the hand *around* the threads, the nexus-point that I use to mark 'here' on the bundle of colours. And the next person, and the next: each a clustering of threads, a nexus on the *same* bundle of threads. The same threads pass through all of us: I'm no different from them, they're no different from me – with a suitable combination of twists and turns in time and in the cross-warp of wyrd, we could see that even at the surface we'd be just the same. The separateness, as the Buddhist would say, is all an illusion. And if all is illusion, what then is actual change?

WEAVING A DIFFERENT WORLD

So what's the point of all this? Even if life is supposedly all illusion, it most certainly doesn't *feel* like it. . .

True – I know that only too well. . . What it feels like, so often, is that I have little or no choice, that everything that happens to me is the effect of my being blown this way and that by a chaos of external causes outside of my control. But imagine – *imagine* – that there is no such thing as 'external': that all our experiences come from where we are – where we've *chosen* (if only by default) to be – on that fabric of life, that fabric of wyrd. Our experience is simply the combination of colours, of threads, that we perceive at that point: the sense of its being external is illusory, an illusion of separateness manufactured by the senses.

If every thread passes through every point, every life, then we can reach out in two ways to change our experience of the world. We can follow the illusion of separateness, and try to fix things in the external world – only to find, as always, that 'there's a hole in my bucket', that everything has to be fixed before everything else. Or we can reach *inside* ourselves, to the threads that *link* us with everything else, and work on the same issues there. It's simpler that way: everything's right here within us. And it works: as we look within, and recognise our choices, the outside world changes too – not just in how *we* experience it, but also as others seem to experience it. The separateness *is* an illusion. Weird; definitely weird.

There's always a choice; there's always a twist. With all these twists and turns, we can easily find ourselves in what seem to be loops in time, yet loops that never quite repeat – whole sections of our lives returning to the same experience from different directions. The same kind of partner, the same hopes, the same illusions, the same mistakes. . . until, in Lewis Carroll's infamous pun, we eventually find a way to make the lessons lessen. In the meantime, though, it can hurt; so often it *hurts*. . . But that, it seems, is life. Or fate.

What kind of loops have happened in *your* life – 'the same kind of partner, the same hopes, the same illusions, the same mistakes. . .'? How did you recognise them as being the same – and in what ways were they different? What did you learn anew each time the not-quite-same event recurred? Did you find a way to 'make the lessons lessen'?

The twists seem to bring us back to the same place each time; but an understanding of the nature of these twists of wyrd can also bring us out of the loops – and into a place more of our own choosing. In the same way, as we watch out for the weavings of the wyrd in our lives, we'll find the same phrases, the same expressions, recurring – but always in slightly different contexts. Each time they come past, they'll have something new to show us – even though on the surface they're exactly the same.

And it affects more than just our own lives. All those big issues – war, the environment, the world economy – that seem too vast to change: it's easy to feel a sense of powerlessness, of fatalistic gloom as soon as we think of them. *I* can't do anything about it, it seems – it's the politicians, the unions, the foreigners, the. . . That'll always be so – and true – if I think of them only as external. But 'there's a whole in my bucket': as threads of the wyrd, these issues are also right here inside us, driven by *our* choices – or our avoidance of choices. "I am the wyrd-one", I might say; "issues spiral through me on the threads of wyrd – are unchanged by how much *I* am unchanged. . ." Find the right thread, and face it, and even a trivial-seeming change in what we choose can have ripples right round the world. The issues are unchanged by how much *we* are unchanged: between us all, we *all* create this world of ours.

If we're going to weave a better world, we have to start some-where: so we may as well start here, with ourselves. We change our world by changing our choices: it's as simple as that, and it's worth doing. Sounds easy? To be honest, it isn't. But then neither is life; and the usual way of living, desperately 'fire-fighting' from one external disaster to another, is no way to live at all. . .

It's easy enough to talk about it: to put it into practice, though, is something else again. But it's only then that the changes happen; it's only then that the changes *can* happen. So work *with* the weirdness of the wyrd in your life. . . and let its aliveness unfold!

3

THE SENSES TAKER

Most of the time, we don't even get a chance to experience the world. Habit – the senses taker – tells us what to expect, so we just switch off, and ignore what our senses tell us. So life slips by, without our even noticing. Oh! Where was I? That's another day just vanished – where did it go?

It's the same old street, I see it every day, so why bother looking at it? And I look at the thoughts in my head instead, and they go chasing round, and round, and round. . . driving me crazy. "Why can't I sort things out? What's wrong with me? What's wrong with everyone? Why? Why?" We've been here before. . . now even the thoughts are habits! We can try to break individual habits – smoking, for example – but the hardest habit to break is habit itself.

Why is habit so – if you'll pardon the expression – habit-forming? Because it *seems* to make life easier, less complicated; and it *seems* to make life a lot less work. Habits allow us to run on 'automatic pilot'. But in practice, if we're not aware of them, they tend to make life a lot less in other ways: a lot less interesting, a lot less fun, a lot less hopeful. . .

Habit gives us the illusion that things are predictable, that they always repeat the same way. Once they're predictable, we don't have to bother about them – they're always the same, always will be the same. And since we don't have to bother about them, they slowly cease to exist, as far as our attention's concerned. The problem is that nothing ever *is* quite the same; nothing ever quite repeats. And it's the differences – not the samenesses – which are

15

where the interest lies. Those differences, those often tiny differences, show us where the choices are – the ones we use to move across the threads of wyrd. But first we have to notice them – and for that we have to break the habit of *not* noticing things. We have to get our senses back from the old senses taker.

Most of our metaphors of perception are visual: "Oh yes, I see that", "I'll look into that", and so on. One way to start breaking the habit of habit is to make more deliberate use of other senses. When sitting on a bus, for example, close your eyes, and *listen* to the passing streets; try to identify where you are by the sound, the smell, the taste.

If nothing else, it can make a regular journey a lot more interesting!

When I'm stuck in habit, I'm running on automatic, trying to get through each day with as little involvement as I can. Habit isn't an absence of choice: it's a choice I use to *avoid* making a choice. And I then wonder why I don't seem to have any choices. . . why everyone out there seems to be 'doing it to me'. . .

CHOOSING NOT TO CHOOSE

Habit is a choice that we've repeated so often that it's become automatic. The choice chooses itself: I don't think about it – I just do it, do what the habit tells me. And if my senses tell me that the circumstances are different, that this choice might not be appropriate – well, it's easier to ignore the senses, just stick to the rules, 'the way I know the world works'.

But how do I *know* the world really does work that way? The short answer is: I don't. But I *believe* it does. "That's what always happens to me – that's what I always get." In other words, it happens because I expect it to happen – in many ways force it to happen that way – in order to confirm my expectation, to confirm my belief that the world works that way. Even if I don't like what's going on, I'll still tend, with habit, to repeat the same situation over and over again. It's only if I look – use my senses –

16

to see what's actually going on, that I get a chance to break out of the loop.

Part of this is because I *want* the world to be predictable. It makes it seem certain, makes it seem safe. But it isn't: it's never exactly the same. For a start, *I'm* different: I've changed, a little older, with different experiences, perhaps even a different point of view. So why can't I see this? Why do I keep doing the same old things in what aren't actually the same old circumstances?

What I'm really doing is avoiding some kind of pain – or rather the expectation of pain. Something I 'know' I won't like. How do I know I won't like it, though? Back comes the answer: because I didn't like it before. I remember that I don't like it. But the memory may be wrong, and the circumstances are different: I'll never know unless I let go of the memory, and work with what I have here, now.

For many years I'd refuse to eat any kind of white fish: I knew it was revolting, I wouldn't touch the stuff if I could possibly avoid it. Then one day, at a friend's house, I found myself eating some kind of fish steak, in a magnificent sauce – absolutely delicious. In my habit of avoiding fish, I'd missed out so often on what could have been a wonderful taste, a wonderful experience.

So where did the habit come from? School meals, of course: in particular, a dish we nicknamed 'porcupine pie', a semi-liquid slush of disintegrating potato and some unidentifiable white-fish consisting mostly of needle-sharp bones. Truly revolting. . . no wonder I felt like saying "Never again!" What I refused to recognise, though, was that the taste of fish depends greatly on how it's cooked – it depends on the circumstances. I'd fixed a choice of choosing not to accept what my senses tell me: "What's cooking?" And even when I did have to eat fish, it always tasted revolting – because I *expected* it to be revolting. In the end, I in effect tricked myself into letting the experience be here, now, at the friend's house – finally breaking the habit of habit.

What experiences have you had like this? If the habit ended 'by itself', how and when did it do so?

In following an old habit, I'm living in the past, elsewhere, elsewhen: whereas what's actually happening in front of me is *here*, *now* – and probably completely different, if only I'd care to notice. I need to re-awaken my senses, to tell me what really *is* going on.

But part of the problem is that that's exactly what I *don't* want to do. I can still remember exactly what that stuff tasted like: I don't want to risk tasting *that* again. So I'd rather shut down my senses, and rely instead on the warning from memory. Avoid all feeling: too much risk. The result is that I shut myself into a narrower and narrower range of experience that I'll risk allowing myself – an ever smaller and more limited world.

And I then complain about how boring and limited the world seems to be. . .

Worse still, I shut myself out from other experiences, not because they bring up painful memories, but because I think they might bring up painful comparisons. There are whole sections of the city that I avoid, for example, not because they're dangerous, or because I don't like them, but because I used to go there with my now former partner. . . I'm not avoiding the memories as such – on the contrary, they were good times; it's more that I don't want to face the emotions I expect they'll bring up – the loneliness, the sense of emptiness, of absence. It hurts. . . I don't want to face it.

So to avoid the sense of feeling bad, I avoid the place that seems to cause the feeling – or that I think might bring up that feeling. In the process, I give myself a still narrower world in which to operate – about which I also complain. And tend to blame others for it, of course – even though it's really nothing to do with them. It's *my* choice not to go there, after all.

AVOIDING EMOTION

Any kind of emotion is frightening, it seems: good ones as well as bad. There's a sense of being overwhelmed, that it will never stop, or rather of being dumped in a timeless space where there is only the emotion. Good ones I tend to cling to – this happiness must last *forever!* – and bad ones, like the all-pervading wave of loneliness, I'm terrified will last forever. . . They all pass, of course; but it doesn't *feel* like that. Not at the time.

For a change, this seems to be more of a problem for men: women are more likely to be aware that emotions come and go in waves, while men have less of an awareness of the flow of *time*, and thus have more a sense of being 'dumped in it' at a random level of intensity. But for all of us, emotions of any flavour give us a sense of being out of control. Some people like that feeling: I don't. If I think 'I am' is the same as the 'I' that controls, loss of control means loss of me. 'I' might cease to exist. I get frightened; and when I'm afraid, I close up. No emotions, please. . . More walls. . .

In any case, whilst *we* may like the freedom of feeling out of control, the culture we're in doesn't like it at all. "Don't get over-excited, Chris", says my mother; "Big kids don't cry", says a school-teacher; "What the hell d'ya think you're laughing at?", snarls a passer-by; "You *mustn't* get angry", says a friend. If I'm emotional, I remind other people of *their* walls; they get frightened too, and take it out on me, as the supposed cause of their fear. Walls within walls within walls: a culture of walls. No emotion allowed: it's not considered *decent*.

> If you're on your own and lonely, how do you react to seeing a couple holding hands and kissing in the street? Would you rather they stopped? Or at least went elsewhere?
>
> How do you react to other people being angry? Or upset? What feelings does it bring up in you to see them? Does it bring up any kind of fears, or memories – especially ones you'd prefer to forget?

There's a catch: all our emotions come from the same place – from the heart, we might say. We can't just shut out loneliness, or sadness: we either accept all our emotions, or we have none. The laughter cannot be truly there without the tears; or the joy without the awareness of loneliness. 'Life, liberty and the pursuit of happiness' is rather one-sided: happiness is transitory, like any other emotion, and only exists side-by-side with sorrow. If I hide from one emotion, I hide from them all: if I won't face loneliness, I actually prevent myself from ever being truly happy.

We're encouraged to be emotionless; we encourage each other to be emotionless. So being emotionless becomes a habit: but if we let the senses-taker of habit take away our feelings as well as our senses, what have we left? Not much, is the answer...

Without emotions, I all but cease to be human. I become a hollow shell – as if without a heart, a soul. And I can *feel* that emptiness – and I don't know what to do. So I find myself desperately running around, doing one thing after another to protect myself from any potential emotion in case it might be painful. The result, as one writer put it, is that I become a 'human do-ing' rather than a human being... Hence the sense of power-lessness, of being walled out from the world. But the walls are of my own making: that's what's hard to recognise, that's what's hard to accept.

The way out is to recognise that I'm afraid of those emotions – and do it anyway. Avoiding all pain means that I have no choice about how to handle it when it does come my way; choosing to *face* the pain, to understand more about myself, means that I've also reclaimed more of my sense of choice. Gently, though... gently. I take the risk: I go to one of those places we used to go to together. And yes, it does hurt. But it's not overwhelming: it *does* pass. Then it's gone: and I can find that I do enjoy being there. Even – perhaps especially – because I'm on my own: a very different feeling, which I know I'd never have experienced if my partner had been here with me. And because I *know* it's different, I get to know how *I* feel now, what *my* senses tell me now: and I'm no longer trapped in a memory of the past. The wall has gone...

The text that's in these boxes is about putting these ideas into *practice*. One of the most common habits is to avoid feeling by 'staying in my head': I avoid dealing with the world 'out there', it's too much like hard work, it might be painful, it brings up memories that I don't want to face. . . any excuse will do! So I'll say "I know that", yet all too often what I mean is "I have that information" rather than "I have that *experience*" – which is not the same thing at all. So take the risk: don't just read it, do it! Build a new habit of doing it, *being* it. And notice the difference in experience; notice the difference in aliveness. . .

It does take real courage to break habits, to break down the walls – especially if there's emotional pain attached to them. It's important to acknowledge ourselves for that.

Despite the usual all-or-nothing feeling, it's important not to try to drop every habit all at once: we won't be able to do it, and it's not a good idea in any case. It's always useful to keep some habits going: they help to give us *some* kind of focus! But once we become more aware of the choices and non-choices we make, we can at last begin to decide which habits we want, and which ones we don't. In doing so, we reclaim our power of choice – and realise that we *do* have a choice.

BELIEFS, FEELINGS, SENSES

One of the ways we learn to avoid emotion is to blur the distinctions between beliefs, feelings and sensations: and a key part of reclaiming choice is to reclaim our awareness of the difference! We won't get far in understanding ourselves and our choices unless we do. . . But blurring the boundaries between them has, for most of us, become a habit – another habit that's surprisingly hard to break.

"I know that", I'd say: but I don't – I only *believe* that I know it. "I feel cold", I'd say – when more accurately I *sense* that it's cold. "I think I'm angry" – but how do I *know*? "I'm happy!" – but

21

where do we *sense* this to know it? "I feel confused", you might reply, trying to make sense of all this – but *where* do you feel the confusion? What does confusion *feel* like? What and where *is* 'confusion'?

Part of the confusion comes from a blurring of past, present and future. Within our experience – as children of the Sisters of Time, we might say – these aspects of time may seem to coincide: but sensations and feelings *only* exist in the present. We don't have any choice about them – they simply *are*. A memory, however, brings back into the present a feeling – or often an edited version of one – from the past; a belief may manufacture something that *seems* like a feeling, even though there's nothing tangible behind it; and the future never exists at all, other than as a belief or a 'future-memory', an imagined version of some sensation or feeling that we'd expect to experience when we get there.

The link between them all is an analogy – a common thread of connection. But it's not a literal one: a belief about a feeling – or about what that feeling *means* – is not the same thing as the feeling itself. The only feelings we *know* are our own. For example, if I say to someone "I feel you're being foolish", it's more than likely that I'm actually saying something about *myself*: "I *think* you're being foolish, because *I* feel uncomfortable, and I want to blame you for it rather than accept it as my own" – which is *not* the same thing at all! This 'projecting' of our own feelings onto others is a habit we all learn very early on: and until we can see how and when we do it, and can re-'own' our own feelings rather than lose them to the senses-taker, we'll find it hard to move on. But to do this sometimes asks us to look at things from a rather weird point of view. . .

One tool that can help break this habit of 'projection' is to watch our choice of language. For instance, when talking with or about other people, make a point of using 'I-statements' rather than 'you-statements' – say what *you* feel rather than what you think

22

the other person feels. What difference does this make to your understanding of the conversation? . . .of the other person? . . .of yourself?

Watch, too, for the blurring of time in the way you speak: "I'd feel happy about that" is a *belief*, an 'imagining', not a feeling – it's an expectation of future experience, but feelings themselves exist only in the present. This kind of precision is a bit strange at first, but it brings a lot more clarity to our understanding of 'now'. . .

And another trick, as a friend showed me the other day, is that if we can replace the word 'feel' with 'believe', it's *not* a 'feeling-statement' – especially when it's said about someone else. "I feel happy" doesn't make sense as 'I believe happy" – so it's likely to be a real feeling. But "I feel you're being foolish" could just as easily be "I believe you're being foolish" – so it's probably only a belief. You might be able to describe your *own* feelings that go with that belief: but the meaning often changes if we shift the focus from 'you' – someone else – to 'I'. What happens? Changing your mode of language in this way, what do you learn about *yourself*?

Ending the confusion takes practice – a deliberate choice to re-create our awareness of ourselves. But it brings with it a new kind of clarity: a new sense of certainty in the midst of all the weird uncertainties of Reality Department.

And it brings something else that we'll only begin to recognise over time: a strange *sharing* of feelings that's commonly called 'compassion' – linking us with others on shared threads of the wyrd. A different kind of *knowing*. . . Weird. . . And that, once we find it, is a habit that *is* worth developing!

A HABIT OF CHOICE

In breaking the habit of habit, we reclaim our power of choice. What hurts most for me at this point, perhaps, is that I get to recognise that I always *have* had a choice: but I've usually given it away. I've chosen not to choose: so the choice has happened for me. I've followed the loop of wyrd that I'm on – round and round and round. So that perception of powerlessness, about which I've complained so much, has in effect been my own choice – or rather my own non-choice, the result of my evasion of choice. In that sense, I have actually *chosen* to be in this mess that I'm in. It's not a comfortable feeling. . .

All right, so it's my choice that I'm in chaos: so now what do I do? I start to make new choices about choices; building new habits that, for a change, actually *are* useful to me – that's what I do. But before I do that, it's useful to look at how we come to make the choices that have brought us each to where we are now – and in particular how other people, and their ideas of 'right' and 'wrong', have helped to bring it about for us.

4

EVERYONE IS TO BLAME

We all have our habits, our mechanical avoidances of the real world. And that's one very good reason why this world of ours is in chaos: no-one's choosing, to a large extent no-one's even looking. We've all been had by the senses taker. In that sense, *everyone* – myself as well as others, others as well as myself – is to blame for this mess.

But even if everyone *is* to blame, the only person's habits we can change directly are our own. So that's the place we need to start: looking at how we interact with other people's habits, other people's choices.

"YOU CAN'T GET THERE FROM HERE"

By being stuck in habit, we choose not to choose: we give away our power of choice, and with it any real control over our lives. So if we're going to reclaim the power of choice in our life, we first have to recognise how we give it away – and how others have been all too keen to encourage us to do so. We've all done it: we've all had to, to exist in any kind of social environment.

The cultures we've grown up in – family, school, religious background, economy and so on – have all had definite ideas about habits that were, they said, good for us; and others which were definitely bad. A maze of rules, instructions, implications: "Little children should be seen and not heard." "You ought to make way for your elders and betters." "You mustn't contradict the teacher." "Thou shalt fear the Lord thy God, and honour His commandments." Many, many of them, over many, many years.

Some of the pronouncements are just plain daft: "You can't get there from here", someone once told me. But they still have their effects, especially if we were told them repeatedly in childhood.

> For most of my life I've been frightened of police, or almost anyone in uniform. There's never been any obvious reason: in fact most of my interactions with police have been humorous or bizarre rather than threatening! Eventually, though, I traced it back to something my grandmother used to say to me as a toddler: "Now you must be good: because if you're a naughty child, a policeman will come and take you away and *he'll never bring you back!*" Trivial enough, innocuous enough: all Grandma wanted to do was keep us kids quiet for a while. But at some level I seem to have believed it in this absolute sense – "he'll never bring you back!" – for the whole of my life. The fear has become compulsive, an unconscious habit – even though at no time has it had any true connection with reality.
>
> Can you think of similar examples in your own life: childhood commands that you've discovered you still find yourself following compulsively, regardless of whether they're appropriate?

As children, we tend to believe that adults are all-powerful and all-knowing. Somewhere deep down, part of me still seems to believe that those childhood instructions are true – no matter what my senses and my memory may show me. So it takes us a long time to recognise just how many of those rules are not so much fact, as someone else's *opinion*: no more than their point of view. But not necessarily ours. . . that's what's important for us to understand. And, often, it's not been good for *us* at all, though often good for the person who wants us to accept statements like those as rules, as habits for life. There's a lot of *emotional* advantage to the teacher if I accept that I mustn't contradict: his authority is never challenged, he's always certain of his superiority. But unless I *can* challenge him, I cannot learn anything more than his point of view; and neither, for that matter, can he. With these arbitrary 'laws', we all lose in the end.

To learn, we need to be able to question anything and everything, before it gets frozen into the robotic state of habit. But if we're not clear about what we want, about what our *own* rules and understandings are, there'll be no shortage of people to take advantage of that confusion and take the power that we give away: as Joan Armatrading put it, "You gotta be yourself – be more like I tell ya". If 'myself' is defined by what other people want, I'll end up, *by my own non-choice*, as a servant, a slave: I've done that often enough in my life, and it's not a good idea. . .

Most of these external rules that are now habits, though, we learnt at school, or even earlier: so how were we to know then how to choose? After all, we were only children at the time. True: but I'm not a child now – despite the cultural pressures on me, or on us all, to remain children for life. I can observe; I can watch for clues. And the most important clue is in the way these disempowering 'rules' are phrased. Almost always they'll contain certain 'magic' words: 'must', 'ought', or 'should'. Or 'can't' – "you can't get there from here".

"You ought to do this. . ." "You must do that. . .", "You shouldn't do this. . ." "I wouldn't do that if I were you. . ." Think of some examples of these from your own life: do you recognise how they disempower you, how we give our power away when we accept them? How do you feel about that?

And think of some examples of how you've given these kind of 'rules' to others: how do you feel now about having done that? Can you see why you used these phrasings?

Phrases like this are meant to entrap, to bind, to enslave: words as subtle chains. When I look back and see how people have done this to me again and again throughout my life, I get angry – very angry. How dare they do this to me!

Then I remember that I've done it to others, probably just as much: and I then feel foolish, a child caught in the act.

And in both cases I've chosen to do it, chosen to accept it: a habit of enslaving, a habit of enslavement. Why?

TYRANT AND VICTIM

The simple answer is fear. Lots of it. Fear drives us all, whether we recognise it or not. It's fear of uncertainty that pushes us into developing the security-blanket of habit in the first place. And it's fear of others that leads to this maze of 'musts' and 'oughts' and 'shoulds': I don't have power *over* others, but if I can ensure that those others are not powerful either, they can't threaten me. Not so much power over others, as power *under*: a systematic habit of disempowerment. So I'll tell them they *should* do this, so that it doesn't threaten me; and they'll reply that I *ought* to do that, to make sure that my existence won't threaten them. What they're actually afraid of may have nothing to do with me, in fact may well be linked to long-forgotten childhood fables – "if you don't behave, the bogeyman will *get you*!" But the fear is real, and acted on accordingly: "you mustn't come near me", "you shouldn't do that", and so on. You can't beat a childhood monster – but you might be able to trap it in a web of words. . .

The end-result is that *no-one* is powerful (or rather, only those people outside the reach of a barrage of 'shoulds' and 'shouldn'ts' retain their power – and they're often exactly those who, in the culture, we'd prefer *weren't* powerful!). We're all hopelessly confused by a maze of childhood instructions that have little or no connection with reality. So with no-one able to make a decision, in case it threatens someone else's fears, we end up with the worst of everything: a kind of lowest-common-denominator of a world.

We seem to live in an all-pervasive atmosphere of fear – a state which, unfortunately, is actively encouraged by most political systems and most of the major religions. But that's hardly surprising: our religions and politics arise from the same fears anyway. As a result, we tend to fall into a kind of tyrant-or-victim cycle, oscillating between the roles of persecutor and persecuted: individuals, groups, cultures, whole nations – even the God is ultimate tyrant or ultimate victim.

We'd recognise this scenario most often in a physical sense: war, brutality, force, violence. Yet physical assault is, if anything, the rarest form it takes: far more often the true violence is emotional, mental, spiritual. Righteousness that rejects another's point of view as 'wrong' is just as much a form of tyranny as physical violence: "Peace on our terms" is no offer of peace, but a declaration of war; "There is no God but mine" is an assault on the soul; and a come-on followed by a callous rejection is little short of a rape of the heart. Fear leads to righteousness, which itself comes from fear – the fear of uncertainty that leads to the desperate need to control.

A common form of tyrant/victim violence is the 'Devil's Alternative', the 'no-win' – 'heads I win, tails you lose'. Here's one friend's example:

"It started off pleasantly enough: a few of us having a discussion at my home. But one woman failed to get her way, built it up into an argument, and then started yelling at me: 'Have you got what it takes to be my equal without violence?' – this being screamed repeatedly just inches from my face, even when I tried to back away from her in the room. If I answered 'Yes', she just repeated the question; if I answered 'No', she mocked me, and then repeated the question. And all the while the others just stood around in confusion, telling me at times 'You ought to see her point of view. . .' After several minutes of this, with panic rising, I answered her question in what still seems to me an appropriate manner: I slapped her face, once, hard – something I've never done before or since. It stopped the verbal assault, of course, but it took me weeks to recover: I felt violated, self-humiliated, all those emotions, the equivalent response to rape – which, in an emotional sense, was exactly what it was. And the woman has usually referred to me since as 'the man who hit her' – a man who resorts to violent assault against women, she says. But I'm still trying to work it out: who was the victim; who the tyrant? Who really *was* the violent one?"

Think of some similar incidents in your own life. Who was the victim? Who was the tyrant? And who was responsible for the incident: who, ultimately, was to blame?

It's much easier to accept the rôle of victim: we can blame the tyrant then for 'doing it to me', we have a reason then for our righteous indignation, our pain, our hurt, our anger. But in fact, if we're honest, we've played both rôles, probably equally: victim leads to tyrant leads to victim, an echoing cycle of unclaimed anger. And a victim needs a tyrant just as much as a tyrant needs a victim: in each rôle we're being dishonest about our true motives – most usually, we're looking for someone to blame.

No-one seems to *choose* to be a tyrant, to *choose* to be a victim: but somehow we all manage to become so. How? Who's responsible?

WHO'S TO BLAME?

'Finding out who to pin the blame on' is an ever-popular game – a bit like 'pin the tail on the donkey'. *Someone* must be responsible: who is it? At the first stage, it's always someone else, especially if you're the victim: the tyrant did it to me, the tyrant must be to blame. After all, what they did *hurts*: I can't be responsible for that, surely? 'Round and round in the usual old game; you take the credit, and I take the blame.' Or is it 'I take the credit and *you* take the blame'. . .? We always prefer to feel that it's someone else: I always want to say "it isn't *my* fault". That's the usual perception, anyway: but it's never quite as simple as that.

Think for a moment about the chorus to a rather coarse old song:
"It's the same the 'ole world over:
it's the poor what gets the blame,
it's the rich what gets the pleasure –
ain't it all a bleedin' shame?"
It may be true – we could argue about that indefinitely! – but if it is, how did things get that way? Whose fault is it? And would

EVERYONE IS TO BLAME

> you consider yourself as 'the rich what gets the pleasure', or 'the poor what gets the blame'?

Another 'solution' to the issue is to take the whole blame on ourselves: "it's all my fault". Sometimes this is a more mature approach, in recognising the choices we do all have in these games; but often it's a habit of the 'professional victim', or someone who's learned or been trained to be the scapegoat for the family or community. Self-scapegoating is all too common, and unfortunately is encouraged by the Christian tradition – the self-sacrificing urge to emulate 'the one who dies to take away our sins'. Once the behavior becomes ingrained, it's a very hard habit to break – and intensely self-destructive. And it's no more realistic, in terms of finding who's *really* to blame, than the more public hunt for scapegoats.

It's also a habit that others may be keen to encourage – precisely because *they* can then avoid the blame. In many tyrant/victim scenarios – as in that example earlier – it's common for the victim to be urged, by others or their own conscience, to take the whole blame on themselves, and 'see the other person's point of view'. The victim is not only beaten up – in whatever sense – by the tyrant, but by themselves as well! The tyrant's actions may very well come from *their* confused response to a maze of childhood 'shoulds' and 'can'ts' and 'oughts', and may well be stuck in depression, paranoia, loneliness or whatever: but it doesn't help if the victim is made to feel responsible for what is actually the tyrant's cruelty.

Whatever drives it, that cruelty is still a *choice*, even if it comes from habit, or from past pain. To be a victim is also a kind of choice, though at the time it's extremely hard to see how or why. It's everyone's choice, everyone's responsibility – usually through the non-choice of habit. And it does no good to anyone to allow the victim to allow their conscience to tear them apart, if the tyrant is not encouraged to make any comparable move – because today's victim will often be tomorrow's tyrant, and so the cycle goes on and on. Eventually, someone *does* take responsibility enough to face the fears that drive the cycle: and it stops. Suddenly a sense of quiet: no blame. But it's *not* easy; it does take courage. . .

Blaming, whether of self or others, is a peculiarly evil habit: a denial of responsibility, a false separation from reality. It's not so much that we say "Yes" to the evil, but that we so rarely say "No". As a habit, we choose by not choosing; we follow the habit of avoiding choice, then look for someone else to blame. But it is still a *choice*: in a sense, we can't blame *anyone*. If we think in terms of wyrd, a life-path as a series of choices, everyone and no-one is to blame. In the complexity of that fabric of interweavings, we all choose, between us, and collectively, to get what we get.

NO-ONE IS TO BLAME

The more we look for someone to blame, the further we get from any chance of finding a solution. That's true whether we tend to blame others, or blame ourselves. The best way to understand this is to let go, let go the control, let go of the anger, the desire for revenge and all those other very real feelings attached to blame: they don't actually help in sorting things out. Let go, go wider. Be compassionate to ourselves, and to others: we're all in this mess together. Just accept, gently, that "things are the way they are because they got that way": once we can start to accept that, we can begin to move onward – and out of this torturous cycle.

Go back to an example of some tyrant/victim scenario, one where you were (nominally) the victim. Remember the sense of hopelessness, the anger turned in against yourself; *feel* those emotions again. It's not comfortable to do so: but do so anyway.

Then, within your memory of that time, think wider, of the overall situation, the choices on the threads of wyrd that have led each participant to that point. What anger is the 'tyrant' expressing, is trapped in? What are others around not facing? What are *you* not facing, to have led you there? And let go, let go. . .

☞

Now turn it round: choose some incident where *you* were (nominally) the oppressor, and reconstruct that in the same way. It may be embarrassing, but do it anyway.

And, within your memory of that time, think wider, of the overall situation, the life-path on the threads of wyrd that has led each participant to that point. What anger are you, the 'tyrant', expressing, are trapped in? What was the 'victim' not facing, to have led themselves there? What are others around not facing? And let go, let go. . .

Consider it to have been everyone's choice to be there – often by default, by choosing not to choose; but everyone chose to be there, chose to do what they did there. Everyone is to blame; no-one, individually, is to blame. What difference does this make?

We're *all* to blame; so no *one* is to blame. That's hard to grasp, in a world in which every effect supposedly stems from a single cause. And even harder to accept! But let go, let go. . .

Everyone is to blame; so *no-one* is to blame.

It's important to recognise that no-one is to blame; but it's also important first to recognise that that's so only because *everyone* is to blame.

Ultimately, there *is* no blame: the world is as it is because, between us all, we chose it to be so.

The next question is obvious. If we made the world so, and we don't like it, what are we going to do about it? More to the point, it's useful to ask ourselves, "what am *I* going to do about it?" – because the only person we can each change directly is ourselves.

5

I AM WHAT I AM

Instead of spending energy looking for blame, it's far more useful to use it to do something about what happens in our lives. So consider this possibility: if we each weave our lives, our fate, on the threads of wyrd, and every thread passes through every one of us, then in changing ourselves, we change everything and everyone else. And everyone else does the same. That's why things get so complicated: but it also means that we *always* have a choice. The world we have derives from a web of choices: yet the easiest place, almost the only place, I can start changing those choices is *here*. In *me*.

Becoming aware of my choices, I reclaim responsibility – literally, 'response-ability' – for what happens to me; I reclaim not so much power *over* my life, but power *with* it.

By breaking the patterns of habit, we reclaim the true power of choice; and by cutting free of the web of other people's 'shoulds' and 'oughts' and 'can'ts', we start to create a life that's actually worth living. It's not a quick process – have no illusions about that! – but it's well worth doing. Perhaps the *only* thing that's worth doing. But be warned: it can certainly be weird at times. . .

WHOSE LIFE IS IT, ANYWAY?

The first stage in reclaiming that power is to reclaim the energy and aliveness that's locked up within us. And a good place to start is to get angry. Very angry. We're going to get angry anyway once

34

we realise just how much our power, our sense of self, has been stolen: so we may as well do it deliberately first. . .

The important trick is not to get angry *at* anyone – either others or ourselves – but just to use anger to reach the passion, the energy that's currently locked up into fighting ourselves.

As a child I was fascinated by facts – an avid collector of not-quite-useless information. As a result, I'd find I *knew*, without needing to look up or guess, an answer in the somewhat competitive family discussions. For the others, this was almost annoying: my mother, for example, would often comment, "Oh damn the child – Chris's got it *right* again!" So which message was I supposed to believe: get the wrong answer, and be told I'd failed; or get the right answer, and be told I shouldn't? And I wasn't allowed to withdraw from the discussions, either – "you shouldn't sulk!" No wonder I'm confused and self-doubting! And recognising it now, how much these unintentional attacks have crippled me, I get angry. Very angry. "Whose life is it anyway! How dare they!"

And let go, let go. . . because it's equally true that I let it happen. And there was no malice: it simply was what it was. I *believed* the 'no-win'; I allowed myself to be locked up by it.

So it's time I unlocked myself from it, isn't it?

Think of some similar no-wins in your own life. As you recognise how much they've trapped you, reach into the anger. . . Then let go, let go. . . release it. Not *at* anyone – just recognise it, allow it to be; and release it.

Herein lies a problem: how to release anger – or even to get at it at all. We're all conditioned not to express emotions, especially anger or rage. And we have to find a way to release it which does not consist of dumping it on someone else, or turning it back in again on ourselves.

Don't ignore the anger: it's there, and it won't go away by itself. If we feel apathetic, a sense of "Why bother?", that's often because of this social conditioning. It locks us up: in effect, we're in a jail of our own creation, one we've been encouraged to build by our own and other people's fears. "There's no point, it doesn't make any difference", you might say. But saying that is *why* there's no point, is *why* it doesn't make a difference: the energy is locked up into keeping us locked up.

So: if we reach inside and look at some of these no-wins, we'll either find a surge of anger, or a surge of apathy – which is actually the same thing in a different guise. Bring it out: if it comes in the form of apathy, break the habit of apathy, and *do* something with it! Jump about a bit; yell; put on some music, loud, and dance it out. Or a common technique is to prepare the scene beforehand: roll up an old newspaper into a club, place an old telephone directory on a cushion; then reach into the anger, and shred the directory with the club, blow after blow after blow. Yell, scream, shout: reach in to the anger: then let go, let go. . .

THE 'SILLINESS BARRIER'

It's usual at this point to feel that the whole idea is ridiculous. Silly. It's just stupid, childish. Surely this is a joke?

In actual fact, it's not stupid at all. It's been proven time and time again that this kind of emotional release – releasing locked-up fear, anger, guilt and the rest – is an essential part of the process of an individual's reclaiming power with their life. And it's no joke: it most certainly doesn't *feel* like a joke when we finally allow ourselves to do it. . .

So why does it *feel* so silly to do it – to let go at all? There's some kind of barrier there. . .

This 'silliness barrier' is real: and in no way is it trivial. It can be extremely hard to get past; even though, looking back, it can often seem to have been nothing much. Other people rarely see it as a barrier: "For God's sake just *jump*, child!" – a real barrier of fear, but it's not *theirs*. It's easy to dismiss it as 'a little bit of silliness, that's all' – that's what others might say, and what we ourselves might say afterwards. But it won't seem so at the time

– and not when we're *facing* it: it's important to recognise that distinction!

Not surprisingly, there are many layers to this barrier, all interacting and interweaving like the threads of wyrd. Part of it comes from social conditioning again: Good boys don't do that kind of thing, do they? It's not *ladylike* to show anger, to show aggression. "Don't be so bloody childish", you'd be told, perhaps. But we looked at this in the last chapter: "Children should be seen and not heard"; "You gotta be yourself – be more like I tell ya".

Layer after layer of no-wins, of 'musts' and 'shoulds' – or, more often, 'mustn'ts' and 'shouldn'ts' – all requiring us to deny who we are, in deferment to other people's fears and resentments, trapping us in apathy, in powerlessness. One writer defined resentment as 'a demand that the other feel guilty': we've been taught to feel guilty simply for being who we are. And guilt is an insidious weapon: it's used to get us to beat ourselves up on another person's behalf – often for no true reason at all.

But it's also important to recognise the part our *own* fears play in creating the silliness-barrier. I'm no different from anyone else: I don't like to look silly either. I'm afraid of being embarrassed; afraid of being laughed at. And I'll go to real lengths to avoid finding myself in any situation where that might happen – regardless of whether what I'm doing is actually intended to help me...

This is most obvious in learning new skills: so it's worth remembering that accepting who we are – with all our weaknesses *and* our strengths – is perhaps the most important skill we can learn. There's a specific moment in learning a skill where some new piece of information *fits*: and it's at that moment we hit a milder form of the silliness barrier. We get hit by an embarrassing sense that we knew it all along, that we could have done this part of the skill at any time, if we'd let ourselves – that kind of feeling. And we get hit by a real fear of uncertainty, as the rules of reality change, from "I can't" to "Oh – I can!". So there's a crucial choice-point here, one that's easy to miss: one of the few times we can *see* the twists in the fabric of wyrd.

Some time ago, for a variety of reasons, I decided to learn how to juggle. It's not the easiest of skills! So for weeks I couldn't do it – I could toss two balls back and forth, but not all three. Then just when I was about to give up, it suddenly worked, for just one brief moment: "I can't / it isn't working" and the rest had shifted into "Oh – I can!" – and back again. I found I had a very silly grin on my face – I was embarrassed, even though no-one was there. And I could *feel* the choice: disbelieve the change, in order to prove that the old 'rule' of "I can't do it" was 'true'; or let go – knowing that it probably wouldn't work again for a while – and *allow* the new rule to be true (or at least possible), to expand into a wider skill, wider awareness. But it was a real choice-point: on that occasion the excitement won out over the fear of uncertainty, but I know that on too many other occasions the choice has gone the other way. . .

Reach out to some memories of similar occasions of your own – *feel* that moment of embarrassment, of uncertainty. What were the choices that you made on those occasions – to go with the change, or revert to the status quo? If others were there, how much did that affect your choice?

Even in learning a skill, where there isn't that much of an emotional loading, the silliness-barrier can be significant. In learning to break free of habit and the social version of the senses-taker, the silliness-barrier can be much harder to overcome. But accept it: it *is* there, it *is* real, it's the same for everyone – you're not just being 'childish' when you find yourself backing away from facing it.

What makes it harder here, in reclaiming the energy from old locked-up anger, is the sheer volume of emotion: it can take us by surprise, and there doesn't seem to be an easy way to do it gently. For a moment – sometimes a very long moment – the intensity of feeling can be overwhelming. There's a real sense of being out of control – fearfully, terrifyingly so. And that fear is one of the main reasons why all that anger, all that guilt and the like became locked up in the first place: it was too frightening for us or, perhaps more often, for others to willingly face. But it doesn't just go away if we don't face it: it stays as energy used to fight *ourselves* – which is why we get trapped in apathy, in powerlessness. Our individual power is locked up in there: only by saying "I am who I am" – without blame, and from the far side of anger and guilt – can we reach that power and reclaim it.

But the silliness-barrier is *not* trivial: when you find yourself facing it, treat it – and yourself – with respect. We'll meet it again and again, in many different guises. At some stages, many people – and I've been one of them – do need some kind of help to open the barrier, and a safe and supportive environment in which to do so. But we don't need to worry about that: the strange part about the nature of wyrd, as we learn to trust it, is that when we really do need help, we'll find it *is* there – if only we can let ourselves see it!

THE 'TALL POPPY' SYNDROME

The silliness barrier, or rather the fear that it triggers, is one of the driving forces behind the nasty game of 'power-under' that we saw in the previous chapter. "If I can't ride a bicycle", the reasoning goes, "then *no-one* can: it's not possible. But if someone *did* learn to ride a bicycle, they'd have an advantage over me: so I'd better make damn sure that no-one ever does...". This fear-driven desire to drag everyone down to the lowest common denominator is endemic throughout the culture: in Australia it's known as the 'tall poppy syndrome', the aim being to cut anyone who might be successful down to the same uniform size – while in Britain it sometimes seems more like that the poppies never have a chance to get out of the ground in the first place! Some people make this 'levelling' a way of life, but we all do it from time to time: it always seems easier to cut someone down than to put in the time and effort to climb up to the same level of skill.

> I'd eventually managed to get the juggling to work – only three balls, of course, but I could keep it going for two or three minutes ☞

at a stretch. At this point I was practising every day: so when I had to wait a couple of hours at the airport for a change of planes, out came the balls from my pack. A nice quiet corner. Just getting into the rhythm of it. "Huh! That's not very good, is it?" says a sarcastic voice behind me. Middle-aged businessman; he didn't know how to juggle, and clearly didn't even want to try – "couldn't be bothered", he said, when I offered to show him how. But he was certainly going to be bothered enough to try to convince me that I couldn't – and *shouldn't* – be able to juggle either. . .

Can you recognise circumstances where others have done this to you? And where you have done this to others?

How do you feel – *feel* – about that now? And then let go those feelings, let go. . . things are the way they are because they got that way. What's important is not what happened in the past, but where you take that knowledge now.

And we discover that this *always* happens at some point in the early stages of learning a new skill. It's almost as if the uncertainty attracts it – the silliness-barrier in an *external* form. Weird. . .

And that's exactly what it is: patterns passing by on the threads of wyrd. So watch these patterns as you pass through them; as we do so, we build an increasing awareness of the strange nature of the workings of wyrd.

STRENGTHS AND WEAKNESSES

It's important to go into the anger and the other emotions that have been locked up in fighting ourselves: but it's also important to recognise that it's only an intermediate stage. It's like the concept of blame: only by recognising that we're *all* to blame for this mess, can we move on to accepting that no *one* is to blame – and then release blame entirely. In the same way, we need to accept the anger that's in us, entirely justifiable anger at the way we've been abused by everyone in this fear-driven culture – and then let it go, by recognising that we've done exactly the same to everyone else. We *all* do it: since it's a habit everywhere, it's very hard not to.

Understand this, and we begin to understand the meaning of the word 'compassion'. . .

We learn compassion for ourselves, too – the many different aspects of ourselves. The anger and emotions are not child*ish*, so much as child*like*: the energy and the clarity of the 'inner child'. That child has come a long way, has been through some good times and some very rough ones: but it's still there, wide-eyed, innocent, inquisitive, aware – by nature intuitively aware of the magic of wyrd.

Much of our power and passion come from that childlike state – it's one of our *strengths*, not a weakness. But the culture and our families have usually had very different ideas about what strengths and weaknesses are – usually to their advantage rather than ours. Their definition of *our* strengths and weaknesses is their opinion only – one which often says more about them than it does about us.

Take a brief inventory of what you think your strengths and weaknesses are. Be honest!

As you make the list, listen to the voice that comes with each item – especially with the weaknesses. If you've written that you get tired easily, for example, *who's telling you?* Your father? Mother? A teacher at school? Is it something that your parents always said about *themselves*? If it's not you that's 'speaking', put a query beside that item.

And look to see if others in the family have the same pattern – especially through the generations. You may feel you have the same quick temper as your mother and grandmother, for example: but it may well be something you've not so much inherited as learned to *copy* – nurture rather than nature. In any case, mark it with a query.

Then go through the list again. Take a closer look at each item you've marked with a query (hint: it's likely to be most of them!): consider carefully whether it really *is* a true strength or weakness of your own – or merely something you've learned, or been told so often that you've learned to believe it, whether it's true or not.

☞

It may seem to be true *now*, because it's become a habit: but is it actually part of that clustering of threads that is your deeper choice of *you*? Make changes to each item accordingly.

Review the list again: and note that it may be very different from the one with which you started. It's certainly likely to be a closer picture of who you truly are. . .

Slowly, we reclaim our *own* understanding of our strengths and weaknesses – re-own them as ours. We have certain strengths: so what? They're there to use. We have certain weaknesses: so what? They're there as challenges – something to *do* with our lives! Accept who you are: not someone else's attempt to mould you to their convenience, but who *you* are – "I am who I am". Nothing more, perhaps, but nothing less either.

To acknowledge this, perhaps it would be worthwhile to echo the chant of the cartoon character Popeye – "I yam what I yam!" And dance with the child within for a while. . .

6

AFFIRMATIVE ACTION

It was as children that we learnt many of the habits we now have. And the way we learnt them, in most cases, was through *repetition*. That's how we learnt to walk, to talk, to read, to ride a bicycle: "If at first you don't succeed, try, try and try again". But it's also how we learnt many of the habits that bind us: often in the form of derogatory statements repeated again and again by some authority-figure, like a form of brainwashing, until we eventually learn to believe them.

> An irate teacher at school: "You're stupid, Kelley, you shouldn't ask stupid questions: how many times do I have to tell you that? So – repeat after me – 'Chris Kelley is stupid'. Come on – say it! Louder, child, louder – I want the whole class to hear you!" I stand there, barely able to open my mouth, squirming in shame and embarrassment. . . she's the teacher, I don't have the right or the strength to fight back. And a thought runs through my mind: "If can I learn to be stupid, like she tells me I am, perhaps she won't make me do this again. . ."
>
> Do you recognise incidents like this in your own life? Can you see how easy – and how apparently *necessary* – it was to change your whole way of life, to avoid that kind of repeated pressure from others?

A statement like that may well tell us more about the person saying it than it does about us – a teacher abusing his authority in order to avoid answering awkward questions, for example – but once we've learnt to believe them, we *believe* them. The statement eventually becomes something that we believe at an unconscious level – a habit of thought, a habitual way of thinking about ourselves. From there, precisely because it *is* unconscious, it becomes a self-fulfilling prophecy: "What I tell you three times is *true*", as Lewis Carroll's Bellman put it in 'The Hunting of the Snark'. And then we're stuck with the results, for life – or until we can learn how to unlearn the habit.

It can take a long time to unlearn habits. . .

THE CURSE OF BELIEF

Belief is a peculiar kind of magic: a habit of thought, an idea that becomes real by filtering reality. With a different belief, we not only change our perception of the world, but our actual experience of it. I experience the world as I believe it to be: I find experiences that confirm the belief, and tend to ignore those that don't. It always seems easier to find 'proof' of destructive beliefs than of constructive ones, so a repeated statement like "You're stupid!" can soon create a downward spiral, a self-confirming curse – even though it was never actually true to begin with.

Once I've learnt to believe that I should be afraid, for example, I experience the world as if I'm afraid: I *become* afraid, and in return the world becomes a fearful place. And even though the fear is of something imaginary, of something that has never existed as more than an idea, the fear itself is *real*: the results are tangible, in terms of my ability – or inability – to work in the world. Through belief, the untrue becomes true; an illusion – a belief – somehow *becomes* reality.

One famous example was the 'toilet-paper shortage', a few years back. An American TV presenter suggested on his show that there was going to be a shortage of toilet-paper. People took his warning seriously; there was a surge of panic-buying, supermarket shelves were rapidly cleared as people built up reserve stocks. In a matter of days there wasn't a toilet-roll to be had. But in fact the whole thing had been an April Fool joke: at the ☞

---

time there'd been no real shortage at all, and now there really *was* one. The untrue becomes true; an illusion – a belief – somehow became reality.

Can you see the same kind of effect happening in your own life? What rumours – imagined beliefs – do you find yourself acting on? How do you know they really *are* true – or whether they're just self-confirming 'prophecies' that you've been caught by?

In that sense our world *is* an illusion. It's *everyone's* illusion: an interweaving web of beliefs, of filters on reality. If we want to change our world, to improve our world, we need at the very least to change how we see it, what we believe about it. But the only beliefs we can change directly are our own – and even then it's not easy. Those 'curses', those self-destructive beliefs that we were taught as children, will seem to block us at every step: at times they twist and turn against us, like a peculiarly evil and insidious form of magic.

Children believe in magic: the 'inner child' still does – with good reason, if you think of belief as magic.

That's the child's point of view – not child*ish*, but child*like*. So once again we let go... play with belief the child's way, and work with it as if it *is* magic. Yet magic is, well... weird. Wyrd... Yet knowing now something of the nature of wyrd – 'there's always a choice, there's always a twist' – we can use the magic of belief to overcome the tyranny of belief: we can *choose* to twist it into a new and more constructive tool. Repetition – this strange process of 'what I tell you three times is *true*' – is how we were taught the habits that now restrict us; so now, in its turn, we can use repetition to help us break free of them.

AN AFFIRMATIVE HABIT

One way to bring up these habits of thought, and rebuild them, is through 'affirmations' – repetitive statements of intent that tend to highlight our resistance to change. And there's a surprising amount of resistance...

An affirmation (or 'intention', 'postulate', 'manifestation', 'positive thought' – there are many different terms for much the same thing) is just another belief. The difference is that, unlike those destructive curse-beliefs, it's one that *we* choose – as a tool to help us – rather than imposed on us by someone else. An affirmation is an invented belief, repeated over and over again, just like the 'curses', and with the same intention of making the belief into another self-confirming prophecy. Once again, the untrue becomes true – but this time in a constructive rather than self-destructive sense.

To make an affirmation, we simply write out this new constructed belief: for example, "I, Chris, now have total confidence in my ability to do anything I want". We then stop for a moment; listen for a moment; then write down the objections that are likely to come flooding in!

The first of the objections that we're likely to hit is the silliness-barrier – and *hard*. Immediately, the whole thing seems ridiculous, childish, pointless – *silly*. Let alone those bitter memories of 'writing lines' as a punishment at school: "Kelley, write out one hundred times, 'I must not ask stupid questions in class'". . . So we acknowledge the barrier – work with it, work round it: yes, it *does* seem childish – it's *meant* to be, so as to be child*like*. Yes, the statement *isn't* true: I don't have confidence in my ability to do anything I want – but the whole idea is to learn how to *believe* it to be true, so that it has a chance to *become* true. Yes, it does sound ridiculously optimistic: but that's only because we're so used to being forced to be pessimistic. And so on; and so on.

Let go. . . let play. . . let the magic of belief break the tyranny of belief. . .

There are so many beliefs that cripple us, it's difficult to know where to begin! But try taking a repeated experience that the world seems to confirm as 'true' – for example, "I never get any credit for what I do" – and view it as if it was the result of a

☞

---

self-destructive belief that you hold at an unconscious level: "I don't deserve credit for what I do". Imagine that it's a belief you've learnt, or been taught, through constant repetition or constant example – which you may even know to have been the case. To counteract it, turn this belief around – "I do deserve credit for what I do" – and repeat it to yourself. Often! After all, the destructive belief was repeated to you often enough. . .

To make this an affirmation, put yourself into this new belief: "I, ___, deserve credit for what I do". (And sometimes in the second- and third-person forms – "You, ___, deserve credit for what you do" and "___ deserves credit for what he/she does" – because that's how the old belief was given to you.) Write out this statement on a piece of paper; as you write it, affirm it to yourself as being *true* – say it aloud, perhaps, put some emotion into it. Then wait for a moment. See what objections come up – "People don't like me, that's why I don't deserve credit" – and write those down under the affirmation, slightly to one side. Then write the affirmation again; then the objections. Repeat this sequence at least a dozen times.

Listen carefully to the objections – can you sometimes hear someone else's voice saying them – the person whose belief it was in the first place? And can you see how bizarre and unreal some of the objections turn out to be?

Let go. . . let play. . .

It *is* important to regard this as play – which, to the child, is its real work. It's a good idea to treat the whole process like a piece of magic, as a piece of ritual – buy a new book to write these affirmations in, use your best pen, write in a quiet space, perhaps light a candle first. . . It's the 'inner child' we're working with here, so we appeal to the childlike nature of the child within us!

The usual recommendation is to do this with only *one* affirmation at a time, twice a day, for at least two or three weeks. (If that seems a lengthy process, remember that it's quick by comparison with the months and years of repetition through which we first learned each 'curse' that restricts us now.) It *does* work – though, as is typical with wyrd, not often in the way that we expect. . .

What we *can* expect, at the very least, is change: if nothing else, affirmations can be a good way of breaking 'stuckness' in our lives.

It seems to be important to *write* these phrases and responses: speaking them, even aloud, does not seem to be enough. Perhaps writing is a way of driving the new beliefs into memory, driving them back into our deepest self, in much the same way as it's usually easier to remember a lecture from written notes even than from a tape-recording. I don't know: all we know is that it *is* so. Part of the magic, I presume.

Watch how the resistance arises – our *own* resistance to our actually living our life your own way. "It can't work", for example; "I don't deserve that, that would be too good", perhaps; or "It doesn't happen anyway, and I can't see how it could be possible, so it can't be possible". Again and again we'll find it breaks down to a simple statement, a simple belief: "It's not allowed for me to be *me*". But if that's so, how come other people are allowed to do what *they* want in life? That's worth looking at for a while.

Take one of your resistances that comes up regularly – "I don't deserve to be happy", for example – and apply the same process as for affirmations, but in reverse. Write out that statement in the same way as an affirmation – and then note the (more conscious) objections that come up to the statement. Wear down the resistance by showing, slowly, that it's absurd. "If I don't deserve happiness and affection, how come other people do deserve it?" "In which case, what is there that's so specially different about me that means I alone don't deserve to be happy?" And so on.

Can you see that the resistance is, in essence, a belief? One that is actively harmful to you? And one which, in all probability, you've been taught – for someone else's benefit, not your own?

Work at it for a while. You may even begin to see where you learnt the habit, and why: "I mustn't be happy because my big sister hits me if I show I'm happy", for example. Habits learnt

---

> very early, beliefs that are usually no longer relevant, but which we all still act on now. . .

One reason why it's useful to look at the resistances in this backwards way is that most of us look at the negative side, the weaknesses, first – and believe them. There's often a strong cultural pressure to do so: being positive or optimistic is considered egotistical, or naïve, or both. It's not acceptable, not *done*, to accept ourselves as we are: we're soon made to feel pretty uncomfortable if we don't put ourselves down – as we saw earlier with the example of the bullying teacher.

But just remember: 'Whose life is it, anyway?'. It's *your* life: it's your right to reclaim power with your life. And this is one way to do it – to put new changes, new beliefs, into action.

INTO ACTION

Think of this as affirmative action – but there also needs to be an emphasis on *action*. If we only write the new beliefs out as affirmations, and then just sit on our backsides, waiting for things to happen by themselves, we're believing in the wrong kind of magic. . . What we're doing with the affirmation, in effect, is lifting a thread of wyrd to the surface, to look at it and see how we've usually pushed it away from our lives. But that, on its own, changes nothing. We also have to find a way to *connect* with that new thread: having written "I now have confidence in my ability", for example, I have to go out into the weirdness of the world and *find* that new confidence, find our connection with it. Let ourselves find it – or perhaps let it find *us*.

So go looking – but without looking. Try to find it – but without trying. It does take a bit of practice. . .

> An affirmation itself is no more than a game with beliefs, a 'head-trip': to be useful, it needs to be grounded, brought into connection with the version of reality we share with everyone else. So having written out a series of affirmations, do something ☞

to 'earth' it, to honour and affirm the change in your intention. Almost anything will do: but do *something*. Put yourself in a different place or different situation for a change. Don't bother trying to *think* through what the best response would be – just follow a whim, an impulse. The wyrd thrives on *difference*, not sameness. . . thinking, on its own, will only give us 'more of the same'.

And then watch what happens: see what Reality Department gives you back. Watch the feelings, the emotions, the uncertainties that arise as you do these 'active affirmations': think of these as resistances, just like those that came up on paper as you wrote. What do these tell you?

Sometimes deciding what to do to act on an affirmation is a bit like looking for a dim star at night – it's not as simple as it seems. For a start, we sometimes have to put ourselves in a different environment: in the glare of the street lights of the city, it's hard to see *anything* of the sky at night, let alone a barely-visible star. If we don't do anything, if we don't try – don't even bother to stick your head out of the door – we'll never see the star: the chance will simply pass us by. Yet if we do look in the obvious way, straight at it, it disappears – and the harder we look for it, the *more* it disappears. The trick to seeing it is to look away slightly, to look not *at* it, but *near* it – look at it without looking at it – and let *it* come to *us*. It's much the same putting these affirmations into action: we have to do something, but somehow let the results come to *us*.

One way in which the results may come to us is not at all what we'd expect: namely in the form of some incident that acts like a test, a challenge. For example, if your affirmation was "I now have confidence in my ability", you might hope for people turning round and telling you how wonderful you are: but don't be surprised if, instead, some stranger comes up with *exactly* the same kind of derogatory remark that put you down in the first place. It's a test, a challenge: and you'll notice, by your reactions, just how much you've allowed your beliefs to change. . .

It's weird – but that's how it works, that's how it is. That, after all, is the nature of wyrd!

After a while working with affirmations, we can begin to see some changes – some of the old, evidently self-destructive patterns begin to weaken, until they're nothing like as compulsive as they were. For example, I recognised that I'd always viewed being on my own as a punishment – "Go to your room!", my parents would say – which had led me to cling on to others, especially parent-figures, to prove that I wasn't considered 'bad'. . . and kept doing this compulsively well into adulthood. Recognising this as an old fear, I turned it round and made it into an affirmation, "The more I, Chris, enjoy being on my own, the more I can enjoy being with others", and worked with it each evening for a while. It wasn't until about a month later that I noticed I wasn't going out much in the old compulsive "Got to see someone or I'll go crazy!" mode any more; instead, without my particularly doing anything to make it happen, people were coming to see *me*. In fact I was getting annoyed that I didn't seem to have enough time on my own. . .

The point was that I'd *always* needed time on my own – but I wasn't allowing myself to get it, because I was afraid of it, of what alone-ness symbolised. But the wyrd knew what I needed, so to speak. . . so it's given me enforced periods of loneliness many times in my life! One way or another we always get what we need: but it may not be in the form that we want. . . With the weirdness of wyrd, there's always a choice, but there's also always a twist.

More accurately, the wyrd seems to give us always what we *say* we want – which may not be what we *think* we want. As long as we're stuck in habit, and in unawareness of our needs and of what we're asking for, we can hardly complain about what the wyrd ends up giving us – if I outwardly say I want company, but am inwardly screaming for time on my own, it's hardly surprising that the results in my life are a mess!

So to give those affirmations something on which to work, and to help the web of wyrd to give us a more worthwhile way of living, we need next to gain more clarity about our wants and needs, desires and intentions – and the subtle distinctions between them.

7

WANTS AND NEEDS

What do you want? What do you want out of life? What do you want *now*? Do you know?

If you do, you're doing well. . .

And what do you need right now? Do you recognise any difference between wants and needs?

If you do, you're doing well. . .

Most of us live in what is known as a consumer-society. The whole point of such a society is to encourage us to consume – consume food, resources, time, anything – as much as possible. The more we consume, the more we are considered to be successful: the true mark of success is 'conspicuous consumption'. Everywhere we go, and in almost everything we see, there's another message of 'consume! consume!': whatever we want, we ought to have it, we *should* have it. If we have enough money, of course. Otherwise, we can want all we like, but we can't have it – whether we need it or not.

It's a weird way to run a world. . . but it's the one that we have, so we'd best find a way to deal with it!

WHAT DO YOU WANT?

It's not easy to make a distinction between want and need: from what we learn in this culture, they seem at first to be the same. But it is important to us to be able to use the two terms to describe different expressions of the power we're reclaiming from within us.

Wants and needs are different. Yet both are somehow undefinable: it's difficult to pin either term down. We can see that they have different priorities – need usually seems more important than want, somehow – but it's confused, confusing. And to add to the confusion, the two words have become part of the weaponry in the old game of power-under that we saw earlier: "I *need* this, whereas you only *want* that, so I *should* have priority over you. . ."

"I don't care what you want, I need you to do this!" How often has someone said that to you? And how often have you said it to someone else?

Think of some examples. What was the distinction between 'want' and 'need'? And how much was the power-under game being played in each case?

The dictionary isn't much help, either: according to one, need is 'that which is necessary', whilst want is 'something needed'. . . About the only distinction given is that need 'arises from the facts and circumstances of the case', whereas a want is more 'something the *absence* of which is *not* desired' – an odd way of putting it. With all the confusion, it's probably best to invent an arbitrary distinction of our own: so we might say that 'a want is *the outward expression of an inner need*'. And whilst the needs themselves come from a variety of levels within us – needs of the body, the heart, the mind, the soul – they're all expressed outwardly as things or actions that we *want*.

We need food, shelter; we need to love and be loved; we need things to make sense, to have meaning; we need to have purpose and a sense of fullness. These are all real needs: to survive, we somehow *have* to service them. If we don't, we die – or at best we exist rather than *live*. An unserviced need comes back again and again: it demands our attention. And that demand for attention is expressed outwardly as an ever-changing stream of wants.

But if I don't know my inner world enough to know what the true need is, I'll have no way of understanding what my wants are

54

about. All I know is that I want *this*; then I want *that*; then I want something else – with no connection, with no apparent rhyme or reason.

There always is a connection between the inner need, and what we find ourselves wanting: but it's often neither obvious nor literal. Instead, it usually comes through the weird dream-like form of metaphor. For example, my child-like self, for a moment, needs mothering: and to me it might be expressed, in metaphor, as a desire for the sweet taste of mother's milk. But since I fail to grasp that it *is* a metaphor, I take the message literally, and find myself wanting something sweet and sugary and liquid – a can of Coke, for example. Which doesn't service my underlying need, of course. . .

> These unserviced needs easily and quickly become unconscious habits – ones that are anything *but* easy to recognise or to stop. When I'm lonely, for example, I tend to go out shopping – looking for some external 'thing' as a token to prop up my sense of self. Or if I'm depressed, for example, or avoiding doing some boring task – 'wanting Mummy to do it for me', in other words – I start eating. A compulsion to eat, and eat. . . food as a metaphor for sweetness, as a metaphor for mothering!
>
> Do you recognise within you any compulsive habits of this kind? Can you see the metaphor – different for each of us – that points to the actual need in any of them?

These too-literal habits don't satisfy my inner needs, though they *do* service the underlying drive of the consumer-society. . . because the message comes back again and again from that inner need, until the next transitory need comes by. All I can see is the outward form: I want, I want, I want. . . a sense of being driven, out of control, addicted. . .

WE ALL WANT MORE MONEY

These habits become the compulsive substitute for servicing a need – each habit backed by all the force the commercial world can bring to bear on it. As soon as we find ourselves wanting something – in other words responding to a present need – all the old unsatisfied ones pop up again and get in the way. In the clamour and confusion, the present need is unlikely to be satisfied, since it will almost certainly be given something it doesn't actually need – which then leads, of course, to another want. Under these circumstances, it's hard work to bring any habit under conscious direction. It always seems much easier to rely on some external factor to discipline the wants – and we then complain, of course, that it does so!

In the consumer society, the primary limiting factor is *money*. We always want more money: ask anyone what they want most, and it's likely the first answer you'll be given is 'money'. "If only I could win the lottery, I'd. . ." Sadly, it doesn't work: in our culture it's all too true that needs do arise from the absence of money – 'a want is something the absence of which is not desired' – but the presence of money, by itself, rarely solves anything at all. 'More money' doesn't serve our true inner needs, but just gets swallowed up in more and more wants – the same pointless process as before, but on a larger scale.

In principle, every monetary transaction could be replaced by the phrase "What do you need?" – a simple process of trust, of honesty. But only in principle – it seems highly unlikely in practice!

But why? What are the fears that prevent us from reaching that level of simplicity? Can you recognise some of those fears within yourself? Look for a while at the distortions that a money-based economy creates: for example, that the closer we get to tangible work, the less we get paid – the extreme of which is the unpaid work of mothers. . . can this really be said to make sense?

Look around you, at the reality of this black joke we live in: the old communard slogan, "From each according to ability, to each according to their need", has become twisted by a world-full of 'between-takers' – the literal meaning of 'entrepreneur' – into the cynical "From each according to facility, to each according to their greed"... It's clear that no-one, individually, is to blame, yet it seems there's no other way to do things: like it or not, we're *all* tied in to supporting this mess. And even if we want to opt out, we can't: we're trapped in it – "There's a hole in my bucket, dear Liza, dear Liza..."

But we've heard that before: the answer would seem, then, to be to look at the *whole* in the bucket, to look *inside*, through the threads of wyrd, to reach a saner connection with the whole.

WHAT DO YOU NEED?

Within the culture in which we live, we're trapped by our wants: whatever we have, we'll always want more. As in the power-under game, our own energy gets turned against us, re-woven into a web that enmeshes us all. And as in that game, we break free not by fighting against it, but going deeper *into* it – deeper into ourselves, to find our own part of the game.

We want something; money seems to allow us to get it. So we all want more money – but what do we want it *for*? What's the underlying *need*? Could we serve those needs without this never-ending stream of material things? Remember that what we seem to want is often a *metaphor* of what we need – especially if the need itself is of the heart, the mind, the soul. So when we find ourselves in a new compulsive habit, it usually means that we're failing to grasp what we're being told from within: if so, it's time to look a little deeper, into the threads of wyrd within us.

> Talking this through with a friend, she admitted to owning a sizeable collection of negligées – not one of which she'd ever worn. "I keep on buying them", she said. "I know it's because I want someone to tell me I look beautiful, and sexy, and exciting. But they never have – perhaps because I've never had the nerve to wear one...!" We all need to be loved, admired: but often the need is better served by loving and admiring *ourselves*, rather

than by rushing from shop to shop, trying to find something that money can't buy. . .

If you find yourself wanting something compulsively – a new car, for example – look closer at the need behind it. What does the car *represent* – a need for recognition, perhaps? Look deeper: look into the weird twists through which your true needs make themselves known.

When we want something, it's an outward expression of an inner need. When the need is physical, there is usually little difficulty in connecting need, want and action: if I'm hungry, I look for food. I eat. No problem. But we have other needs too: and that's where the problems start.

Consider all those different needs: not just of the body, but the desires of the heart, the will, the passion of the soul. Think about the many ways they combine: body and mind as the need for recognition; body and heart in the need for touch, for pleasure; mind and soul, in the need for validation, for meaning, the sense that "I've done something useful with my life". These are all *needs*. They are part of us all; on the threads of wyrd, they pass through us all.

The problem is that to a large extent we can express these needs only as outward wants, as things we can act on – something in the physical, tangible, shared reality. We can't act on a metaphor: I can't eat my words, though I've often tried. . . A metaphor has to be deciphered, translated into appropriate action. If we don't decipher it correctly, we get into a crazy loop of cravings, doing the wrong thing again and again. If I'm lonely, I eat, and eat, and eat, because I'm hungry for company; someone else might not eat at all, though, because *their* metaphor is that they're starving for company. And as the old song goes, "Money can't buy me love". . . certainly not on my income, at any rate!

WHAT DO YOU WANT FROM ME?

The real problem is that we're used to relying on *others* to service our needs. Again, we learned this as children – partly because, as children, we had no choice in the matter. We *had* to have support then, or die: a child, perhaps even an adolescent, cannot really care for itself, let alone a baby. But it takes a deep awareness to be able to support another person's needs, even those of a child.

The simple, literal, physical needs of food, warmth, shelter, most people can manage to supply; but beyond that, at the deeper levels of emotion, mind, spirit – especially emotion – it's a sad fact that few people can cope. I remember seeing an American report, for example, that said something like 90% of all US families could be considered toxic, in the sense of being inadequately supportive, or even outright destructive, at the emotional level. In this culture, most people have too many troubles and emotional needs of their own, to be able to support even a baby fully – let alone anyone else. We rarely get what we *need*: in fact, if we're not careful, we end up – even as children – living to service other people's wants.

For me, there's a painful personal example: setting myself up as scapegoat at school, from childhood right through to adolescence. Well, the other children wanted someone on whom to take out their frustration, didn't they? For whatever reason, it seemed natural for me to take on that rôle: but I've been learning how to recover from it ever since. . . And the main reason I was sent to that school, I'm told, is because my grandfather demanded of my parents that 'your children should follow the family tradition'. . .

Many parents act out their wants by trying to live vicariously through their children. A son is told that he must 'follow in his father's footsteps'; a daughter is forced into a career she doesn't want in order to 'raise the family status' – or perhaps prevented from going to college "because you ought to be a good wife and mother". You wouldn't be offered a choice in the matter – you'd be told you *must* want it, you *should* want it, it's 'expected of you'.

Did this happen to you? Is your career or life-path one that you chose, or was it chosen for you? Is it what *you* want – or what

---

someone else wanted, what someone else taught you to want?
And is it what you want now?

We end up being focused outward – either trying to live for others, through others, or both. And often with no idea of our *own* needs at all. This just doesn't work: other people aren't necessarily very good, or even capable, of servicing our needs, and often don't know what *they* want, either. Yet in many senses it's dangerous not to know what we truly want – dangerous for everyone concerned!

Some needs always seem to have to be focused outward. The quest for love, for example, is what gets us most into all this mess. We all need to be loved. As children we have to look to others for love – even though they're rarely much good at giving it. . . When that love we need is not forthcoming, we devise all sorts of methods to gain a little bit of attention instead – "Look at *me*, Daddy, I'm here!" (or "Look, Mummy, I've fallen downstairs". . .) – in the hope that it might attract some love.

It doesn't work. Love comes in the moment, from the heart. . . it can't be given on demand. But attention – physical action – can: and demands no emotional commitment from the giver. So attention becomes confused with love – an unsuccessful substitute for love, since attention alone doesn't service the need. Yet in time the childhood habit sticks – we cry out for attention whenever we feel a need to be loved.

In many countries you'll see what one friend sarcastically refers to as "pick-up trucks with hormone trouble" – small utility trucks with big tyres, big sound systems, expensive paint jobs. . . That desperate need to show off. . . Look closer, and you can see the thought behind it: "Look at me! Look at me! If the girls notice my truck, they might notice me, and perhaps I can *make* them love me. . . But I have to get in there before everyone else. . . So look at my car. . . look at *me*!"

What do you do to get attention – particularly in relationships?

☞

> Does it actually get you what you want? Or does it only, by the usual weird twists, get you the *wrong* kind of attention?

Another habit to unlearn. . . About the only way to do that is to break free from the senses-taker and watch closely – watch how we act, watch to see whether what we get back is what we truly want.

And just in the process of watching, things change. By being conscious about our choices, about what we do – but without appearing to change them – the results change. On their own, apparently. It's weird, but that's the way it works. . . just watch, watch. . .

WHAT DO YOU NEED FROM YOU?

If we rely on others to give us what we need, we're trapped: being dependent on others makes us an easy mark for the power-under game. But in a sense, if we rely on others, we cannot afford to let *them* be free either: we have to trap them, to tie them to us so they'll always be there to give us what we need – or what we think we need. Our neediness drives us into 'co-dependent' relationships, where each party is acting out the other's expectations: and that can include all kinds of abuse if attention has become confused with the love we crave. All too often, as John Bradshaw put it, we don't have relationships, we take hostages. . .

That's behaviour we've carried over from childhood. But as adults we do have the option to no longer rely on others: we can learn to give *ourselves* what we need. Since we cannot rely on others to love us – it's not that they won't do so, but that they can't – we have to learn to love ourselves.

> We can use the twisted sense of wyrd to help in this: whatever I'm asking others for, especially at an emotional level, is likely to be a reflection of some way I'm not loving myself. For example, if I find myself angrily thinking "I need more respect from others",

what I'm actually saying is that I don't respect *myself* – which is probably why they don't respect me!

Do you recognise how this happens in your life? Try turning these thoughts round in an affirmation – "I, ___, now truly respect myself and my abilities", for example, or "The more I, ___, respect myself, the more others respect me" – and watch how the resistances come up, showing how you've learnt not to love yourself! How do you turn these resistances round?

This isn't easy. And often it *hurts*. . . Giving to others is easy; taking is even easier, since what you're doing is giving the absence of something in return to what you've been given. But giving to ourselves means not giving out, but giving *in* – a form of surrender. And that's risky. . . frightening. . .

It'd be so much easier if we could always get others to give us what we need – but it doesn't work. We can't rely on it: and when we need love, for example, we *need* it. Since the only person who'll always be with me is me, the only person I can rely on loving me is me. Accepting myself, loving the whole of who and what I am – "I am what I am!" – gives me freedom of choice, gives me the power to be *me*. It gives me the choice to be independent, yet interdependent, as and how I choose.

But don't expect others to like it! If we've been caught up in a relationship with family, partner or business colleagues, that's co-dependent – and in this culture most are to some extent – they are not going to want us to break free. They *need* us to be dependent, so they can depend on us: they dare not let us have any choice in the matter. For a while, we're likely to find every weapon in the power-under game being thrown at us: we'll be accused of cruelty, treachery – "How could you do this just when we need you?" – selfishness, stupidity and almost anything we'd care not to name. It can hurt, and hurt a lot, but wait it out: use it as an excuse to look deeper into what *we* need, rather than what others want from us. Take it, perhaps, as the wyrd's way of showing us that we're on the right track in finding our own path through its web?

"I'M A SUBSTITUTE FOR ANOTHER GUY. . ."

Much of this weird behaviour comes from the fact that we're usually trying to borrow other people to substitute for old unsatisfied needs. Time after time, for example, I'll find I'm relating to some man not as himself but as a 'Daddy-substitute' – which at some level he'll *know*, and won't be pleased about at all. . . But we all do it: as one writer put it, it's as though we're running around with great armfuls of masks and costumes, asking every passing stranger "Put this on for me! I want to see if it fits!" – with each mask or costume representing the expected supplier of some old and probably long-forgotten need. It's usually unconscious, but it's there, all the time. Again, a weird way of running a world. . .

What's embarrassing is that so many of these needs are amazingly trivial. A need for approval, for an ego boost to get over self-doubt, in some minor incident in early childhood: "Daddy, look at me!" But Daddy didn't look – for perfectly good reasons! – and I've been looking for approval ever since, from every person I can hand the 'Daddy' mask-and-costume set to. . . asking them to be 'a substitute for another guy', as the old Who song puts it. Crazy! But there are hundreds or thousands of these old 'lost wants': and all of them firmly rammed down into the unconscious layer precisely *because* they're so 'silly'.

Perhaps it's traceable back to that "Oh damn the child – Chris's got it right again!": but after all these years I still seem to spend an inordinate amount of time trying to get approval from others for my ideas. If they don't even respond, I can be depressed for days. I *know* it's silly, I know it *shouldn't* affect me: but it does. Every time. . .

Do you recognise a repeated pattern like this of your own? Does it seem childish, silly? What do you do about it – pretend it's not there, for example?

Silly or not, they're still very firmly there – and they crawl out of the woodwork, demanding my energy and attention, every time I want anything now. And there's often no way I can get the person I originally wanted to service them to do so: I'm many years older, and many of the people concerned are either dead or thousands of miles away. Yet if I can trace back to the original need and *consciously* satisfy it – *consciously* provide a substitute – the pressure, the driving urgency, just evaporates. Gone. It's an amazing sense of relief. . .

It's also not easy, because of our old friend, the silliness-barrier. Finding a conscious substitute for an old childhood want often means consciously being childish – which is usually one of the things we most fear. Giving out is easy, taking is even easier; but receiving, especially from ourselves, means giving *in*. Surrender. And that's not easy at all. But that's often what we most need to do. Learn to play again. . .

In this bewretchedly serious world, when did you last allow yourself to be childlike? To skip down the street? Build a sandcastle? Read a children's story? Curl up with a teddy-bear – your *own* teddy-bear?

If you haven't done so for a long while, do it. Face the silliness-barrier, and do it anyway. Treat playing as a kind of affirmation, giving the play as a conscious gift to the child within you – and as with affirmations, watch your resistance to letting go! What happens? What memories and resistances come up?

Most of us need a safe space, or safe company, with whom to let go. Being with children is often the most popular excuse. Think of the absurd things people say to babies – how many other times will you hear serious adults talking absolute nonsense in public! But it's easy for this to become a new way of trapping others into living for us – remember the infamous "it's a model train set for my son, honest. . ."? Instead, we do it consciously, as a way of giving to *ourselves* – then if others want to join in, that's fine.

It's interesting – weird – to see how others *do* want to join in. . . but someone has to take the risk, and be the first to play. It does take courage – no-one is any too keen to be thought of as weird in the wrong sense. . .

Another weirdness is that while the "wear this mask for me" substitute game creates all sorts of problems when it's unconscious, it's quite a different matter when it's done consciously, with awareness.

Many forms of therapy are based on this experience – especially as they provide a safe space for doing so. By exchanging masks – often literally a mask – deliberately with someone else, we not only get a chance to uncover and release old needs, but also to see who the other person truly is, behind the masks we give them.

For most work like this you need a partner, and usually some direction; but some you can do on your own, with *yourself* as your partner. Make or buy a few masks, showing different characters – there's a beautiful Victorian set available at the moment, for example. Try some on: pick out one that seems to be *you* at the moment. Look at yourself in this mask in the mirror. What does this character – this you – want from you? What do you want from the person behind this mask? What do you feel? What memories of old needs does this bring up?

Consciously using – rather than unconsciously abusing – other people as 'substitutes' to release old needs can be an enlivening and empowering experience for everyone concerned: one that really can ease the confusion, and get closer to the aim of a better world for us all.

TAKE AIM. . .

Wants hit us in the moment – and as far as possible it helps to respond to them in the moment. (If we try to push them away – "not *now*!" – they have a nasty tendency to hang around forever, as another hard-to-get-rid-of habit.) But it's also important to build some kind of clear longer-term aim: "It's dangerous not to know what you truly want. . .". By now we can recognise that externally-defined aims like 'more money', 'a bigger car' – or even 'a better partner' – are unlikely to be useful: we can't rely on others, or things external, to give us what we need. An aim has to be centred, grounded, in who *we* are.

> A comment: "What is your aim in life?" is rarely an easy question to answer – most of us spend our lives trying to find out! But do you have any sense of direction, any pointers – especially once you detach from aims given to you by others? What would you choose? And how would you know you're on the right track?

Once again the nature of wyrd complicates the issue: there's always a choice, but there's always a twist. Whatever track we think we're taking, it always twists and turns. Very often we find that a step that fits the logic of what we're doing doesn't work; whilst an apparently backward step turns out to be the best thing we could do. It's never easy to make sense of it.

But perhaps it's best not to try to make it make sense. It doesn't: so don't worry. What we *can* do is work by the feel of it: act, follow what seem to be our needs, our wants – and then see what we get, see what the wyrd gives us. What it gives us is what we *actually* ask for, not what we think we ask for: it's up to us to notice the difference, and change what we ask for accordingly. It's a strange juggling act. . .

When our wants and needs mis-align – such as when we've interpreted a need's metaphor too literally – we get stuck in childishness. We run around looking for attention – overgrown children in fancy dress or fancy cars – when what we really need is love. Especially self-love, self-acceptance: and that's hard, because once again it requires us to give *in*, to surrender to ourselves, without needing to rely on anyone else at all.

There's a magic moment, a real sense of power, when all our needs align: body, heart, mind and soul, all leading to action. It works: in that moment, there's no doubt about it. But it requires that we respond *in the moment*, responding in a way that is not childish but child*like*, trusting that whatever we want in that moment is right. And to get there we have to reach past the silliness barrier, past the social ostracism that would describe us as 'weird', and move to a state of 'fool-hardi-ness' that is not out of control, but somehow beyond the need for control – a different state entirely.

But that childlike-yet-not-childish state is in some ways the opposite of the casual ease of the child. It demands from us vast resources of courage, of fearlessness, of self-awareness – simply to let go. In reaching to reclaim our own power, releasing our need to control may be the hardest lesson yet.

8

CONTROL AND OTHER MYTHS

We all crave for control – control over our lives, a control that would give us certainty over what happens to us in our lives. And we want it, and want it, often desperately.

A pity, then, that it does not, and cannot, exist.

Control is a myth. An illusion. A pleasant-seeming illusion, a highly desirable illusion – but an illusion nonetheless.

Control, if it existed, would be a state of absolute certainty, absolute predictability. But no such thing exists: there is no shortage of proof of that as a fact, from the esoteric uncertainties of quantum physics, the bizarre twists of chaos mathematics, or the mundane realities of Murphy's Law. We can often create an illusion of control – control in technology, control in politics, control in our own lives – but we can do so only by narrowing down the range of possibilities in a way that becomes further and further separated from reality. And even if we do manage to build that illusion so well that others believe it as strongly as we'd like to do, there's always some random weirdness that will break it down – more often sooner than later. The semblance of control is rarely more than a *belief* that we're in control – wishful thinking rather than reality.

> Are you truly in control of your life – in the sense that you could and did predict everything that has happened and will happen to you? If not, who *is* in control?
> If you'd say 'others', such as parents or politicians or abstract
>
> ☞

entities like multinational corporations, look more closely: do the people involved actually have absolute certainty about what will happen? Do they really have control over *their* lives?

If not, who is in control of *anything*? Who or what is actually in control?

The feeling that *no-one* is in control is frightening. The desire for there to be *someone* who's in control – since clearly we aren't – often leads us to search for certainties in religion. But even this doesn't give us what we crave: we'd be told, for example, that "even the Will of God may be perverted by the machinations of the Adversary in the hearts of men" – which translates into normal language as 'there always will be uncertainties'. According to the Norse tradition, even the gods were subject to the twists and turns of their fate, the results of their choices in the web of wyrd. There's no escaping Fate; there's no escaping uncertainty.

Control is either absolute, or nothing: if it's not absolute, it's not control. But reality is infinitely complex, and infinitely sensitive to its infinite conditions: absolute control would require us to control everything, everywhere and everywhen, past, present and future. So control is impossible: a myth, a joke. To seek for control is to seek for an illusion – an illusion for which most of us, unfortunately, spend most of our lives striving to achieve.

We cannot control: though with awareness we can *direct* what happens to us – the distinction is subtle, but very important! But before we can reach that way of relating to reality – one that accepts it for what it is – we first have to let go of the desperate need for control. And to do that, we first have to understand why that need is there in the first place.

FEAR IS A FOUR-LETTER WORD

There's a simple, one-word reason: *fear*. Lots of it. So much fear that we'll often deny it exists at all. . .

Fear focusses our attention on anywhere, anywhen *other* than the here-and-now. Fear, in effect, is another form of belief: that something we *don't* want is at risk of happening. The more we don't want it, and the more uncertainty about the when, the where and the likelihood of its happening, the more afraid we're likely to get. And the more afraid we get, the more we think it's likely to happen – in fact, the more likely it *is* to happen, because of the self-confirming nature of belief.

That desirable myth of control seems to offer a way out: "I'll damn well *make sure* that it can't happen!" So we build walls, restrictions, limitations on reality. But since control *is* only an illusion, we have to build more walls to protect us from seeing that those walls are only illusory, and then walls within walls within walls – until we forget what it was we were afraid of in the first place.

> When you find yourself controlling – for example, minutely planning every detail of some future event – what are you afraid is going to happen? What are the controls for?
>
> When you get to that event – if it happened at all – did it happen the way you planned, the way you expected? What was different? How come you hadn't allowed for the difference?
>
> Take a specific example – either your own or, if you don't want to face that, someone else's – and look at the fears that drive the need for control. How far down do you have to go to reach the fear at the root of it all?

All that we're left with is the certainty that we *have* to control – and we're usually careful never to wonder *why*, because that might mean that we'd have to face that well-defended original fear all over again.

The core fear will usually turn out to be some central self-doubt, a 'curse' that someone else has taught us to believe, as we saw earlier. And – for all our controlling – until we do face that fear, the fear is controlling *us*. If we're not aware, everything we do can be driven or distorted by a handful of long-forgotten fears... definitely weird!

In the other extreme, we can use fear as a *substitute* for control: we can use fear itself as an excuse for avoiding fears, avoiding facing up to real issues in Reality Department. Instead of trying to impose our internal point of view on the world, we hide until the issue finally comes up – is imposed on us by *external* events – and are then forced into 'panic mode' in order to deal with it. This may get the job done, but it's hardly efficient. . . And we might spend so much of our energy avoiding the issue – looking again and again at the washing-up we don't want to do, for example – that it can be said to be controlling our lives.

> I hated doing my accounts. I'd do anything to avoid them. They'd sit and fester – a puddle of unchecked invoices – for months. Until tax-time came – then all hell broke loose! Panic! Everything stopped: it's gotta be done *now!* It would have been a whole lot simpler if I'd spent a little effort over the months keeping everything tidy, everything under control. But I didn't: I relied on the vastly magnified fear at the time instead to control *me*, since I didn't want to 'control' myself. And perhaps also because, ultimately, I was afraid of the metaphor of being 'called to account' for my life as a whole. . .
>
> What issues do you find yourself dealing with only in panic-mode? Can you identify the core fear behind the evasion in each case?

For a long while I ran my life like that, in a permanent state of panic, and using a vast intake of coffee – 'liquid fear' – to keep me going. Another hard habit to break! In part it can be a peculiar kind of laziness: a colleague, perhaps unkindly but accurately, once commented "You're just a bag of flab held together by fears – the moment you drop control, you collapse in a heap on the floor. . .". But the root *is* always fear: fear of failure, even fear of success. And behind those fears will be some kind of curse-belief like those we saw earlier: most of which break down to the belief that "I'm not allowed to be me".

Control comes from the opposite direction: because we're afraid, we want to make sure that others are not allowed to be themselves, or that reality is not allowed to be as it is. We want to disempower them, to create the illusion of being powerful ourselves. We want power over them; if we can't have that, we'll play the power-under game as hard as we can. There's an old saying that "Where there is fear, there is power; where there is power, there is fear": power and control may be what we see at the surface, but fear – a seething morass of fear – is what lies beneath it all. Until we face those fears, *no-one* can be truly powerful: none of us can reclaim the power of choice with our lives. To move on, we need to re-define our understanding of power.

I WANT TO BE POWERFUL

When there's so much fear that we deny it exists at all, we'll usually call it 'power' instead. The drive for power – or rather, the 'disempowerment of others' that we *think* of as power – is inextricably interwoven with the need for control. To be powerful in this sense, it seems, is to be 'in control' – we feel certain of having our needs met, whatever they might be. Power seems to give us the ability to control, to have power over events: and the more powerful we are, the more we're in control. We're told that power even makes people love us: "power is the ultimate aphrodisiac". To be powerful is to be called a *success*. If I'm powerful, I can do whatever I want: and woe betide anyone who gets in my way.

And I *feel* powerful: "Nothing and no-one can stop me now!"

The opposite, to be 'out of control', or subject to someone else's control, is to be powerless. I'm told I'm a *failure*: I *feel* I'm a failure; I feel shame, embarrassment, futility – all of which reinforces the feeling of failure. If I'm powerless, I'm at the uncertain mercy of someone else's power: I have no guarantees whatever of having my needs met. And that's frightening. I'll do anything I can to prevent that. . .

It's not surprising, then, that we all want to be powerful. We'll fight each other – to the death, if necessary – to become powerful. Or we'll manoeuvre, lie, cheat, cajole, manipulate, *anything*, to prevent others from having power over us. And all because we're so afraid that we've forgotten we're afraid. . .

For certain 'powerful' people, the fear that drove them is obvious: the dictator whose rivals all met with fatal 'accidents', for example; the politician who surrounded herself with 'yes-men'; the tycoon who lived in morbid seclusion. Think of some other examples. Why is it obvious to us – but almost never to them – that their behaviour is driven by fear rather than true power?

Since the threads of wyrd pass through each of us, somewhere in you will be the same fears (though probably to a lesser degree!). Put yourself in the place of those people; reach inside yourself to look at those fears where they pass through you. Do you recognise them as your own fears? If so, are they hard to face? What kind of behaviour, what kind of 'power', would enable you to avoid having to face those fears yourself?

It's often hard to grasp that this kind of power is an illusion – especially if you're looking at the wrong end of someone else's belief that "power comes out of the barrel of a gun". Yet in the long run, that's all it is: an illusion, based on unacknowledged fear.

The real problem, perhaps, is that this 'power' seems to be a means of dumping our fears on other people: if we're 'powerful', our fears become someone else's problem. We've seen this already as the tyrant/victim game: what happens is that the victim starts looking for someone else to be a tyrant to, on whom to dump their hurt and fear; the new victim goes looking for *their* victim, and so on. In no time at all, a climate of fear can build up: not one in which people are powerful, but in which *all* are ultimately powerless – including the original tyrant.

Since what we're afraid of is fear itself, we rationalise the fear. In the same way that love becomes confused with attention, love can become confused with fear. The 'Big Brother' syndrome: we don't fear the tyrant, instead we say "we love our great protector"... And the tyrant, in turn, is convinced that people love him *because* he is powerful: if he too believed that 'power is the ultimate aphrodisiac', he may well have started out on this road because he felt it was the only way he would find the love he craved. And yet that 'love' is an empty shell, giving nothing: he will always be trapped into wanting more, and more, and more.

Go back to the pick-up-trucks-with-hormone-trouble scenario we saw earlier, with its obsessive mode of display: can you see in there the same confusion of love with power – the notion that power alone can keep people producing 'love on demand'?

Listen to the lyrics of a few popular 'love songs': look at how much they encourage this muddling of love, power and fear. Phrases like "I'm gonna make you love me", or "You're mine, all mine" equate love with *ownership*; and "Since you've been gone, I can't go on" or "I can't live without you" are paeans of praise to powerlessness – or an attempt to regain power by power-under, by manufacturing guilt.

How often have phrases like these been said to you, in your relationships? And how often have you said something like this yourself? Was this done as a means of control, so that wants – romance! love! schmaltz! – would be met? If so, did it *actually* satisfy the need?

Power is equated with ownership, the *right* to exploit without reference to anyone else. Employment is equated with ownership: as your employer, I'm deemed to have the *right* to have power over you. So if I employ you, it's easy for me to believe that I *own* you – not merely the use of some of your time, but your body, your mind, your soul – and thus you must surely *want* to do my every bidding, follow my every whim. My wish is your command: you must satisfy my every need! But as the employee, of course, you might not be too happy about this point of view: so you may well either fight to gain power over me, or seek to destroy my power with every trick of the power-under game.

None of us wants the responsibility – the blame – for what goes on; but all of us want control, the semblance of power. "Round and round in the usual old game – I take the credit and you take the blame". . .

Does this sound familiar?

In the midst of that kind of mess, very little gets done: everyone's too busy playing power-games. It almost seems like the definition of power is 'the ability to avoid work' – 'winners' are those who get others to do their work for them, by force, trickery, manipulation or otherwise.

So it comes as a surprise to discover that the formal definition of 'power', from physics, is 'the ability to do work'. In all those power-games with power-over or power-under, no-one is actually being powerful in any real sense. What they *are* doing is wasting everyone's energy – and disempowering us all in the process.

In the end, that kind of power, like control, is based on illusions. If we're going to get any work done – if we're to reclaim the power of choice with our lives – we're going to need something more realistic than that. We're going to need a very *different* approach to power.

A DIFFERENT KIND OF POWER

In a way power-over and power-under are two sides of the same coin – traditionally the male and female forms of power, in fact. Both of them are rooted in fear; both are concerned more with disempowering others than with empowering ourselves; both make it far harder to get work done; and both are based on an absence of *trust*.

It's trust that makes the difference. With trust, power becomes empowering. The threads of wyrd pass through us all, and always loop back to where they started: to try to fight someone else through power-over or power-under is ultimately to fight ourselves. So instead of fighting futile battles against the wyrd, against the nature of reality, we let go, and *trust*. At that point, by letting go of power, we reach a different kind of power – one in which we actually do have 'the ability to do work'.

We let go; but we don't let go so far as to collapse in a heap on the floor. Knowing what we want, we state the direction in which we want to go, provide the energy to get the process started, and then trust the wyrd to bring us to where we want to end up. We may get there by some surprising routes: but we do get there. Whereas if we try to control not only the direction but the route as well – controlling every step of the way – we somehow miss the point we're aiming for: there's always a choice, but there's always a twist. And if we're not clear about what we want... well, we could end up anywhere – which is what happens all too often, of course!

This distinction between controlling and directing, this balance of letting go without letting go, is hard to describe – yet we've all had experience of it. It's like looking for a parking bay in a crowded city: if we don't try for one, we won't get one; if we try hard, forcing our way around, pushing others out of our way, we'll probably end up with a parking ticket rather than a meter; whereas if we're clear about what we want, but let go of defining the *form* it should take, we find ourselves in a parking place almost without noticing it. Weird – but it works. Trying without trying; 'doing no-thing', as the Taoists would say.

What are some examples of your own? Go back to one of those examples. Can you remember feeling the lack of trust, the fear of uncertainty – and letting go anyway? And the surprise – joy, even! – when things 'worked by themselves'?

The usual approach to power is about being prepared against surprise: we try to control every eventuality, we leave nothing to chance – we hope. But as one engineer commented, "Mother Nature loves to throw a surprise party": reality is full of surprises, always will be full of surprises. Yet surprises can work both ways, to our advantage as well as to our detriment: if we only allow things to happen in expected ways, we're limiting the chances for things to work out on their own. So we'd be far better off instead preparing *for* surprise – working *with* the twists of reality rather than against them. And in any case, surprises are where the interest lies, the excitement lies. A life without surprises is a pretty boring one...

True power comes when we face the fear – accept it for what it is – and allow for surprises. The state that the writer Starhawk describes as 'power-with' arrives when we trust others – co-oper-ation leads to an extraordinary power and multiplication of energy, especially when we help each other to work on the fears that would otherwise lead to a pointless power-struggle. And the other state she describes, 'power-from-within', arrives when we finally trust *ourselves*.

Power-from-within flows from the heart, from the whole core of someone's being – and still leaves room for everyone else, in fact *includes* everyone else. Someone who has that kind of power seems to glow, seems to radiate light, an ease, a certainty, in everything they do in life. They don't control: instead, they *dance* with life. People are drawn to them not out of compulsion or fear, but from sheer delight. In that sense, power-from-within probably *is* 'the ultimate aphrodisiac'. . .

Compare those four forms of power: power-over, power-under, power-with, power-from-within. Who do you know that epitomises each of those forms of power, that makes that form of power a way of life?

The same threads pass through each of us: so reach into your memories and recall a time when you felt each form of power within yourself. How does each *feel* within you? Feel the fear that's behind power-over, power-under; feel the power and strength, the fear*less*ness, from which power-with and power-from-within wells out. And note how power-over and power-under keep your focus and attention 'out there', on the external world; whilst power-with and power-from-within come from and help to reinforce a more definite sense of *self*.

If that's so, who are you? "Who am I?" Look deeper into these threads for an answer. . .

A willingness to trust leads to a sense of *empowerment*, of 'discovering' power that lies within, a power that we all share. A power that is powerful *because* we share it: as another writer put it, this deeper power is 'the ability to empower oneself and others'. Since the threads pass through us all, there's ultimately no difference between 'self' and 'others': empowering others *is* empowering myself, empowering myself *is* empowering others.

But we always have a choice; and there's always a twist. If we give in to the all-pervading fears – which always seems easiest – and strive for power-over or power-under others, we pull everyone down, *including* ourselves. Somehow, it always loops back – if only in that the whole culture becomes more fear-ridden. Yet by looking within, by trusting others, by trusting who *we* are – "I am what I am!" – something else comes through: something else that makes it easier for *everyone* to reach that same power-from-within. That seems to be where the true power lies.

Or perhaps only part of that power. For many people, there's also a clear sense of a 'higher power', from whence their power comes. A power so strong that they feel they act simply as a channel, a conduit, like a dancer swept up in the energy of the moment. A power that's not external, but deeper within, somehow intensely personal; and 'higher' not in the sense of an overlord, but rather as greater, wider, wiser. More aware. More connected with totality; more closely connected with the infinite interweavings of the web of wyrd. And as such gives us a sense of certainty, an ability to trust – and to act on that trust, as a way of life.

> Do you have a sense of a 'higher power' within you – a Weaver of the wyrd? If so, how do you know when it's there, when it's available to you? Does it happen only in some activities – in your art, or exercise, or some aspect of work? Or only when you're drunk, perhaps!
>
> What do you *feel* when you 'let it work through you'? In what way are you different when it does so? In what way are you different so as to let it do so?

In principle we all have access to this kind of power within, this link to the threads of wyrd. For some it's a way of life; but for most of us it's more something of which we only get occasional glimpses. Like the dim star at night, that sense of connection is *there* – and then it's gone, as soon as we try to look at it.

Whatever it may be, our awareness of it *is* intensely personal. If we try to describe it to someone else, we soon get into tangles of confusion. The term 'higher power' is no more than a meta-phor: a personal label such as 'God' or 'my guardian angel' may mean nothing to anyone else, since they may not – cannot – have our personal experience of what it means to us. It's important to recognise, then, that for each of us this power is ours – and ours alone.

Yet the alone-ness itself can bring new fears – of loneliness, of isolation, of responsibility. Which, if we're not careful, brings up new needs to control, to dominate – and brings us right back where we started. . .

NEW AGE, NEW ILLUSIONS?

The old religions resolved these fears by resorting to power-over in a different guise: only one 'higher power' permitted to exist, labelled as God, Allah, Buddha or whatever. "*My* way is the *only* way" – the origin of all religious wars. And its root is fear: "if I can convince others that what I believe is true, then perhaps it *is* true. . .". Another variant on the old game of "what I tell you three times is *true*", all mixed in with another infamous fear that "my place in heaven is dependent on the number of souls I can convert to the true faith". . .

As the old authorities have faded, the self-styled 'New Age' has come to the fore. Rightly, there is once more a free and open discussion of a personal connection to 'higher power', and of a right – if not duty – to affirm oneself within the world. A new freedom to be ourselves, to be who we truly are.

It's unfortunate, then, that so much New Age material instead re-affirms the same old fears, the same old illusions – in fact encourages them to grow. . .

All too often there's new aggrandisement of power-over, bu-ried beneath a veneer of novelty: one well-known writer, for example, claims that his book on affirmations "serves as a magni-ficent and devastating battle-plan whereby you will learn to expand your personal power and win back absolute control of your life." We're told that we should "mould reality to suit our positive ends" – and our personal point of view, of course, is always 'positive'. That others might have a different point of view is to be ignored: for "we are Children of the Light", which presumably means that all others are in Darkness. . .

It's perhaps too easy to be cynical about it all. Within that mass of 'New Age' material there is undoubtedly much good sense – true gold amongst the dross. But we do need to use a great deal of care – especially since so much of it is little more than a new way to sell old fears in a pretty gift-wrapped package.

So much of religion is centred around fear of death: dealing with perhaps the most total and inevitable of all uncertainties. One well-known New Age solution is to declare that death does not exist: we can, it's claimed, be physically immortal – but only if we deny death's physical reality. This seems a little unrealistic. . . If denying our fear of death consists of refusing to face it, we in effect spend our lives in service to it by committing ourselves to avoiding it; whereas if we accept that fear, dance with it, we *live* each moment as it comes. Another twist in the web of wyrd. . .

It's rarely helpful to become preoccupied with death; but it can be useful to reflect on its reality every now and then. What fears come up for you? How do you face them? In what ways does living *with* those fears make it easier to *live* – to be *alive*?

The New Age provides no more certainties than the old religions did – probably even less, if anything, considering its all-too-casual attitude to discipline and sheer hard work. And I know I'm no guru either: I'm *me*, with my strengths, my weaknesses, my all-too obvious failings. I don't have all the answers – about all that can be said is that I may sometimes have some useful questions. . .

Ultimately, the only guru we each have is ourselves. Oh, we can borrow other people for help from time to time: but they can't do the work for us. This section of the wyrd that I call 'me' is mine to deal with as best I can: it's my problem. To find out what I'm supposed to do with it, it's up to me to look inside, to call up that 'power from within' – and to do that I have to trust. Then, somehow, without knowing how, I'll *know*. And no, it isn't easy. . . letting go is never easy. . .

A TIME TO TRUST

We can't control anything – or we can try, but it doesn't work. What we can do instead is *direct* what happens: make choices, act on them, see what we get. Make choices; knowing that we can never know, we trust that they *are* the right choices; and see what we get.

This is the aspect of wyrd that used to be known as 'providence'. Literally, it is 'that which provides' – when we trust it. If we can't trust it, we find ourselves reverting to control: and control, by the usual weird twists, ends up never quite providing us with what we need.

To let go control, we somehow have to let go the fear that underlies it. That's *not* easy. We never do have 'power over' our fears; we never do conquer fear. But we can learn to live with it; learn to *face* fear, learn not just to accept it but dance *with* it. And even use its energy to help us – much as we used the energy of anger to release us from the power-under game – to get us moving, to reclaim our power of choice.

There's a strange inversion, when accepting being scared puts us in touch with the sacred: our own true power *from within*. But to reach there we have to trust, trust ourselves and the interweavings of the wyrd. It's time to let go: let go of fear, and much else that holds us back from being who we are.

9

TIME TO LET GO

In some ways there's no difficulty in knowing when it's time to let go: we let go when we get fed up of holding on! Or sometimes the wyrd will get 'fed up' on our behalf, and dump us in some place where we have no choice but to trust – we've all had experience of that. Either way, at some point – usually quite suddenly – we find ourselves facing the reality that the old way of working on the world, the ordinary, 'normal' way of control, of fear, of power-over and power-under, just doesn't work any more. Or rather we recognise that it never *did* work: that sense of control, of power, was never more than an illusion. It's not a very comfortable realisation, but it is a realistic one! Time for a change. . . time to let go, and start again a different way.

We can't *make* change happen: it happens in its own way, and in its own time, weaving through on the threads of wyrd. It's not in our control – it never has been. But we *can* direct the process. Even though there's always a twist, we always have a choice: it's up to us to choose which way we want to go.

It may seem that change happens because we do something new, but often that's only because we've made space for it by letting go of something old. There has to be space for the new to enter into our lives, to unfold itself in the space that's created. Part of the preparation for change consists of extending some kind of invitation: we need not only to allow change but *welcome* it. That's not always easy: one reason why we so often try to fill every possible gap in our lives with activity or habit is because we're afraid of change – yet sometimes the wyrd will make space for us anyway, whether we like it or not. . .

Part of the fear of change is that since there's always a twist, we can never be certain what it is that we're inviting. What if we're only making room for something worse? "Better the Devil you know than the Devil you don't" – especially if the new 'devil' seems to be a void, a yawning chasm of nothingness.

Facing that fear does take true courage: but fears can take up a lot of space that could be filled with other, better, things. Like laughter, for example; or joy.

By letting go of fear – by *trusting* – we create space for what *we* choose to be in our lives. The catch is that we have to let go completely, let go *unconditionally*, without attachment to any outcome. If I'm only willing to let go when I'm certain that my wishes will be fulfilled, I'm not actually letting go: all I've done is find a different way of controlling – the same old illusion in a different guise.

So we have to take the risk, have the courage. And trust. Trust to make that jump into the unknown. . .

NON-ATTACHMENT, NON-DETACHMENT

This business of letting go of attachment is like the silliness barrier all over again. From the other side it seems easy: "Why don't you just jump?" But it doesn't *feel* like that: the fear is real. . .

About the only thing that makes it easier is recognising that the other way – the way of control, of slavery to an endless stream of wants – just doesn't work. Like the Red Queen in Carroll's 'Alice', it leaves us running ever faster and faster, just to stand still. "The more you want, the less you get" – or rather, the more we end up drowning in a sea of *things*, none of which actually give us what we need.

But first we have to make space to see this: which isn't easy, because we're usually very careful *not* to make space to see it! Recognising what's actually going on would break the whole illusion: and none of us like our illusions shattered. So the first step is to *make* the choice, *create* the space: and watch what comes up. . .

The classic tool for creating space is meditation: sit quietly for a few minutes in a quiet space; relax; watch the breathing go in and out, in and out; relinquish control, and watch the thoughts go by.

That's the principle, anyway: the practice isn't quite so easy! The habit of filling every scrap of space is so dominant – because of that fear of change – that thoughts and images come crowding in the moment there's a gap. "Breathe in. . . breathe out. . . breathe in. . . breathe out. . . oh bother, I forgot to put the cat out. . . no, he can wait. . . I wonder whether George will wait for me tomorrow. . . Damn! Start again: breathe in. . . breathe out. . . breathe in. . . that film was good. . . must see it again sometime. . . *Damn! I keep* losing track!" – at which point you'll be in anything but a relaxed meditative state!

The trick is to not worry about the way thoughts come crowding in: they do. For everyone. So when your mind drifts off from the task of creating space, bring it back *gently*: without hurry, without pressure, without blame. It does get easier with practice: but in the meantime it's useful to look at the fears, the habits, the effort to control even this. You can't fight control with control – so relax, don't try, just let go, let go. . .

It's a kind of spring-cleaning of the mind: and it's often surprising what comes up. The sheer amount of *stuff* in there. . .! The same is true with all those things I own: this house-full of stuff I rarely use. But I cling on to it. . . it's *mine*. Partly because of memories I don't want to lose; partly because I use it to define 'I', a substitute for *knowing* 'I'. . . the end-result, though, is that there's little or no space for anything new – and in a way, very little room for *me*.

In one form of a *visualisation*, we get into the same meditative state, quietly watching the thoughts go by: and then deliberately fill the space with an image or a question, some issue on which we want to meditate. To an extent, this is what we've been doing ☞

with affirmations: "they give the old toothless dog in my mind something to gnaw on", as one friend put it. So perhaps reflect for a while on your experience of "the more you want, the less you get": hold that paradox in your mind. What ideas, images, memories come up about that? Watch them, watch them as they go by. . .

We get stuck in the loop of 'the more you want, the less you get' because, as we saw earlier, the feeling of 'wanting more' usually comes from a need which is being responded to inappropriately. A want, you'll remember, is the outward expression of an inner need. We misinterpret the meaning of the want, interpreting it literally rather than as metaphor; what the need gets from us isn't what it needs; so it repeats the want, in the hope that we'll get it right this time. But if we don't stop to listen – if we don't create the space in which to listen – we'll just repeat the loop: "same again, please!"

In time, we get attached to that way of doing things: we *have* to do it this way, we *must* have that toy, that food, that job, that car, that person as prospective partner. If we don't get it (or them), we're stuck. To get out of the stuckness, we have to let go: we have to release the 'attachment'.

This is where there's usually a lot of discussion about 'non-attachment' to things, to people, to expectations. True non-attachment is an idealised state in which we let go completely, release our fears, trust entirely to the fates or the wyrd. A state of enlightenment. . .

Even in the classic descriptions it's recognised that it's anything but easy to reach that state. But it's made even harder by the way non-attachment is usually described.

Non-attachment does indeed mean letting go. But it's *not* the same as 'detachment': in letting go, we don't just drop everything and walk away. It's not necessary, or even advisable – quite apart from being an absolutely terrifying concept for most of us! Perhaps a better way to understand it is to recognise that non-attachment is the same as '*non*-detachment': neither attachment *nor* detachment.

It's a bit like looking-without-looking, or trying-without-trying – that state of 'doing no-thing' which we need in order to see a dim star at night. We don't just let go: we still have choices – even though there's always a twist. What we let go of is not the choice, but the fear: make a choice, and then trust that the wyrd will bring us what we need.

We're back to another of those child*like* states – a state of optimistic trust. Imagine, like a child: we make a wish, and then see what the fairies bring us. But do it without controlling, without demanding it be a particular way or form – let it be a surprise, a happy childlike surprise. Play with it; play with the twists of the wyrd – and let go.

For example, modify the image that we meditated on above: give the old toothless dog something different to gnaw on. Make a wish: think of something you'd really like to happen, something you would *choose* to have happen. Build a clear image of it in your mind. In your mind, write down the wish on a piece of card. And imagine a pink balloon, a light helium-filled balloon, tugging gently on its string. Tie the wish-card, that wish you'd dearly like to happen, to the string of the balloon. And let go, let go; watch it lift up into the sky, and drift away on the threads of wyrd.

Don't just forget the balloon, though: remind yourself of it each day. Where is it? Where has it landed? Who's read your message? How is it being acted on? Yet still let go. . .

You've let go: you're non-attached to the wish. You're also non-detached from it: it still has meaning, importance for you. Trust that somehow, in some way, there will be a response.

And watch how, *over time*, the wyrd responds to the wish.

Try it. Watch what happens!

It's important to recognise that the choices *are* always ours: without that, we lapse back into that irresponsible 'laziness' mode, in which we rely on panic and fear about 'external' events to get us going again.

And it's important too to let go of how or when the wyrd

should respond. It works in its own way, in its own time: trying to control it, getting attached to some abstract idea of perfection, just makes things worse in the long run. So let go, let go: neither attached, nor detached, but non-attached, non-detached, accepting it as it *is*.

"NOBODY'S PERFFECT"

Accepting things as they are is not easy. It never is. We all want instant change, instant perfection, even instant enlightenment. And strangely enough, we don't get it. . . except that sometimes, even stranger, when we give up we find we're already there. Odd. Weird, in fact. . .

We've all been taught that people and things 'ought to' be perfect, work perfectly, according to some abstract ideal of perfection: the 'Laws of Nature', the 'Will of God' – or the ideology of the Party, perhaps. These ideals, however, are always abstract, and arbitrarily exclude the bits we don't like: uncertainty, unpredictability, or the aspects of our own nature that we'd prefer to forget. But reality, the web of wyrd, is neither arbitrary or abstract: it simply *is*, including *everything*, whether we like it or not. If we don't accept reality for what it is, and how it is – including those bits we don't like – sooner or later we'll find ourselves in trouble. The demand for perfection can be a problem.

In many ways that demand is actually another form of power-under. We're required to reach and maintain some arbitrary state of perfection: if we fail to do so, we must classify ourselves as 'failures'. But it is, by its nature, an impossible task: if we accept the demand, we lose before we even start. It's valuable to *aim* for some kind of perfection; but the demand to *be* perfect is best understood as yet another way to trap us into disempowering ourselves for the dubious benefit of others.

Perfection is a cruel all-or-nothing game: whatever we do, we're failures. By striving for the arbitrary perfection, we push the ☞

perfection of *ourselves* away. We push even *living* away – that sad cry of "If I'm so wonderful, why am I still lonely?"

There's a simple test that can help us to let go: if someone demands that you be perfect, are they themselves perfect in that sense? (A hint: in *every* case you'll find they aren't. . .) Are they themselves truly striving for that perfection – or are they only demanding that *you* do so? If it's the latter, it may be that they're only playing the power-under game, trying to dump their own fears on you: if so, let it be their problem rather than yours. . .

And in either case, look again at what you're being asked to do. Is it what *you* want, is it what *you* choose? Give it to the 'old toothless dog' to work on for a while. What answers, what images, come up?

The quest for perfection is just that: a quest. It's a process, not a state; becoming, not being. The perfection is in the maintaining of the aim *towards* it; but none of us – *none* of us – ever achieve it. 'Nobody's perffect': so don't worry about it. Just *be*. Find more who *you* are, what *you* choose: that, in itself, is perfection.

The quest for perfection is perhaps best understood as a dance of awareness. It comes and goes – make space for it, allow it to come and go. And when it goes, we use some kind of discipline or system – that arbitrary description of perfection, of 'how it works', of 'how it ought to be' – to remind us of our aim. If necessary, pretend! "If you can't fix it, fake it", to show us what we're aiming for, to show us how it could be – that's what we're doing with affirmations, for example. But it is important to re-member that we *are* only faking it. . . it's only part of the process, not the end in itself!

We never *do* reach perfection: it's a goal, an aim, rather than an achievable target. We improve by allowing things – and ourselves – to 'not-work', to work in *un*expected ways. When things don't go according to expectation, that doesn't necessarily mean that anything's wrong: it may just be that the wyrd is taking a different – and probably better – route to our intended aim. We don't *know*. And holding on to 'knowing', to certainty, is another form of control that we need to learn to release.

LET GO OF KNOWING

Most of us have a strong *need* to know that things are working – mainly because it's so hard to trust that they are. So it's hard to let go: but notice, slowly, how often some 'bit of good luck' turns out to lead nowhere, and how often some apparent disaster turns out to be 'a blessing in disguise'.

A long time ago, at the far edge of a village far away, lived an old woman and her young son. They were poor: her only possession of value a beautiful horse. "Surely you'd be better off if you sold it?" said the villagers. But her only reply was "Maybe yes; maybe no. . ."

One day the horse was gone. "It must have been stolen", said the villagers, "You're crazy, old woman – you should have sold it while you had the chance." Yet her reply was the same: "Maybe yes; maybe no. . ."

But a week later, the horse was back – and it had brought a dozen wild horses with it, back to the woman's paddock. "What amazing good fortune!", said the villagers. And again the woman's reply was "Maybe yes; maybe no. . ."

Her son began training the wild horses. One of them threw him: he landed badly and broke his leg. "He'll be crippled for months, and he's your only help", said the villagers. "What bad luck!" But once more the old woman replied "Maybe yes; maybe no. . ."

The very next day, the villagers were in despair: an army recruiting party had passed through, conscripting all young men for service in the latest of the king's incessant and bloody wars. Only the old woman's son was spared, because of his broken leg. "We'll never see our sons again!" cried the villagers. "How much more fortunate than us you are, old woman!" And for a change, her reply was slightly different: "Maybe yes; maybe no. . . I do not know; do you? Does anyone? It does not help to judge too soon: it always changes. As time passes, we will know: but until then, maybe yes, maybe no. . ."

Over the next few days, try watching events like that old woman. Watch your judgements, your assumptions, your expec-

☞

tations about what's happening: and, gently, let go. Compare later the expectation with what actually happened: notice the difference! So let go, let go: "maybe yes; maybe no. . ."

In hindsight we can see a pattern; but at the time we simply don't know. There's no way we can know. So rather than worrying over whether each little incident is a 'forwards' or 'backwards' step, it's more useful to pay attention to the overall flow, the overall sense of the direction of events. And note the choices that *we* have in that – maintaining our own aim towards a better life.

Remember too that if we only allow things to work in expected ways, we're limiting our chances of their working. But as far as the culture we live in is concerned, things *only* work in expected ways: we're supposed to interact with each other only through what we might call 'double-entry life-keeping', treating everything in life as if it was part of double-entry book-keeping.

If I give something to you, I feel that you owe me the same in return: you must at some time repay me in exactly the same way and kind – "not a penny more, not a penny less". And we do this not just with money, but with emotions and almost everything else. It's a crude way to make things seem fair while at the same time avoiding the need to learn who or what or when to trust. We expect our 'just reward' – or perhaps our 'just punishment' – in a strict book-keeping of credits and debits. But reality, once again, simply doesn't work that way: life is far more weird than that.

For most of my life I indulged in a habit of 'trying to buy being liked': I would give, and give, and give, in the hope that this would somehow *make* people like me. After all, I'd given things to them: so now they owe me a favour in return – that's fair, isn't it? It took many years of emotional bruises – "why is everything so damned *unfair!*" – for me to recognise that reality doesn't quite work that way. . .

Look at some of your own patterns, your own habits, your own expectations of fairness: how much do you demand a perfect 'double-entry life-keeping' from life? How much do you expect it of others?

I give, you take – but you don't give me anything in return. Hey! That's damned *unfair*! That's how it seems – we certainly complain about it enough. . .

Yet even at a cursory glance, life isn't 'fair' in that simplistic way. With a better understanding, though, we can see that there *is* a kind of feedback, a kind of balancing of the books: but one in which, as we'd now expect, there's always a twist. It does all seem to loop round: but often not from the direction we'd expect, or in a form that we'd always recognise. It may well come back from someone else entirely – and often not until we actually need it. It's up to us to see it as such – and act on it.

> A while back, a colleague and I were presented with a professional bill that was far higher than we'd expected. It was wrong, *unfair.* "We're not going to pay that!" But there was a sense of a comment on the wyrd, a kind of message that said "*Don't* argue about this one – just *do* it". So we did. Just after coming back from the mailbox, after mailing the cheque, the phone rang. An unexpected job. For exactly the same amount as the bill. . .
>
> Weird. . . But sometimes this happens so often, and seems so ordinary, that I can only comment "Ah! Normal Rules!" when it happens again. . .
>
> What experiences have you had like that – the weavings of the wyrd? How did you recognise them? How do you know when to trust them? And do they seem extraordinary, or ordinary – or just plain weird?

The key issue is trust, combined with a kind of inner message from the wyrd – which is always there, if only I'd care to listen. But it's not easy to listen, because I'm still usually expecting things to be fair, to follow the crude simplistic rules of 'double-entry life-keeping'. If I'm not listening, I'm only allowing things to work in expected ways – which means they often can't work at all.

What it comes down to is that to connect with the wyrd we have to disconnect from this culture's notions of 'fair' and 'unfair', and instead re-learn how to trust: who, what and when. Instead of giving away virtually at random – which is what I'd been doing in the buying-being-liked mode – I have to learn to *sense* when it's appropriate to give, and when not to. When I think back, I can see that many of those people that I gave and gave to, and later blamed as being unfair, I actually can't blame at all: I was giving the *wrong* thing, in the *wrong* way, to the *wrong* people. Trying to control them, in fact: trying to trap them into giving to *me* – which could hardly be called trust. . . In that sense, they weren't 'doing it to me': they just took what I gave them, and walked away – often with some confusion and surprise, as I remember now. But under the circumstances, that was a perfectly reasonable thing for them to do!

I can't blame others for my own unwillingness to set 'boundaries' – my own limits on what I'm willing to give, and how and what I'm willing to receive. That's up to me: I have to learn how to trust *myself*, my own inner knowing, as well as that of others. As we learn to trust, and as we learn to get the balance right, we connect with the wyrd: and slowly, steadily, strangely, things begin to work in unexpected ways as well as only in expected ones. But if we don't – if we try to control, or hide in the crude fair/unfair of 'double-entry life-keeping' – the end-result is always some kind of pain, some kind of suffering. About which, of course, we then complain. . .!

AN END TO SUFFERING

Pain is something else we try to control – or, more to the point, try to lock out of our lives. We don't want it! Though we'd more often put it in a more positive-looking light, and say "I want to always be happy"; but in fact it comes down to the same thing. We don't like to face it, either in ourselves, or in others: it just hurts too much. Yet suffering of various kinds and at various levels is a real part of life: and if we try to avoid it or ignore it, eventually the wyrd will find a way to *make* us face it. We have a choice; but there's always a twist. . .

We'd *like* to put a nice, solid, permanent boundary between ourselves and pain of *any* kind, emotional, physical or whatever.

92

A lot of New Age material claims to do that for us, which unfortunately is downright dishonest. For example, the obsession with 'positive thinking' – "I only accept positive things in my life", one woman said to me recently – can easily become a new form of controlling, a new way to avoid reality. And while the concept of boundaries is important (as we'll see later), it's now routinely abused as a new way of blaming, to dump fears on other people – "how dare you overstep my boundaries!". The search for enlightenment too often degenerates into a new style of 'endarkenment' (Charles Tart's delightful term!); it's often forgotten that the closer we get to 'the Light', the larger the shadow grows. . .

The 'old' age has left us with problems enough, though. Most traditions regard an acceptance of a certain amount of suffering as a necessary reality – "you have to go through suffering to become more whole". And that's probably true: but some traditions – especially Christian or Buddhist – go to an extreme, presenting suffering as a *virtue*. To be in pain is to be considered more worthy of God, or closer to Buddha. . . Even if we disregard the cynical power-politics that's often been behind it, this still leaves us with that infamous holier-than-thou syndrome – an absurd aggrandisement of suffering for its own sake.

There's an interesting story on this in Richard Bach's book "Illusions". The mechanic, the 'reluctant messiah' in the story, asks his audience if they would do anything, *anything*, that God commanded. "Of course! Of course!" is the reply. For example, if God asked them to suffer great pain, excruciating torture, to prove their faith, would they do it? "Yes!", reply the people, "*yes! YES!*" But what, asks the mechanic, if God's commandment was that they should be joyful, happy, free: what then? And there is utter silence. . . .

A question: if 'God's commandment' to *you* was that "you should be joyful, happy, free" – what would you do? And how hard would it be to believe that this really *was* 'God's commandment'?

A clue to what's actually going on comes from what one writer described as "that special attention which is the prerogative of the miserable". If – as children – we're upset, or hurt, or in pain, we get more attention. Attention isn't quite as good as love, which is what we really want: but it'll do. So we can 'buy' attention – so the thinking goes – if we're in pain: and if necessary we'll create the pain *ourselves*, in order to get the attention we crave. It's another variant on the game of trying to buy being liked: another form of 'double-entry life-keeping'. It doesn't work: but we think it *should*. It *ought* to. And if people won't give us the attention that's our 'just reward' for being miserable, perhaps our suffering will convince God that we ought to be given some kind of special attention – in the next life if not the present one. . .

A more realistic view is that suffering is simply part of reality. It *is*. It's often also the only thing which will break our complacency, to get us to *feel* once more. And only by reaching the depths can we reach the heights: they're inextricably interlinked.

A common myth about great art is that it comes only from great anguish, from tortured emotions or deep suffering. It's more accurate to say that it comes from an *intensity* of emotion – for which suffering can be a key that opens the door. It's not the only one!

We can reach the same intensity with other emotions: anger, excitement, laughter and, especially, love – other keys to the same door. A door that opens onto true creativity, and a knowledge that we're *alive*.

It doesn't *have* to be suffering! Cast back your mind onto some memories – feel the aliveness that comes when we let go, and let our emotions be what they are.

Without compassion – a shared understanding of emotion – it's hard to reach much of an understanding of life: especially other people's understanding of life. Art, and the spiritual paths, are deeply concerned with understanding, and with compassion. We don't *have* to experience pain and suffering in order to have compassion – we just have to find *some* way to reach that compassion. It's a fact, though, that most of us seem to learn only through personal experience... the trick would seem to be to keep the experience down to manageable proportions!

One of the classic New Age mistakes is to forget that a small amount of pain can relieve a great deal of hidden pain. Much of our suffering has its roots in old fears or old wants, still crying for attention in the background. Facing those issues with tools such as affirmations brings those old issues right back up to the surface, and often they *hurt* – but only for a short while. Then we finally let them go, releasing them like that imaginary pink balloon – followed by a deep, deep sense of relief... And while it may not seem so at the time, the pain *is* only transitory: it does help to remember that.

And within the wyrd, certain kinds of pain can twist into totally different emotions: heavy exercise may seem like the tortures of Hell, for example, but the exhilaration afterward makes it all worthwhile! But it takes courage to accept it, and to trust that the pain will pass, and will take us where we need to go.

Refusing to accept any pain can leave us in an empty search for an ever-elusive 'happiness'. But when we take the risk, and trust – when we include everything, and allow all the emotions, 'good' and 'bad', to be as they are – we find that we've also let go of suffering. And with that we reach a quite different state, far deeper than happiness. At the far side of suffering, when we allow ourselves to include everything, what we discover is *joy*. And that's when life really *does* become fun!

10

ALL THE FUN
OF THE FAIR

Life *can* be fun. It certainly may not seem like it, when everything's gone wrong and we're back into 'living in the dark' again.
But once more the key is in how we see things: it's a matter of our
point of view. If we have fixed ideas about how things 'ought' to
be, we're likely to be in trouble when we meet up with the twisted
reality of wyrd. . .

So play with a different point of view for a while: play with the
idea that this reality isn't meant to 'be' anything at all. It's no more
than a quest, a game, a joke – though often one with a twisted sense
of humour behind it!

Life as a fun-fair. . . a weird place, where we find ourselves
"searching through these carousels and carnival arcades" (to
quote Mark Knopfler) for no apparent reason. Flashing lights,
raucous noise, distractions everywhere; chaos and confusion.
Voices yelling, screaming, laughing, crying. . . tears for fears, or
sheer exuberance. We paid our entry fee on coming here: now all
the rides are free. Which one shall we choose next? – the choice is
ours!

There's only one catch: we're part of this crazy circus. We can't
just stand aside and watch: we're *in* it – "the hell if you're willing,
your name's on the billing", as the old Donovan song puts it.
There's only one way in, and only one way out. . . in the meantime, we're *here*. So we may as well enjoy it!

It's only a game. That's all this is.

Why? We don't know. And it doesn't *matter*. It *is* – that's all.
And it's the only game in town – the only game there is. So we

may as well play it for all it's worth! Take it seriously, but not *too* seriously – it *is* only a game, after all. . .

So lighten up. . . be 'enlightened'! Choose your own rides: and join in the fun of the fair!

RIDING THE ROLLER-COASTER

Look around at the fair. To the left is the carousel, its old gallopers reminding us of the 'good old days'. Beside it is the Tunnel of Love, as tawdry and tinselly as ever – if we're not in that mood, we might feel it's a little overrated! To the right is the Ghost Train, in whose atmosphere of gloom and doom we've already spent a disordinate amount of our time – despite its being nothing like what it used to be. . . In the background is the circus tent; behind us are stalls selling a wide variety of sickly candy – anything *but* a wholesome diet, your parents would say! – and over there is the hall of mirrors. But first let's go on forward to the biggest ride of the lot: the Scenic Railway, the roller-coaster.

There's no doubt that life is like a roller-coaster. . . one moment we're up, the next we're way, way down. . . And back up again, with an unexpected jolt; then down again into the darkness, with people yelling all round us in an odd mixture of fear and enjoyment. And this is supposed to be *fun*? Well, yes: it is, if we let go of holding onto everything. But at the same time there are some things we *do* keep hold of in this wildly lurching world: your seat, for example! The one constant in all this is ourselves, twisting and turning through space and time: so what do we *feel* here?

Up and down, up and *down* again; then a sudden swing round a corner – almost felt like we were going off the rails then. . .! This whole thing is so rickety, it hardly seems possible that it can all hold together: but it does. Somehow. . . Gawd only knows how!

But watch the emotions: a swirl of fear, then exhilaration – an ever-changing torrent of feelings. As fast as they come, they're gone: if we try to hold onto any one, we get run over by the next, welling up from within at the next move. We can't control them, either: we can look ahead to see what to expect, from the way the rails are going, but expecting and *experiencing* are two very different things... emotions literally 'move outward in the moment'. Yet we can *watch* them, passing through us, passing by, without holding on to any of them, without letting any of them grab hold of *us*. In there, somewhere in there, is a real sense of aliveness, a true sense of power as the power within flows through. Not a transient happiness, not mere ephemeral fun – but *joy*. "You must have chaos within you to give birth to a dancing star. . ."

I suppose I'm hardly one to talk: last time I went for a ride on the roller-coaster at Luna Park, I was too busy trying to make sense of how it worked, to take much notice of what was going on around me! Being 'in my head' was a way of avoiding being there in body, I suppose: another habit, another trick of the senses-taker. . .

But a suggestion: this is probably a good time to go out to a real fun-fair, and put some of this into practice. *Experience* the analogy: the fun-fair as a microcosm of the wider world. Yes, I know the fairs are tacky, expensive, and often don't seem to be much fun – especially if you're on your own. It's hard work to *make* it fun. But then so is life, isn't it? It's all in your point of view. . .

All the rides are like this. We choose them, too: crazy obstacle courses, or some absurd box lurching, twisting, stomach-wrenchingly swirling from side to side in the sky. But what do we do if it suddenly stops being fun, if it all gets too much? Once we're on the ride, we're on it: we're committed. No matter how rough, we can't get off until it's finished – not without getting *really* damaged rather than merely shaken around a bit. . . So what do we do?

Wait it out: that's all we *can* do. We can't blame anyone else for it: *we* chose this ride, after all. . . But we know it *does* come to an end: everything, whether 'good' or 'bad', comes to an end eventually. If we need to, we can recover then. But in the meantime, while it's still going on and all seems just too much, the only essential is not to panic. That only wastes energy, scatters it everywhere but where it could be some use. A few tricks can help, to keep the panic at bay, together with a little discipline: look straight ahead, for example, and keep breathing in long, smooth, deep, regular breaths. We don't try to control the fear, but work *with* it: stand back from ourselves, so to speak, and watch the emotions passing through, neither attached to them, nor detached from them, but 'non-attached'. All that standard stuff: mystical-sounding clap-trap that always seemed quite useless – until we discover we need it *now*!

Just like the rest of life, really...

And the fun, the joy, is not in the action but in the *process*. Not in holding on to any one emotion or action, but in *all* of them. In *being* them, rather than doing; in being *alive*. There's a lot to learn in the fair...

THE HALL OF MIRRORS

After a few rides, we'll need a rest: take a break to clear the dizziness and the scrambled sensation in the guts. Wander into the hall of mirrors, perhaps. But is it any better in there?

Reflections. Everywhere we look, there are more reflections of ourselves. And distorted reflections at that. As our point of view changes, so do these images of ourselves: here, there's a 'me' that's stretched; there, there's another that makes me look as fat as I sometimes fear I am. In another, a matched pair, I see myself reflected and reflected and reflected from alternating sides, on and on into infinity. And over there is one that's really strange: at first I can see myself quite clearly, but upside-down; but as I get closer it suddenly goes all chaotic and confused, and then reappears the right way up, but somehow stretched and magnified. Odd... I don't quite know whether to laugh or be frightened: there's something a little weird going on in here...

Again, a bit like life...

I look around my home: a mirror of my life. Reasonably tidy, a bit cluttered, probably just too much *stuff*. Books and papers everywhere, system manuals side-by-side with books on psychology and magic. A computer printer that's been awaiting repair for weeks; flowers in a vase that have probably been dead even longer; and of course a puddle of unfiled invoices in a corner. But the floor is clean, the washing-up is done, the bed made; and over there is the Chinese streamer with its coloured threads drifting in the breeze, interweaving like the threads of wyrd. And my grandfather's brass microscope on the top of the bookshelf, a friend's painting on the wall: old memories. All pretty much a reflection of me, I suppose.

How does your home reflect you – your state of mind, of heart, of being? Look around you: see the reflection in where and how you live. And see how what it is reflects in you, in what you do, how you live. Accept it for what it is: "I am what I am!" – if we want to change it, we first have to recognise what it is. . .

The nature of wyrd itself suggests that life would be like that: everything a reflection of everything else. Since the same threads of life that make up the wyrd pass through everywhere and everyone, 'out there' would naturally be a reflection of 'in here'. And the bits of ourselves we don't like will tend to be even more prominent 'out there' precisely because we're not looking at them 'in here'. We can access the same stuff either way: it often *seems* easier doing so by looking at the outside reflection – by looking at what's going on in the world 'outside' of us, the world that seems to be 'not-I' – than by delving deep inside. We can choose – as long as we remember that it's all the same stuff. The inside is the outside is the inside: what we see is always a reflection.

But there are two important catches. One is to recognise that much of what we see is our 'projection' onto the mirrors: the more we dislike something, and the more we hide it in ourselves, the more it will appear outside, to maintain the balance of the reflection. Whichever way it comes, it'll be an issue that our wyrd requires us to face. We can't escape our wyrd: there's no evading the Fates. So we can face it either as happenings 'out there', apparently outside of our control; or we can deal with the issue 'in here', by finding the courage and the awareness to look at what we're *actually* asking for from life.

It's our choice: it's *always* our choice. But since it's our wyrd, there's also always a twist. . .

And that's the other catch: all those mirrors 'out there' distort things, to a greater or lesser degree. Things also change according to our point of view: depending on the kind of mirror, the reflection may change as we move, but it'll still be distorted. Rather like the relationship between want and need, the mirrors often reflect in metaphor rather than literally: it's up to us to interpret the metaphor, to make sense of what we're being shown. With practice, we can learn to interpret even a wildly distorted mirror: but it's easier to start with those that are reasonably predictable!

Some distorting mirrors are like 'yes-men', in that they only show us what we want to see, whether it's true or not; others always show us up in our worst light. Neither are much actual help if we're trying to work out what's going on around us. But that's often all we'll get, if we ask others to help as mirrors: because of all the fears that are floating around in the culture, people are often afraid or unwilling to tell us the truth that they see. A true friend, then, is one who'll risk reflecting back exactly to us what they see or feel, with compassion yet without 'protecting' us from realities that might hurt.

So try what one colleague calls a 'reality check'. If you feel you're *certain* about something – particularly an intuitive certainty – take the risk, and talk to your friends about it. Ask them to respond in the moment, without thinking: not their considered thoughts, but their immediate responses to *you*. Watch the mirroring in action: let go, treat any criticism not as an attack, but as a reflection of your own *inner* uncertainty, echoing through the wyrd. What do you learn?

In the end, there's almost no point in arguing with people, or fighting with them over what is true or not-true – because what we see 'out there' are mirror-masks, reflections of our own *inner* selves! Fighting with others is as foolish as fighting with our own reflection in the mirror. It is 'out there', of course: but it's also 'in here'. And it's often far more effective – if not necessarily simpler, at first – to deal with the issue inside, by looking within, rather than by struggling in futility against the chaos and distortions of the outside world.

Everything around us is a mirror, reflecting the threads of wyrd that pass through us all: the outside is the inside is the outside. But we do usually have the choice of which mirrors we wish to face: it's important to choose with care. There's always a choice; but there's also, as always, a twist. . .

WALKING THE TIGHTROPE

Perhaps a little bewildered, we leave the hall of mirrors by what looks like a back door. As we blink in the suddenly bright light, the door slams shut behind us: then we realise where we are. A tiny platform, high above the circus ring: and the only way out is by walking the tightrope! It's a long way across on that wire: but it's an even longer way down if we don't make it. . . There *is* a something like a safety-net down there, but it's mighty small: and even if we *do* land in it, there seems to be some kind of weird contraption attached which would put us right back on this rickety little platform again. No easy way out: it's either across. . . or down. . . Some puzzle!

The wyrd has a habit of dumping us in the infamous sink-or-swim scenario, apparently to force us to learn the hard way some lesson we've been avoiding. I have many memories of situations like these – particularly from the haphazard way in which I used to run my business. *Somehow* I survived them all – I've often no real idea how! But looking back I can see in each case the aspect of reality that I'd left out of balance: the aspect of myself that I was refusing to face in the hall of mirrors. One way or another, it seems, the wyrd would find a way to get me to deal with it. . .

☞

---

placing me back on the platform at the beginning of the tightrope again and again.

But oh! the embarrassment in looking back at some of those issues! Definitely some sizeable examples of the silliness-barrier there. . .

Think back to some examples of your own. What kind of weird hoops and balancing acts were you put through before you got the lesson? And what did you learn?

How do we get across the tightrope? The short answer is '*very* carefully. . .'! But it's not just a question of balance. There's also a matter of timing: if we go too fast, we'll almost certainly slip somewhere; yet if we go too slow, trying to control every fraction of every move, we'll also fall. Reality has its own ideas about timing, and won't wait for us to catch up!

A nice illustration of this – given this circus metaphor – is juggling. In principle, it's extremely simple: you throw one ball in the air, and catch it; then another; and another. The problem is that you have to do this with all three at the same time: and they won't wait! The trick is to let go, to *allow* yourself to catch them without trying to control the process; and also to allow things to 'go wrong', too, especially while you're learning. Try it sometime!

And there's also a matter of commitment: once we start, we have to keep going. In fact trying to turn round and go back is probably the most dangerous thing we can do – but that's exactly what we'll try to do if we panic. That's one reason why so many of us – I, for one – spend so much of our time avoiding commitment. But the wyrd has that habit of throwing us in at the deep end if we wait around too long – and we find then that we're committed, whether we want to be or not!

"How on earth did I get myself into this mess? More to the point, how do I get out of it?" A familiar feeling, perhaps?

For many issues, we don't actually have a choice about whether we face them: the wyrd will make sure of that. It seems to be our fate: we can't evade it – the same issue just keeps coming back and back, harder and harder, until we do finally face it. But we do usually have some choice as to when, and how – as long as we do take that choice before the wyrd takes it for us. If we're honest, we *know* we can see – or sense – these situations coming; we can feel that sense of 'impending wyrd'. And it would probably be wiser to deal with it while we have the chance – rather than have it deal with us, so to speak. It's a long way down otherwise. . .

The balance of how we deal with issues is important, too. It's easy to overbalance: if we go too fast or too slow, if we don't keep awareness of what we're doing, or if we try to control, we'll lose it. What happens next depends on how badly we've overbalanced. . . most often we only know about what's happened when we land in the net! But it's a long drop, and the ropes can be harsh: we'll be lucky if we get away with only a few bruises. Sometimes it can be a lot harder than that. . .

> Quite often, with hindsight, we can interpret some 'misfortune' – an accident, an illness, an end to a relationship or a business – as a weird kind of message, forcing us to face an issue of our own. Time to slow down, *deal* with it; rest, even. I can certainly see how I was so afraid of loneliness that I wasn't giving myself the time alone that I *needed*: so the wyrd gave it to me. I didn't exactly like the *way* it gave it to me – some very painful times there. . . but I have to admit that it was the only way I'd have faced it. My choice, either way, I suppose. . .
>
> Think of an example of your own. What was the message there? (Remember that it may well have been in metaphor – 'hungry for company', 'starving for company' – so you may need to look deep inside for an answer.) What did you learn? And how would you get the message back to the wyrd that you'd rather learn it a different way next time?

Each issue we have to face is our own personal tightrope. We can't ask others to do it for us: it's our problem, our own fate, our own wyrd. If we cling too much to others, or allow them to cling to us, there's no way we'll be able to balance on the rope: then we're *all* in trouble. And some of us may miss the net on the way down. . . we've all seen examples of that. . .

This *is* a tightrope. But like the tightrope, there are well-understood ways to tackle that balance. We learn to be aware, for example, that it is indeed a long drop: we don't deny that fact, but we also don't feed it with our fears. So we don't look down: we'll only panic if we do! The way to deal with the tightrope is to get a clear direction of where we want to go – that tiny-looking platform on the other side – then look straight ahead, just place one foot in front of the other: and just keep going. In many ways that's all there is to it.

It really *is* a bit like life!

BRING ON THE CLOWNS!

On the ground at last: relief! But who are those weird people in the shadows? Uh-oh: it's the clowns – and it looks like they think we're part of the act! That's *another* fine mess we've gotten ourselves into!

This whole tangled, tortuous mess of life is just a chaos of clowns. It *is* a joke, there's no doubt about that – though often one in dubious taste. It may not seem much fun at times to be on the receiving end of yet another one of life's custard pies, though the watchers may well think it's hilarious – perhaps especially as they're not the ones it's happening to at the moment! But we'd better get ourselves in the right frame of mind to enjoy it, because it's slapstick time, whether we like it or not. . .

So often we'd like things to be ordered, controlled, sensible, *rational*. We don't want things to be silly and stupid: we want things to make sense, to have a reason, a meaning, a purpose.

The short answer is: they don't. Life *is* also crazy; life *is* also stupid; life *is* also pointless. At the least, it includes those aspects into itself: so it won't always make sense.

Life *is*. That's all. . .

Everywhere is chaos: and there's no point in complaining about it. It *is*. In science, for example – or at least in engineering – there's probably only one true law: Murphy's Law. But being a law, it also applies to itself, and usually cancels out – so what we think of as 'order' is better understood as chaos cancelling chaos. Not so much probability theory, you might say, as improbability in practice... And there is, of course, a twist, as the new mathematics of chaos demonstrates: evolution is 'chaos with feedback', simple systems can be surprisingly complex, complex systems surprisingly simple, different processes can follow similar patterns, and similar-looking processes follow very different ones. As one writer put it, "behind apparent order lies an eerie kind of chaos; yet behind that chaos lies an even eerier kind of order". So even the chaos is weird!

The ordinary turns out to be weird; the weird twists of wyrd turn out to be the ordinary, the normal reality of life. And we thought this was *serious*? It's time we took some lessons from the clowns!

Yet behind it all there *is* 'an even eerier kind of order'. And we can use that to *enjoy* the weirdness, rather than trying to fight against it. It's not always easy; and it is, of course, weird. We've come a fair way along it already: but now it's time to put it more into practice. So it's time to leave the circus and the fun-fair, and return from the metaphor to our everyday world. And move onward within it, steadily, each in our own way, one step at a time.

11

ONE STEP AT A TIME

Back in the real world, after our foray into the fair, we can stop and take a look around at our own version of reality. But for many of us, it may seem at first to be a nasty surprise. . . All the same old problems, still there: but now they seem even *worse*.

I think I'll just give up and go to a monastery or something. Or just give up entirely. . .

Stop. Wait a moment. Things may well *look* worse: but that's only because we can now see how bad they always were in the first place. There has been a big change, a vast improvement – but as yet it's mostly in our ability to see what's going on, and to understand some of those weird and tortuous twists in what is laughably called the 'normal' world. The real changes can't happen without that wider awareness. It's unfortunate, though, that as a side-effect things often appear almost unbearably awful. And we want to change it all *now*. Desperately. A new sense of panic.

If that's what's happening now, don't worry! In the normal warped way of wyrd, it's an indication that things are getting *better*, not worse. We're no longer 'numbed out': and while it means we can now feel a lot of the old long-forgotten hurts – with all too much clarity, perhaps – we're no longer at the effect of them in the same way as before. We've broken loose from the rigid mould of our old conditioning. And in actual fact the worst is probably over: we've done the hardest part, which was to get started at all.

Most 'self-transformation' books tell us that our aim should be to 'get rid of' our patterns – all our old fears and such – that we dislike. This happens, unfortunately, to be impossible: if we try to follow that advice, we're going to be deeply disappointed. The reality is that these old patterns keep coming back again and again – and they always will. The senses taker, the silliness barrier, those obnoxious games of power-over and power-under that everyone plays – they'll always be there. They're part of the wyrd: regardless of whether we like them, they're aspects of us all. And at first sight that seems to make the whole idea of personal growth a pointless task.

But as long as we face these patterns, and face the fears that drive them, they *do* get easier to deal with: they never *quite* disappear, however hard we try, but they do become less and less of a problem. And the reason they reappear is that they always have something new to show us. By our accepting their lessons, they change – as Ram Dass once put it – from being house-guests we can't get rid of, to visitors we can safely welcome in for tea – knowing that they will move on, and sooner rather than later. "Ah, sexual *perversity*!", he said, as an example, "haven't met you in months! Do come in, the kettle's on. . .!"

In time we can accept *anything* that comes to us on the web of wyrd. In time. . . but it probably won't feel like that now! It takes practice: and practice often means allowing things to go wrong in order for them eventually to go more right. That's why things may well seem to be going even more wrong than before. If that is the case, accept that it *is* only a stage, a temporary part of the process. And it *is* survivable: all we have to do is keep going, keep going, one step at a time.

A STATE OF SURVIVAL

Even if it's not painful now, the important point is to keep going when it does become so. Which it will: it does. It's part of the process. It comes, and it goes: we need to remember, then, that it *does* go!

Looking at old issues will bring up old hurts – long-forgotten, perhaps, but still lurking in the background, and still in the way until they're dealt with. Most often, they're dealt with simply by looking at them, and letting them go. But since it's only too natural to avoid pain, and avoidance seems the obvious choice, the tendency will be to run away back to the old numbing habits – especially if, as per our cultural conditioning, we translate 'more painful' as 'more failure'. Yet it *is* only temporary – *if* we keep going. Once we've started on some metaphoric tightrope, we must keep going till we've crossed it: if we stop – if we panic and try to turn round on the tightrope, so to speak – we risk being frozen for a while in a kind of limbo state, where the old hurts are staring us in the face again but nothing is moving. And that's not comfortable at all.

What matters here are those often-hyped qualities of 'self-esteem' and 'a positive attitude', which essentially come down to a sense of trust and optimism about ourselves in the long term. We need a sense of direction, of clarity about our long-term aim. And also we need to remember the crucial distinction between happiness and joy: happiness is ephemeral, and cannot be held, whereas joy – riding the roller-coaster of emotions – can last the rest of our lives.

As the old story tells us, we enter the stream of life when we're born, and our life flows onward from there. Change is the only constant in our lives – a stream of ephemeral incidents, flowing down to a greater ocean. So imagine life being like a river, flowing from the mountain to the sea: with rushing torrents and wide stately curves, with steep canyons, open meadows and stagnant bywaters. And imagine yourself floating down this river, as a leaf, a stick, a boat – choose! What part of the river are you in now? And how do you enjoy it?

On your journey down the river, what do you encounter? Are there obstacles in the way, like rocks or a waterfall? Are you in the main flow of the river, or stranded in some side-current?

We flow with the river: we have no choice about that. But we do still have choices. We can waste energy in a futile fight against the river, for example; or be pushed along, inert and passive, at

☞

---

the mercy of the whims of Fate – and complain about our powerlessness. Or we can choose to work *with* the river's flow: action at the right moment – and only then – can give true direction to our path in life. But how do we choose? How do you know when it's 'the right moment'? Meditate on that for a while.

The way we act is important. It's not action in the usual sense, but rather something that flows from a receptive awareness – a state of being rather than doing. At the beginning, this 'receptive action' is easily confused with passive inaction: it's another of those subtle but crucial distinctions that can take a long time to learn. With practice, we do get the balance right – and the wyrd gives us plenty of practice, whether we want it or not!

FACING FRUSTRATION

The hard part, perhaps, is accepting that it *is* only one step at a time. We all want it to change *now*. And it doesn't. Change happens when it happens: "I'll get there when I get there – not before, and probably not after", as I often have to remind myself. . . We can place the invitation, so to speak; but after that we have to wait, quietly, receptively, listening – as the Taoists would say, "we can't push the river". Even if we try to force change, this often prevents or delays it, just as trying to prevent change often brings about that very change. Weird – of course.

It's worth remembering that the three 'Sisters of Wyrd' are the sisters of *time*: their names mean 'past', 'present' and 'future'. We can't fight the Fates – which means we also can't fight time. If we have to wait, we have to wait: there's nothing we can do about it. But we're not used to waiting: we're all trained to *action*, thinking always in terms of *now*. The result is often chaotic, especially in two modes which another friend describes as 'White Rabbit' and 'ice-cream'. In the former ("I'm late, I'm late, for a very important date") we confuse the present with the future, and get stuck in ineffectual panic; while in the 'ice-cream' mode ("want it *NOW!*")

we confuse the future with the present, and get stuck in angry frustration – which again achieves nothing.

We get frustrated because it's the wrong time, or the wrong person, or the wrong situation. And it's easy to reach out and blame the 'other' – whatever it is – rather than recognising that it's actually our own expectations that are at fault. It *ought* to be this way, it *should* be this way, we'd say: but whilst those words may be magic in the power-under game, Reality Department takes no notice at all! By assuming that our expectations *are* reality, we disempower ourselves again: so somehow we have to learn to deal with it, and reclaim the power of choice that we lose to it so easily.

I've been painfully familiar with frustration-anger: ranting and raging for days on end at snail-paced bureaucracy, for example – dammit, I want to get *on* with my life! But it's a very specific emotion: I can feel, even while it takes me over, that it comes from the head – from my fixed expectations about time – and is quite different from the true and powerful anger that wells out on rare occasions from the heart. And because it *is* a specific emotion – one I can recognise only too well – I've come to use it as a clue that tells me that I *can't* do anything about the situation. It's not in my control: so I simply have to wait, whether I like it or not. . . another lesson from the wyrd!

Is this familiar? How often do you find yourself 'run over' by this kind of anger? How do you deal with it? How do you bring yourself back out of the 'ice-cream' mode while allowing the situation to work itself out?

Frustration-anger is childish, which is one reason why it's difficult for us to admit to it – the silliness-barrier again. The way out is to develop that child*like* awareness, watching, watching in amusement and wonder. Just stand back and watch, like a child, as we go through our usual loops. . . and slowly, for example, we can see the subtle difference between when something isn't working because we're not trying hard enough, and when it's not working because we're trying too hard. With that awareness, we can recognise when we don't *need* to try harder in some situation –

111

because trying harder would only make things worse – and so release the frustration, the pressure to 'do it *now*'. But it takes time, and practice: it's important to give ourselves that time, and allow things to 'go wrong' in the meanwhile. It's not easy, of course. . . easier, in fact, to get stuck in frustration about still getting stuck in frustration!

Some of the tricks and techniques that we've learned so far can help. We can use affirmations, for example: "I, ___, now release my frustration about ___". We know perfectly well that it isn't true at the moment: but the point of the affirmation, and similar tools of the mind, is to place the invitation so that it can become so – especially if we've learnt a habit of believing that it can't be so. And it's useful to look back at that discussion about 'everyone is to blame': in some way we've chosen – if only by default – to get ourselves into this situation, so what can we learn from it?

Most important of all, though, is not to berate ourselves over the fact that things – or we ourselves – haven't yet changed. It's all subject to the wyrd, to the 'sisters of time': we must place the invitation, but change happens when it happens to happen – not before, and probably not after. Change is secretive: it only seems to happen when we're not looking. And whilst the moment of change is instantaneous, to get to that moment takes time. Another weird paradox to ponder, perhaps?

PANICS AND PRIORITIES

In a way, that 'ice-cream' mode is self-centred, focussed on our *own* expectations of time: "*I* want it now". The 'White Rabbit' mode, by contrast, is focussed on our beliefs about other people's expectations of time: "I'm late, I'm late" is 'other-centred' – if it's centred at all! Rushing around trying to do everything at once, we'll be lucky to get anything actually done at all: there's a real danger in scattering our attention at random – and losing our sense of self in the panic.

The word 'panic' is linked to the Greek prefix 'pan-', meaning 'everywhere' – and in panic our attention is everywhere, anywhere but *here*. In what ways do you find yourself falling into panic? How do you recognise that state? And how do you reclaim your sense of self and purpose, in order to get anything done?

It's interesting to note the roots of panic, as described in Greek mythology: it's a response to the nature-god Pan, whose name also means 'everywhere'. More accurately, it's a failed response: if your courage failed when you found yourself facing Pan, you'd fall into a state of panic – rushing to be everywhere but here! The way to face Pan, in that tradition, was to be clear in your purpose, and use his enormous energy – the energy of everywhere, all focussed on *here* – to help you in your task.

That concept of Pan as 'everywhere' is useful in other ways. He represents the interweaving of everything and everywhere in *here*, and here in everywhere and everything: in fact one way to understand wyrd, if you're more familiar with Greek mythology, is to combine the imagery of the three sisters of Fate with that of Pan – especially his wry humour and love of life, so different from the cold and dispassionate Moirae!

A very masculine symbol of the ubiquity of nature, Pan also represents power, a power without limit: but we first have to have a focus for that power, since true power, as we've seen, is strictly 'the ability to do work'. And because he symbolizes everywhere and everything, he also tends to represent what Jung describes as the 'shadow', all those fears and unacceptable aspects of ourselves that we don't want to face. So his most common depiction now, as 'the Devil', is actually the symbol of the shadow that we're usually too frightened and too dishonest with ourselves to face: it's hardly surprising, then, that so much of our culture is best described as 'pan-demonium' – 'demons everywhere' – a permanent state of panic!

Panic also has a weird counterpart: inertia. When there are so many changes that have to be made, each of them dependent on the others, and each of which has to be done *now*, which one do

we do first? "There's a hole in my bucket, dear Liza, dear Liza...".
So which one does get done first? The usual answer is: none. A
real barrier of inertia. . . often linked to a sense of futility, of
hopelessness.

We've tried panic: it doesn't work. Now we're stuck. That
strange state of 'stuckness': a kind of frozen fascination, an actively passive nothingness, like a mouse cornered by a cat. It's
actually the same energy that drives us to action, but now turned
inward against us: the so-called fight-or-flight syndrome is more
accurately 'fight or flight – or freeze'. The moment we look out
from that space, everything screams for attention – now, *now*,
NOW! – and we're quickly overwhelmed. Inertia and lethargy are
a kind of escape from the panic: but nothing gets done, because
it's an 'escape' into nothingness.

The way past that wall of inertia is to take things one at a time.
Not nothing, slumped in hopelessness; nor everything at once, in
a chaotic panic; but just *one* step at a time. Often, any step will do,
as long as it's a step: "the journey of a thousand miles begins with
a single step". And this is where that stuff about 'listening to the
inner self' comes in: the outer analytic awareness can only focus
on one thing at a time, which is why we get lost in chaos so easily
when we try so hard to control; but while the inner awareness
can't focus in that way, it *can* maintain an overview of the twists
and turns we need to maintain direction. And to listen to that inner
awareness, we have to slow down, be quiet, be still – which is in
any case a good way to reduce the grip of panic. "So what do I do
now?", I might ask myself. "Oh yes – the washing-up. . ." If I'm
stuck in lethargy or in panic, even completing that task can be
considered a major achievement!

It's important to develop a vision of what we want, so as to give
that inner awareness a direction in which to aim, and from which
to derive priorities in the moment. When we're half-drowning in
alternate waves of lethargy and panic, this is not exactly easy! But
think of it in terms of choosing which of the threads of wyrd we
each relate to best, which ones feel right to us – and then allow
ourselves to weave across on the warp of wyrd towards them. If

we can maintain that vision – never easy at the best of times! – each choice then becomes a deliberate move towards that goal, though it's not so much the goal that's important, as having a goal at all. Given the twisted nature of wyrd, the true 'towards' choice may well seem to be one that takes us further away: and that's when a trust in our inner awareness becomes important. But learning – or re-learning – to trust is not a quick process; and in any case is hard, since its choices so often seem so wrong. . .

Here's an exercise on visions and choices – lovingly lifted from a certain well-known workshop!

Imagine yourself in twenty years' time. What are you doing in this 'now'? Where are you? Who is around you? What do you look like? How have you succeeded in your aims? How do you feel? Let the feelings wash over you.

Now come back, to ten years from now. What are you doing? Who are you with? Who are you now? What choices are you making that will enable you to reach that self you saw ten more years into the future?

Now come back another five years, to five years from now. Again, who are you? What choices are you making? What are your priorities here?

And come back, to just one year from now: who are you now, what are your choices now?

So come back to *here, now*: what are your choices, your focus for your interweavings with the wyrd? Remember that what you're doing *now* will in some way determine the person and life you 'saw' in twenty years' time; though remember too that while there's always a choice, there's always a twist. . .

Every one of our choices is part of the path that leads us to where we want to be in five, ten, twenty years. Everything matters: every choice, however trivial, is still a real choice on the wyrd. To keep out of the panic state, and maintain our priorities, we need to find a way to keep that quiet focus, of trying without trying. Listen to that inner awareness that *does* connect with the web of wyrd – and accept whatever it is that we get.

So what do I do now? Oh yes: the washing-up. . . Just what I don't want to do, of course: but that's what I've got!

RE-ACCEPTING SELF

Part of accepting what I have is accepting that I have myself, exactly as I am in each moment. Once again, "I am what I am" – and that includes all my many and evident imperfections. I dislike them, I'm embarrassed about them, I try to hide them: but at the moment they're part of me, whether I like them or not. As long as I maintain some kind of focus, some kind of direction, and allow them to change more to what I'd like, they will change – in time. The 'in time' part is perhaps the hardest to accept. . . but change happens when it happens to happen – not before, and probably not after!

We can't *make* things change; likewise, we can't make *ourselves* change. All we can do is provide the invitation, the direction, and a certain if undefinable amount of effort: and we then have to accept a wait of a certain if undefinable amount of time. Changes happen suddenly, secretively, unobtrusively, partly to keep at bay the fears that make up the silliness-barrier: we don't so much break a pattern as discover that it's 'suddenly and silently vanished away' – we no longer react to something in the old habitual way. As before, change happens not because we find something new, but because we let go of something old – usually because we finally accept that the habit doesn't serve us any more.

> Change won't happen while we watch: so one of the tricks to change involves what we might call 'conscious forgetting'. I'll work through every angle of some problem, without aiming for any real resolution; and then move onto something else, and quietly forget about it. Later on – it may be minutes, hours, days, weeks later – I become aware that there's been a change: and often it takes some effort to work out what the change was *from*! I don't really know *how* the change has happened; but by allowing

for change, then forgetting that I'd done so, the change somehow worked itself, without my conscious involvement at all.

Think back on some old patterns that have already changed for you: when did you notice they'd changed? Had you forgotten they were once a problem? And having remembered, and thus perhaps re-awoken it, how do you set out to forget it again?

There's a beautiful old Quaker story that describes this kind of change, but with a typical wry twist. In the early days of the movement, a true gentleman would never be seen without his sword – it was his mark of honour, of pride – but Quakers, with their commitment to pacifism, would not wear them. One new member, William Penn (later famous as the founder of Pennsylvania), found himself caught in internal conflict: his principles told him to get rid of his sword, but his pride wouldn't let him – and he could not make himself change. "Wear thy sword while thou canst", was George Fox's cheerful advice. Don't worry about it, don't struggle, don't try: if you're committed to the change, sooner or later you *will* find that it's happened. But in the meantime, "wear thy sword while thou canst": enjoy your sword while you have it, for one day it will no longer be there!

It's useful to keep a diary, to keep track of the changes in our dialogue with the world – and note that it's essential to record what's seemed good and successful in the day as well as what went wrong! The diary then acts as a proof that change can and does take place – something that can be very useful in those times when it seems the blackness and bleakness will never end. . . Those 'endarkenments' do pass, in time, but it can seem an unbearably long time: and so something of our own, like a diary, will prove to be a real help in a way that nothing else can do. It can be very consoling, for example, to discover that an old pattern that's re-surfaced and we're struggling with now was far worse and far more dominating a few months back!

A diary is also a way of re-accepting ourselves, and of watching our changes as we interact with our wyrd. "I am who I am – even though I don't understand who I am", as I found I'd written in my own diary a while back. Accepting the totality of who we are also gives the wyrd a kind of starting point on the threads, from which to weave in a change: so if we try to deny our faults and failings, we actually block the possibility of change.

We change all the time in any case. I look back at photographs taken of me at various times in my life: and even in the most recent ones I can sometimes barely recognise who I see there. "Who *is* this? I *think* I've seen them before. . ." And yet it's always been the same me – constantly changing, yet still somehow identifiably *myself*.

> For each of us, our face is a record both of the continuity of 'I' and of the constant changes that pass by on the wyrd – "It's written all over your face", someone might say. So look in a mirror: who is this stranger that you see? Have you met them before?
>
> Look at that face for a while: what do you see written there? What are the feelings that are written on that face? Emotions on the surface: "I am what I am". If you can, acknowledge those emotions by acting them out: release them from the face, and let them fly free. And watch the changes. . . watch the changes over time in this built-in 'diary' of your own.

I am who I am, constantly changing, yet always the same: it's important that I accept that. Some changes happen whether we want them or not: we can't evade the Sisters of Time, for example. But to make changes that we want, we have to be committed to them – and then allow each change to happen in its own way, and in its own time. And with that choice, that commitment, there's also a weird twist: to release something we don't want, don't like, we often first have to enjoy it, to love it for what it is. So "wear thy sword while thou canst" – enjoy who we are in each moment, for that moment will not return again!

THE PROCESS OF CHANGE

Change is always weird. It's a process, a state of becoming rather than being: and we pass each of our goals long before we recognise that we've done so. And yet it all takes time: its own time, not ours. All we can do is provide the direction, the energy – and then wait. Waiting is not easy. . .

It helps, though, to have an understanding of the weirdness of change – not just in theory, but in practice. The more we try to control change, the more we try to impose some kind of order, the less it happens – except for changes that we don't want. True change has to be invited, encouraged: and it thrives best in the kind of quiet chaos that can, paradoxically, demand of us an intensity of courage. "Behind apparent order lies an eerie kind of chaos; yet behind the chaos lies an even eerier kind of order" – and that 'eerier kind of order' is weird. Wyrd. So by placing ourselves deliberately in an atmosphere of wyrd, we give ourselves the chance to take an active role in the change. By letting go of the fear, the need for control, we give ourselves the choice to reclaim a different kind of control with our lives. But it is a choice, of course, that always has a twist. . .

In the next few chapters we'll look at some ways to work with wyrd in practice. Some of them work well for some people, others prefer others – we each choose our own wyrd – but it's worth while to at least *try* each one.

In each case, look at the techniques it uses to connect with the web of wyrd; look inside, to that inner awareness, to see if they feel right for you. Put them into practice, and see what happens: it's important to watch the results, but *don't* try to make them fit some kind of explanation – you'll miss the whole point of it if you do. Change thrives in chaos; explanations are an attempt at order; the two don't easily mix!

In reaching out to work *with* the wyrd, it's important to be aware that many of the techniques we use can bring to the surface old obstacles and old patterns – and sometimes that will hurt, because old emotions will come up too. Let them happen, and let them go: they do pass. But in a way this is often an indication that change *is* happening: the old habits fade, the old stuckness is released, and we're free to move again. By keeping careful track of the changes, and developing that quiet space of inner awareness, we learn to know – not merely think, but *know* – when it works and when it doesn't. And that's definitely enlightening, in every sense.

But it can also, at times, be frightening: the wyrd is, after all, weird, and we all have our own fears about that. The wyrd connects us with everything, everywhere, everywhen: and we all have things that we'd rather not face! So there's often a sense of being tested: and as with Pan, it's important that we keep our courage, or we'll collapse back into panic. As long as we maintain that inner awareness, and that acceptance of "I am what I am", we can *always* survive the 'test' – though sometimes it's hard to believe at the time. The way to cope with it, even in the worst of times, is to remember what we came here for: and just keep going, keep going – one step at a time.

12

WEAVING THE THREADS OF WYRD

So far we've talked a lot about wyrd: but what *is* it? The short answer is that it is what it is: there is no such thing as an 'explanation' as far as wyrd is concerned. But while we can't define it, we *do* all have our own experience of it. We're actually very familiar with it, and we have a very clear practical understanding of what wyrd is: it's just that we're not often aware of the fact.

If that isn't obvious, just think for a moment: when and where and under what conditions do you use the word 'weird'? Wherever you do, that's also wyrd. It's as simple as that. . .

So how do you use the word 'weird'? Think back on some experiences that you would regard as weird – preferably your own experiences rather than someone else's. Why would you describe them as weird? And was there any particular feeling or sense of awareness that suggests that you should describe them that way?

Build a new habit, perhaps, of noticing when you describe something as 'weird': look at the circumstances, the feelings, in each case as you do so. And use it to expand your understanding of the nature of wyrd: your connection with the tortuous nature of totality.

What we most easily recognise in something that's 'weird' is the twist, the surprise. "It's weird, meeting you like this", you might say; and they'd reply, "That's weird, we were just thinking of you". But it's not so easy to see the subtle web of choices that links the weirdness together: there's always a twist, but there's also always a choice. One of the most important results of re-connecting ourselves with wyrd is that we discover we're not solely at its effect, 'at the mercy of our Fate': so we learn to recognise that we do have choices – and can thus reclaim them as our own.

But that disturbing sense of 'weirdness' that accompanies our contact with wyrd – "it sent shivers down my spine", we might say – makes it hard to see the choices we've made that have led us there. And again the wyrd interweaves through everything, often showing us things we don't want to face: "that old guy was really weird", might be your response to the frightening glimpse of totality represented by the antics of some strange old man. It's not comfortable to face your connection with him: him as part of you as part of him, all inextricably interwoven on the wyrd.

Comfortable or not, that's wyrd: it is what it is. We can't control it: it *is*. And yet it's often the only place where we truly have a choice. To reclaim those choices – to re-empower ourselves, to reclaim power with and within our lives – we have to face our fear of the wyrd: and we do that best by working *with* its weirdnesses, rather than trying to fight against them!

A WEB OF CONNECTIONS

To work with wyrd, and to see it in action, we have to learn a different way of seeing – although more accurately we need to re-learn it, since it's a way of seeing that we knew well as children. We need to be able to see connections, patterns, samenesses within differences, in a way that at first seems quite alien to our usual concept of cause-and-effect. But this is true in science too: to understand the concepts of chaos, researchers had first to develop an eye for pattern – especially pattern that appeared on different scales at the same time, and what one writer described as "a taste for randomness and complexities, for jagged edges and sudden leaps". Chaos is weird – is wyrd – and full of strange connections: so much so that we need a different way of seeing before we can see them.

We usually only see separateness, difference, in self, in time, in space: the sense of 'I' and 'not-I', for example, or the way we distinguish *this* object from *that* one, or that event *then* from this event *now*. We analyse, break things apart into components, describe chains of cause and effect, refine probability into predictability. It all gives a satisfying sense of certainty, of security.

It happens to be wrong. Or incomplete, rather.

The separateness is only one side of the equation, so to speak. It's like a threadbare fabric, consisting only of the weft: it has a shape, but there's nothing holding it together. It's the cross-warp of wyrd – those weird, improbable connections – that weaves in the connectedness, and makes it into a whole.

The improbabilities blur the boundaries. Remember the Möbius loop that we saw earlier, for example: the strip of paper obviously has two sides, yet the loop as a whole, through an improbable twist, has only one. There's no set point at which it changes: the boundary is blurred. In effect, each point is both on the opposite side *and* the same side as every other. And although every point is different, every point passes through every other point. It's weird – wyrd.

All these weird happenings in our lives are much the same: both separateness *and* sameness, connectedness, at the same point. We're used to having one *or* the other: having both together is what makes it seem 'weird'. And to regard it as ordinary – to *experience* it as ordinary – takes a little getting used to!

In wyrd, the inside is also the outside: we can experience others 'out there' or 'in here', and feel the connection and the separateness at the same time. The easiest way to do this is to indulge in the age-old game of people-watching – but with a subtle difference.

Choose a café – my own favourite for this is one in the city's legal district. Sit quietly in a window, and move yourself slowly, gently, into an awareness of wyrd. . .

Allow the boundaries to blur: the shapes of passers-by become silhouettes, a two-dimensional array of shapes that merge, split-off, merge into other larger shapes. . . Allow the

☞

boundaries of time to blur: watch the shapes woven by those people in their pathways through space and time. . .

Look again at the clientele, the passers-by: so many of them in ritual dress, clothes as labels for masks. The lawyers and barristers in their formal wigs and gowns; the businessmen in the corner, in their crisp suits and ties, bragging about the 'killing' they've just made in a deal. The secretary stomping by in shoes that are 'killing' *her*: tight skirt, a mask of make-up, papers clutched in front of her. And the old man, limping, sweeping the pavement outside. Stereotypes; each one acting out an archetypal thread in the fabric of life.

But they're all there inside you too. The patterns of the wyrd echo on every scale: the things you see about each person here are metaphors for how the same threads pass through you.

The barrister, releasing her long blonde hair from under the formal wig; and the lawyer, almost a 'beard with man attached': in what ways do you conceal or express your individuality? Watch them change masks as they shed their layers in the café: what masks do you wear in different surroundings?

The businessmen: yes, they're self-serving, uncaring, aggressive, greedy – and, incidentally, evading reality, because they're drunk. But how do the same adjectives apply to you? You wouldn't be able to see this in them if it wasn't there in you. . .

The secretary: you can feel, without trying, that none of this fits her. Reach out, feel deeper, and you may well find yourself sharing her anger: she hates these clothes, this job, the people who stare at her – but she's told that she 'has to' do this. So reach deeper again: what masks do you wear because others say you 'have to'? And what are you 'holding to your chest', as a shield against the world?

And what does the old man tell you? Where are you limping inside? Where is this road inside that you're sweeping, slowly, painfully – and which you know no-one notices?

Drink up your coffee: time to go. And as you leave, look back through the window at the place where you were: and see yourself sitting there, looking through the window at yourself, like you have done at all the passers-by. The observer and the observed, interlinked on the threads of time – and wyrd.

The boundaries blur; yet there are still boundaries. Other people are still 'other'; yet we can experience the sameness within us. Non-attachment, we might say, that's also non-detachment. That's wyrd.

When we finally allow ourselves through into this awareness, it's a truly enlivening experience – among other things, we *experience* the end of the myth of separateness, and with it find a release from that crushing sense of isolation that pervades our culture. But there is a catch: non-detachment *must* also be non-attachment, especially when it comes to building an awareness of other people and their feelings. Without maintaining a clear sense of separation at the same time as building the connections, there's a real danger of 'enmeshment' in everyone else – and a risk of losing our sense of self entirely.

I learnt this the hard way a long while back, as a student in London. I went on a strict vegetarian diet for a while, 'to improve my sensitivity' for some experiments I was doing – and couldn't work out why I felt so ill every day. The answer was that I'd succeeded rather too well! As part of the practice, I was reaching out, feeling my connection with everyone else, even while sitting on a bus: so I was sharing that person's headache, the next one's sore knee, the next one's dislike of her job, and the man beside me's argument with his wife. Being 'attached' to everyone, I took it all on as part of me. . . and experienced it accordingly. *Not* a good idea: that experiment came to a very quick end! We'll come back to this issue in more detail later on.

THE ORDINARINESS OF WYRD

It's important to realise that these experiences are nothing special. They may be weird, but so what? The wyrd itself is entirely ordinary – a part of the ordinary world that we've forgotten to see, perhaps, but ordinary nonetheless. Once we stop looking only at the separateness of things, and instead remember how to see in a way that's both non-attached *and* non-detached, the wyrd once more becomes part of our ordinary, everyday world – and we can then learn to work with it.

> To not see wyrd, despite its effects being all around us, is a habit we all learn in this culture: and it's that, and the strange – literally 'weird' – feeling that we get when it forces its way into our awareness, that makes our experience of wyrd seem so 'extra-ordinary'. Like most habits, this one tends to block our ability to see what's going on around us – and blocks our awareness of wyrd, making its 'un-ordinariness' into a self-confirming myth.
>
> One way to break the habit is to go back and deliberately re-view some of your experiences of wyrd as if they're part of your ordinary world. Those weird coincidences just become 'Normal Rules'; the weird antics of that old man become a normal reflection of your own fears, echoed by him through the wyrd. Allow these things to become normal, ordinary. Seeing them this way, what do they now show you? What can you learn from them?

The wyrd is entirely ordinary: we usually don't see it because we've *learnt* to not see it. The only thing that's unusual about our usual experience of wyrd is that in some weird way it's managed to work its way through our defences against it! Once we re-learn how to see it, it sometimes seems surprising just how common it is, rather than how rare: but it shouldn't seem surprising at all, considering that wyrd is the interweaving of everything, every-where, everywhen. . .

In particular, it's important to understand that having 'weird experiences' doesn't make *us* special – or anyone else, for that matter. It's an easy mistake to make. In the past, whole religions have been constructed from some minor interaction with the wyrd that's been exaggerated out of all proportion; in the present, we see it most often in fundamentalism and much of the New Age movement, and their obsessions with 'received truth' and the (egotistical) rôle of 'the Chosen Ones'. But once we get a grasp on the *ordinariness* of wyrd, this loses its entirely unwarranted glamour. Something's weird, you say: so what? It's nothing new. People have always experienced weird coincidences and 'channelled' information, people have always had strange meetings with strange entities: the history books are full of them. So it's nothing special: it's just wyrd, doing its usual weird interweavings; the 'strange entities' most often just 'id-entities with mistaken identities'. If we're ever in doubt, it's useful to remember the old Zen saying: "Chop wood; carry water. Enlightenment! Chop wood; carry water. . ."

Wyrd is nothing special: it's nothing to get frightened about, and in a way it's also nothing to get excited about. Sure, it's weird, but so what? – it is what it is, it does what it does. But it can be useful – if we know how to use it. And that, in the end, is all that matters.

What makes it hard is that wyrd so often speaks in metaphor. Those 'received truths' of which so much is made in New Age circles may be weird, for example, but in fact the interpretations are rarely wyrd enough! They're too literal: they don't allow for the twist that's always there in our interactions with the wyrd. As with wants and needs, the metaphor – the twist – has to be translated before we can put the information to use.

To take one example, we could look at a fairly common experience, that of 'past lives'. The experience – a very real and definitely weird experience – is of seeming to live in another body, another space, another time, at the same time as in this one: and often of recognising, in some weird way, other people you know in 'this' life. In some cases the information brought back can be linked to tangible archaeological finds, or other evidence that couldn't have been known beforehand. So the literal interpretation is that it *is* a past life: one of many past lives, shared with the same people over and over again.

> Have you had experiences that seem to be of 'past lives' – or 'déjà vu', perhaps, which is sometimes interpreted that way? Remind yourself of them. Now re-view them as if they're unusual but *ordinary*, just an ordinary aspect of the wyrd. What difference does that make?

Think for a moment, though: this literal interpretation depends on a very crude and linear concept of time. And the sheer number of reincarnated Napoleons and Virgin Marys and Atlantean priests and priestesses would make anyone suspicious. . . If the wyrd's interweavings in time are as twisted as the sense of humour it certainly seems to have, we can safely assume that for a few of these experiences, the literal interpretation may well be correct – the experience is indeed of *some* past life, though not necessarily linked to any present one other than through the wyrd. But in most cases – certainly from my own experiences – it's wiser to interpret 'past lives' as mirrors of the *present*: reflections of the outside and inside, much as we saw in the café: the apparent past-life-as-Napoleon as an active metaphor for the thread of 'Napoleon' within us. Once we know how to interpret the metaphor, it can tell us much about ourselves that otherwise we probably wouldn't see (or face): but first we have to understand that it *is* a metaphor, and interpret it accordingly.

It's an ordinary experience; it's also weird. The weird is ordinary; the ordinary is wyrd. Because it's wyrd, there's always a twist; yet for the same reason, there's always a choice – one that relates not to some metaphoric past-life, but to the practical, tangible here-and-now. By reclaiming our awareness of wyrd, we can reclaim the choices that are concealed in those experiences – and begin once more to put them to use.

DO WHAT YOU WILL

If we don't see that we have a choice, then wyrd will always seem to be something that's happening *to* us – rather than *with* us. Not seeing the choice, we don't *have* a choice – and the whole weird happening is then 'out of control'. And that's frightening. So we tend to block wyrd out of our lives more and more – not realising that in reality it's there to help us, if only we'd let it do so. The wyrd is the interweaving of everything, everywhere, everywhen: once we choose to look at what it shows us, we'll find that somewhere in there will be not only what we need, but also the way to reach it. The choice is ours: we just have to remember, though, that there's always that twist. . .

Rather than complaining about life or blaming it all on someone or something 'out there', consider yourself the weaver of it. Life as a cloth of choices, conscious and unconscious: which threads do you choose? They're all there on the wyrd. All you have to do is reach out and connect with them, and you'll find they're right there, in your hands. . . and then realise they've been there all along. What do you find?

Because of our interweavings with others' choices, and because of the twist that's always there, our experience is not solely our choice – and yet to a large degree that's exactly what it is. If we won't face the results directly, the wyrd will usually find a way to show us anyway: and then offer us the chance – but with a twist – to choose again. It can take more than a little courage to accept this! But it's important to acknowledge the choices we make: that's why it can be dangerous not to know what we truly want – dangerous for ourselves, and also dangerous for others, as we saw earlier with issues such as blame and boundaries.

Look back again at some of those weird experiences that you've remembered. Re-view them this time as being linked to choices of your own: were you wanting to meet that person, for example, or was there something you wanted to avoid? What were the threads of choice – or avoidance of choice – that made up the weaving of that incident?

The problem is that so many of our choices are unconscious: they're 'made for us' by habit, by fears, by default, by allowing others we assign power-under or power-over to make them on our behalf, and so on. And because they're unconscious choices, they're hard for us to see – or often to accept as our own. By re-connecting with the wyrd, we find out what those choices are – and can thus reclaim the power to change them if we will.

Connecting with the wyrd is itself a choice, a deliberate act of will. We saw this earlier with affirmations: we make the choice – the written 'affirmation of intent' – as an act of will, a deliberate choice. We then let go, without letting go – non-attachment is also non-detachment – and trust the wyrd to work as it chooses. And the results can be magic.

Literally magic: it *is* magic, if we accept Crowley's definition of magic as 'the art and science of causing change in conformity with will'. In this sense, though, magic is best understood as a way of working on our beliefs, which changes our perceptions, which in turn changes our experience: so it's more 'the technology of inviting change' than 'the science of causing change'. We don't *cause* change as such: we choose, and something happens. Not always what we *expect* to happen, though, because there's always a twist. . .

And it's magic in another, quite different sense. The dictionary may define magic as 'illusion and trickery', but that's not what we mean when we describe some special occasion as 'magical'! Magic is also joy. . . the discovery of joy: and that too can be found within the threads of wyrd.

Yet oddly enough, to reclaim that most true of all emotions is a deliberate choice – an act of will rather than an evasion of 'won't'. So to quote Crowley again, "'Do what thou wilt' shall be the whole of the law, ere it harm none". The wyrd is yours, is ours, is everyone and everywhere. The choice is yours – do what you will!

BUT BE SURE THAT YOU WILL IT!

There is, of course, a catch: there's always a twist somewhere! It's not quite as simple as "do what you will", because we're also responsible for the choices: it always loops round in the wyrd. That's one reason why magic is also defined as 'the art of the wise' – because we need to be wise to survive it! And the wyrd doesn't maintain a simple set of accounts, like some kind of 'double-entry life-keeping': it plays subtler games than that. . . "Do what you will", it might say: "but be *very* sure that you will it. . .".

When we talk in terms of magic here, we're not talking about the modern technological magic – the kind that does exactly what we tell it, and nothing else. (Though oh! how often have I heard the despairing cry: "this machine's done exactly what I told it to do – so what on earth did I tell it to do?") The wyrd is quite different, is something deeper, older: and while our usual everyday magic was made with reason, and for a reason, this older magic is simply a part of things. It is not *for* any purpose: it just *is*. "It is magic of the heart, not of the head", as the novelist Alan Garner once put it. "It can be felt, but not known; it may work to your need, but not to your command". And if we try to control it in our usual way, we'll soon find ourselves in deep trouble: we very quickly discover that it has a will of its own.

> Once again re-view those weird experiences: but this time in the sense that 'the wyrd has a will of its own: it will answer to your need, but not to your command'. Remember the confusion between need and want – 'command' – that we looked at earlier: can you see in each experience the wyrd's response 'to your need but not to your command'? And which explains why what it gave you wasn't necessarily what you wanted. . .?

Whether it actually *does* have 'a will of its own' – or whether what we see is just the reflection of our own (child*ish* rather than child*like*) frustration – is a moot point: though since the wyrd is the interweaving of everything, everywhere, everywhen, there's likely to be something resembling 'will' somewhere! But in any case it's long been understood that it's wise to treat it *as if* it has a will of its own – in much the same way as we declare affirmations 'as if' they're true, in order for them to become so.

We can't control the wyrd: we can work with it, but we can't fight *against* it. We can't fight the Fates. . . And we can't *command* it: if we treat it with disrespect, we may well find that "there are memories about the Old Magic that wake when it moves". Sometimes we get exactly what we ask for: so we need to be very careful for what we ask!

We can't control the wyrd: but we *can* direct our relationship with it, our path within and through it. It depends to a great deal on commitment, and on respect – both of the nature of wyrd, and of ourselves – and a willingness to start from where things *are*, rather than where we'd like them to be. Slowly, steadily, we discover that we can indeed do anything we choose. But this is wyrd that we're working with: so there's also always a twist. . . Do what you will, then: but be very sure that you will it!

13

MY WORD IS MY BOND

One way of relating to the threads of wyrd is by formally stating a connection to them: we reclaim our choices by 'claiming' a thread, acknowledging, accepting and inviting it as an aspect of ourselves. We've already done this to some extent with our affirmations: but now we can see that if we're going to get anywhere with them, it involves something a bit more definite than a few lines scrawled in a note-book.

An affirmation is a commitment: a statement of intent, a statement of will. In that sense it's actually a form of practical magic: a commitment to break free of old habits, and move in new directions that *we* choose. As we saw earlier, it's no different from the way we learnt our existing habits of experience: by choice, and by repetition. But because it's a commitment – 'my word is my bond' – and because the wyrd tends to give us exactly what we ask for, we now need to become rather more careful about what we say, and how we say it.

CHOOSING YOUR WORDS

What we say *matters*. It's often difficult at first to believe that tiny changes in phrasing can have such a huge effect on our experience: but they do, especially in affirmations, where we're *committing* ourselves to what those words mean to us.

The wyrd provides us with what we ask, with what we tell it our needs are: the whole point of affirmations is to become more conscious about what we ask the wyrd to give us. But although, from our point of view, many of our dealings with the wyrd can seem tortuous in the extreme, it in fact tends to be entirely literal. In its twisted way, it gives us exactly what we ask – nothing more, nothing less.

One reason why positive phrasing is important is that, to the wyrd, everything we say is an *intention*. If I say "I am searching for my keys", the wyrd tends to interpret that as an intention to *search* – not to find. The twist is that the wyrd will thus give me every help it can in *not* finding my keys – so that I can continue searching indefinitely, as requested. . . So it becomes rather important to watch what we say: "I am finding my keys" is likely to be more successful as an intention, as well as being more optimistic in outlook!

Keep an ear open on what you say, for hidden implications like these. It takes a little practice to spot them: but it's surprising just how many there are in ordinary everyday speech – let alone in affirmations!

In the same way that we easily find ourselves confused by the weirdness of some of the wyrd's metaphors, the wyrd in turn is easily confused by ours. What *we* think of as literal, the wyrd sees as metaphor – being wyrd, it's always expecting a twist along with each of our choices. The problem is that we rarely recognise just how much of what we think of as 'obvious' is actually a kind of metaphor – and thus not obvious at all. As we saw earlier with wants and needs, we actually express most of our needs in terms of metaphor – 'hungry for company' and the like – and if we try to put those directly into an affirmation, we're not likely to get the results we expect!

In general, it's important to check that the thread of wyrd we're claiming in an affirmation is something definite. The confusion is that 'definite' is opposite for internal and external worlds: anything tangible applies to the 'outside', whilst anything intangible – a quality, a feeling and the like – tends to apply only to the 'inside' world. So if, for example, the issue we want to address is about respect from others, it's non-tangible, and thus the affirmation needs to be addressed to *ourselves*: not "I, ___, am gaining more respect from others", but "I, ___, now truly respect myself and my abilities". We could also acknowledge the way the inside is reflected in the world 'out there' – "The more I, ___, respect myself, the more others respect me" – but the focus of this affirmation still remains on the inner world.

If the issue relates to our experience of the external world, it needs to be described in the affirmation in terms of something *tangible*. In these cases the affirmation is usually linked to some kind of visualisation, to give a clear mental image as a 'handle' for the wyrd to work on. It's long been found in practice that there are surprisingly tight limits to what works and what doesn't: we'll look at this in more detail shortly, but as a general guideline, we'll find that we can't visualise ideas – only objects; we can't visualise a quality – only its by-products; and, especially, we can't visualise money – only what we want to do with it. It's important not to mix up the inner and outer worlds: "money can't buy me love", remember!

One further trap is that, as another writer commented, "there is no image for 'not' in dreams": the same applies to affirmations, which are in effect the declaration of our dreams. Negating-words like 'not' and 'no' have a nasty habit of disappearing from affirmations: as far as the wyrd is concerned, "I, ___, no longer wish to fear . . ." is often understood as "I, ___, wish to fear . . .". The usual explanation in books on affirmations is that we're still putting energy into the *idea* of fear – in this example – and it's this energy, rather than the words themselves, that the wyrd picks up. We could argue about this point, as the words themselves *do* seem important; but the general experience that 'negative' wording can be a problem is something to take account of in phrasing affirmations.

Go back through any affirmations you've been doing so far, and review them for any of these subtleties of phrasing: self-sabotaging such as "I am searching for. . .", indefinite abstracts like

"I am becoming richer", or loose negatives such as "I am no longer lonely". In particular, watch out for cases where you're relying on others to provide your *own* inner qualities: the infamous trap of "As I, ___, send out this mental vibration of love, ___ will be drawn to me" – a crude example of trying to use the wyrd as yet another mode of the power-under game!

Does anything in those affirmations you're reviewing need to be changed? If so, in what ways can you see how the former phrasing might have given the wrong message to the web of wyrd? Try out the revised phrasing as a new affirmation: what difference do you *feel* in the way you interact with the wyrd? And what difference can you sense, over time, in the results?

Remember that the wyrd is also ourselves: through the web of wyrd, we're telling *ourselves* what we want. Affirmations are not so much 'the science of taking control of your life' – as several books I've seen would put it – but something more like 'the technology of reclaiming direction with your life'. And these subtleties of language can affect not just us as individuals, but whole cultures and countries. I remember hearing many times in Melbourne, for example, that "Australia rhymes with failure" – which is hardly an incentive to national success! And the right to 'the pursuit of happiness' enshrined in the Bill of Rights effectively commits the entire United States to *pursuing* happiness, and never finding it. We're unlikely to be able to change these cultural curses; but by becoming more aware of them, we can at least reduce their effects on us. Whether we do so, though, is up to us – and to our commitment to ourselves.

A QUESTION OF COMMITMENT

An affirmation is a commitment: a statement of intent, a statement of will. It's not only a form of practical magic: it's a commitment to *ourselves*, to knowing and accepting who we are, who we are becoming; a commitment to the Self that forms a nexus for the wyrd to weave around.

We're not doing affirmations for anyone else: our word is our bond to *ourselves*. In a way it comes to the same thing – the inside is also the outside, as the same threads pass through every one of us – but the focus at this point is on ourselves.

And that's exactly what other people are likely to complain about! As we begin to end old patterns and to reclaim our own focus, the centre of our attention shifts from where it was before – which, according to the rules of the power-under game, will almost certainly have been on someone else. They're likely to notice. . . and respond. . . often not in a supportive way at all.

> Sometimes, though, the response is one of *relief*: I'd been stuck in a 'trying to buy being liked' mode for so many years that it was a real relief to my friends when I finally worked free of it! But it's far more common that as soon as we start to work on our own issues, we find ourselves accused of 'being selfish'. Has this happened to you? How did you respond?
>
> If you're in doubt, remember that you would not be able to help others with their needs if yours are never satisfied; and you can deal with that best by spending time and energy on and for yourself. Power-under is so pervasive that we've largely forgotten what being aware of ourselves is like. . . so sometimes we can even take an accusation of selfishness as an indication that we're on the right track! But it's always possible that they're right – only you can answer that. . .

The usual accusation of 'selfishness' comes in part because we're no longer (so much) centred on others. But there's another subtler part to it: because any move to break free of habits tends to expose – for everyone – the unacknowledged fears that drive the power-under game, there's a real fear of anyone within the culture doing any true work on themselves. This leads to what Alan Watts described as "the taboo against knowing who you are": and enormous pressure can be brought to bear on anyone who breaks the taboo, however unwittingly. When that happens, it *hurts*: and it's hard to keep going, to keep committed to our vision.

The old proverb is completely wrong: "sticks and stones may break my bones" but words most certainly *do* hurt us – especially when it feels like the whole culture is telling us we're wrong, we're silly, we're selfish. Sometimes it's useful to think of this as another test from the wyrd, to get us to prove that we really *are* committed to ourselves, reclaiming our right to our choices. . . We *do* "have a right to be here, no less than the trees and stars". . . .

When the going gets rough again, I often turn to the copy of 'Desiderata' on my wall, from which that last quote comes. For me, it's a kind of affirmation of hope about the world – and the comment that "whether or not it is clear to you, no doubt the universe is unfolding as it should" is a useful reminder when I fall back into 'controlling'!

Do you have a similar small text or poem which you use regularly for contemplation? How and when do you use it? In what ways does it help?

To commit to ourselves is work: sometimes very hard and very uncomfortable work. It's worth it: as we do that work, we *do* reclaim our choices. But it's not at all easy to commit to anything, especially once we realise what the commitment involves: and it's often hardest – *not* easiest – to commit to ourselves. We all have our own fears: in fact most often we can't blame others at all, because all they're doing is reflecting our own fears back at us.

And we have our own resistances to resolving our old patterns and problems: not just because we're afraid of change, but also because we'd then become responsible for them – or rather recognise that we've always been responsible for them. It's much easier to blame others, even if it isn't honest. . .

DOUBT AND DISCIPLINE

Resolving the doubt and self-doubt is really a matter of discipline. Not someone else's discipline imposed upon us, but our *own* discipline – literally being 'disciples' to ourselves – which, if anything, is far harder to accept or accomplish.

Doubt and self-doubt echo back and forth. Just when we think we've finally resolved some issue, up comes another little message from the wyrd to tell us that we haven't. And self-discipline, especially if it's not moved past the level of vague intentions – "I *am* going to do this. . . sometime!" – tends to fade into nothing. All of which suggest, strongly, that we'll never make it, that we're no good, all that kind of stuff. . . after all, there's plenty of proof that it's hopeless, just look around. . .

That's power-under – from others, from the culture, or just as likely from ourselves. All-or-nothing perfectionism is perhaps the most common trap here: "if I see any evidence that it isn't working, it proves it's not possible". The way out is to remember that this is wyrd we're dealing with, not some crude concept of cause-and-effect: so *expect* it to come and go, to fade away and quietly return when we're not looking. The whole point of having some kind of discipline is that it keeps us going in the times when our sense of connection with the wyrd does fade away. Yet at the same time, too much of the wrong kind of discipline – living by the clock, for example – will block the wyrd by leaving no space for it to enter. Discipline is another of these subtle balances – 'doing no-thing' again.

Self-discipline is a kind of dance: a self-imposed timetable that still leaves plenty of room for manoeuvre. It's important to provide some kind of pressure to give the intention that change should happen, but yet not to push it too hard: as the 'Desiderata' puts it, "beyond a wholesome discipline, be gentle with yourself". Many books on meditation, for example, recommend for beginners just one or two sessions a day, to be done strictly at the same time each day: but these should be no more than five or ten minutes each, and an inner silence of even five or ten seconds in that time can be regarded as a major achievement!

> What little self-discipline I have comes and goes – but it does come again if I let it. The wyrd needs space in which to play: panic and aggressive self-criticism only get in the way. I've learnt to wait out all the guilty feelings – "I *should* be doing my
>
> ☞

meditation, I *must* get some exercise today" – and at some point simply *discover* that I'm doing what I need to do once more.

What kind of discipline or regular practice – if any – do you follow? If the answer is 'none', it's worth while choosing something like basic yoga or meditation, and stick to a commitment to it – religiously, we might say – for a minimum of a few months. In reality, almost anything will do, as long as you remain committed to it: what you do is not so important as the fact of doing something at all in a disciplined way. As the discipline fades – it always does after the initial enthusiasm! – gently bring it back: dance with it, allow it to return. . . What happens?

Rather like "wear thy sword while thou canst", the key part of the discipline is not doing but *being*: maintaining the vision, the aim, the target, and not worrying too much about the details of how exactly to get there. This seems strange – weird – because we're so used to 'doing': but even maintaining that focus is hard enough!

Self-discipline is another test of faith, but this time of our faith in *ourselves*. We slowly learn to trust ourselves, our 'providence' to ourselves, by proving to ourselves that we *can* do something: again, it almost doesn't matter what we do, as long as we do *something* in a disciplined way – yet without force, without coercion, and without blaming ourselves (or others) in the times when it fades. And it is, unfortunately, 'slowly': these processes do take time to work! The wyrd "will work to your need, not to your command": and the wrong kind of discipline – 'controlling' – is a little too close to 'command' for the wyrd to be able to respond to our needs. . .

THE ROLE OF RELIGION

When self-discipline becomes a little too hard, it's useful to be able to call on others for help. This is where religion becomes relevant, as shared help from others on a similar path to the Self. As part of our *own* discipline, we might accept what seems to be an exter-

140

nally-imposed discipline of some doctrine or practice: we don't forget, though, that it's our choice to do so.

True religions are far more than mere belief-systems such as the money economy we're all required to believe in, the armchair-psychology of yesteryear, or the fashionable 'instant cosmologies' of so many New Age groups. They deal with the totality of ourselves, as beings of body, mind, heart and spirit: so they all provide, in one form or another, external discipline, guidance, and tried-and-tested tools for working with the wyrd. (It'll usually be called something else: in Christian terminology, for example, wyrd is Providence – and the experience that "the hand of the Lord moves in mysterious ways". But the name we give it doesn't matter – the wyrd is the interweaving of everything, everywhere, everywhen, so it's still the same wyrd, weaving its way through each of us.) Religious rituals are tools for the mind and Self, with the sequence of the ritual providing discipline; and prayer and invocation are, in essence, just another form of affirmations, another form of practical magic.

Perhaps the most important facet of religion is the social aspect. Here we'd find safe space in which to let go, and a community of others who've been to similar spaces and know what the rough times are like. Here too we'd find the concept of 'service' in a true sense: not something paid for, or tendered as part of 'double-entry life-keeping', but a true gift of the heart. Serving others is serving myself; serving myself, in the widest sense, is also necessarily serving others – I find myself reflected in others through the way in which I serve others. Here wyrd and religion closely coincide: the same threads pass through us all.

So as a fiction writer put it, "do not mock the Church and its mummeries: they have a purpose". Religion can have much to offer us: at the right time and in the right context it can be an enormous help.

> For many people, some kind of religious framework provides a structure of belief and faith which forms a focus for their ☞

discipline and a centre from which they move outward. For others, though, that doesn't seem to work: I happen to be one of them. I've often been asked what I 'really believe': but the nearest I can give to a truthful answer would be 'Yes'. Or 'Sometimes'. Ideas and beliefs flow through me in a weird, chaotic way which to me now seems normal: I have no idea which, if any, are 'me'. I *know* that I don't know, and I seem to be able to accept that. . . that's about all I can say.

Do you consider yourself committed to a religion, a belief-system, some specific description and mode of reaching a 'higher power'? If so, look at the tools which it provides you; respect rather than fight against the discipline it offers! And if not, take the risk – and commitment *feels* like a risk – to visit various groups, to listen and to ask their advice: trust your *feelings* in relating with them. . . they all have much to teach. What do you learn?

Religion provides tools, structure, discipline, commitment, community. *But*. . . at the wrong time, in the wrong context and with the wrong people, religion can be an enormous hindrance instead of a help. There's always a twist. . .

Although ritual and religion provide useful tools, it's essential never to forget that all these things are only *tools*. By all means use them – that's what they're there for – but we need to take care that they don't end up using us. A ritual, for example, is a habit we choose: but we've seen earlier the problems that arise from letting habits run our lives without our conscious awareness, and we don't need to get caught in that again! Likewise religions easily become a *substitute* for self – which will eventually put us back in a far worse situation than that from which we started.

And we also need to be cautious about the package-deal manner in which many religions are presented. Religions are products of their respective cultures, much like anything else: so they necessarily reflect not just the best of the respective culture, but also the worst – with nothing holy about those aspects at all. Once we commit to a religion, we commit to *all* of it: so it's wise to look carefully first at what's beneath the surface. . .

The word 'religion' literally means 'to re-bind', which in one sense means 'to re-make into a whole', but all too often instead means 'to entrap'. The emotional and psychological tools and the commitment to service that typify any valid religion have always been all too useful to those whose concept of power we would now understand better as unacknowledged fear; and the routine claims to a monopoly on 'the Truth' are more political than spiritual – or simply a reflection of fear of uncertainty.

So-called state-religions are generally just that: religion co-opted or even created as a tool in service of the state, with institutionalised power-under replacing physical force as a means of control. This affects most major religions: even Catholicism, as a religion, was actually constructed by a committee (the Council of Nicaea) in the dying days of the Roman Empire, specifically as a means of 're-binding' the people to the central authority of Rome. So the test, as always, is to see whether those who would have us commit to their religion really do *themselves* practise what they preach. . . the reality, in most cases, is that they don't. The only recourse in such cases is to go elsewhere. . . or even accept that we have to go it alone.

There are also some aspects of religion that don't become obvious without an understanding of wyrd. Many religions are based on a past or present 'received truth', regarding it – and its recipient – as extraordinary and special: but as we've already seen, 'received truth' is perfectly ordinary *because* it is weird. It can be – and often is – useful, but it's nothing special; as we saw earlier, it usually means a great deal to the person who 'received' it, but not necessarily to anyone else.

And because wyrd is seen as unusual, extraordinary, special, there's a danger of getting lost in weird glamour, in weirdness for the sake of weirdness. Fundamentalist religions and New Age groups tend to make a great play about weird energies, and the felt experience of 'being a Chosen One' that occurs within these groups: but it's usually no more than a minor side-effect of wyrd, which, as we've seen, is perfectly ordinary, perfectly normal. It may well *feel* special, but that doesn't *make* it special – and especially does not give us special authority over anyone else!

True 'channelling', for example, is not about contacting something outside of us, but accessing the threads of wyrd from *within*: and it demands enormous skill and awareness just to get out of the way – both a letting-go *and* an acceptance of responsibility. And it's perfectly ordinary: it occurs in every skill and every form of art, though usually in a less obvious way. Other 'spiritual phenomena' such as prophecy and clairvoyance are routine side-effects of the interweavings of wyrd – they're certainly not proof of 'spirituality'. In most traditions, in fact, they're regarded as a mere passing phase – a distraction, or a trap, on the path to a true and deeper awareness.

Another glamour-trap is the assumption that a foreign religion is necessarily better because it's weird. Westerners who reject Christianity and get excited about Eastern religions often fail to understand that Easterners get excited about Christianity for the same reason: it's different, and therefore *seems* special. Within its original context, the religion is entirely ordinary: sometimes dragging it into a different context produces weirdnesses that seem exciting, but may not necessarily be a good idea – Westerners' confusions over the Indian concept of 'kundalini energy' being a case in point. And given that 'my word is my bond', it's perhaps important to ensure that we know what all those weird mantras and Latin chants mean: what we say becomes our *commitment*, so we need to be careful what we say. . .

I've just spent a pleasant couple of days at a gathering for a well-known Indian guru who's visiting the city. Three thousand people in their best business suits produce a lot of energy when chanting, and the mantra – which roughly translates as 'praise the name of the Lord' – is harmless enough. And for many people there, it's probably the first time they've felt able to let go since they left the Church for the 'Church of Mammon'. . . Plenty of wyrd around: easy enough to mistake it for 'instant enlighten-

☞

ment' – and it's clear, from the excited descriptions of 'amazing energies', that many people have done just that. The more experienced meditators, though, just nod their heads quietly: they *know* – and they listen quietly, respectfully, to the deeper threads of wyrd that their teacher describes.

I learnt a lot from them. . . Not by committing myself to the religion – I'm still unwilling to do that with any – but by being clear in myself that I was committed to *myself*. And listening. . . it takes practice and discipline – more discipline than I'm keen to admit – just to learn how to listen!

In the end, it's always our responsibility. Religions give us a space in which to let go: it's up to us to make sure it's a safe space for us to do so. 'Self-abandon' does not mean abandoning ourselves: we let go *without* abandoning responsibility – otherwise we're giving the responsibility to others, and we can't complain at the results! Once again, "do what you will – but be very sure that you will it". . .

An affirmation is both a letting go and an acceptance of responsibility. We make our choice, and accept the twist: we 'claim' a thread of wyrd, and then get out of its way as best we can, to allow it to work in its own weird way. For each of us, 'my word is my bond', a deep and total commitment: initially to *ourselves*, but eventually, through the web of wyrd, to everyone, everywhere, everywhen.

14

IT'S ALL IMAGINARY

Words are only one tool for working with the wyrd: it also helps to know how to use our imagination in building up a clear vision of what we want. When we remember that our view of the world is to some extent a choice of perception, it becomes clear that through visualisation we can change that perception, and thus the way that we – and others – experience the world.

REAL OR IMAGINARY?

As it happens, there are no historical links between the words 'imagination' and 'magic': but there should be, because imagination, used in the right way, is quite literally magic. In everything we do, we create something from nothing: we pluck an idea out of thin air, and through us it eventually becomes something tangible, or at least exists in a form that other people can share. The intervening stages, which are often forgotten, are the intention to follow up the idea – the *commitment*, as we looked at in the last chapter – and usually a lot of hard work. . . but we get nowhere at all without that first fragmentary image of an idea.

Those images are essential. Everything we do, everything we say, everything we use, was once imaginary. Tomorrow's breakfast is imaginary now; today's was imaginary the day before. Through our work we bring it into a tangible or shared reality: we make it real – literally 'real-ise' it, in the same sense that we talk about 'realising an investment'. But before that, it's *all* imaginary. Everything starts from imagination, visualisation.

Is your current project real, or imaginary?

If you think about it for a while, the only feasible answer is 'Yes': both real *and* imaginary. Every job and every kind of work in essence consists of realising imaginary 'objects' in some way, bringing them into the reality we share with everyone else. Weird, when you think about it!

The first stage of any action is to get a clear image of what we want to do – and to do that we need some way of choosing *which* ideas to pluck out of thin air. There's an infinity of ideas out there: we want to find not just any idea, but an *appropriate* idea, an appropriate image on which to focus our commitment. This is where visualisation comes in, as a structured way of building images, and, as with affirmations, a deliberate connection with the web of wyrd.

But here we hit the same problem as with wants and needs. A want is an outward expression of some inner need: yet very few of those needs are for things that are tangible. In the same way, we can only visualise something that can be expressed in terms of the senses. It's very difficult, if not impossible, to visualise a metaphor: but most things we want are metaphors. Health, wealth, freedom, love, joy: they're all concepts or metaphors.

To illustrate the point, what does 'freedom' look like? How would you imagine freedom *itself*? You'll find that there's no way to do so. . .

Yet what do the *results* of freedom look like? We could visualise these much more easily: and yet they're clearly influenced by our own ideas, our own choices – and thus, as always, there's a twist in every case. . .

We can visualise objects, but not ideas; we can visualise something we want to buy with money, and perhaps money as a pile of notes, but not the *concept* of money; and we can visualise the tangible results of a quality, but not the quality itself. These crucial distinctions are blurred in the way we speak, the ways we express ourselves: and this gets us into all sorts of tangles, with the same kind of misunderstood metaphors as we saw before with 'hungry for company'. So we need to take exactly the same care with visualisations as we have with the phrasing of affirmations – otherwise they'll lead us nowhere.

INVISIBLE IMAGES

The word 'visualisation' gives the unfortunate impression that we're aiming for something spectacular: if we don't get to some kind of New-Age visionary experience, it seems, we're obviously getting nowhere. But as usual, this comes from a misunderstanding of the ordinariness of wyrd: there's nothing special about visualisation, in fact we all do it all the time. And despite the 'vision-only' implications of the term 'visualisation', we don't necessarily 'see' in a visual way: we combine impressions from *all* the senses to build an overall image to present to the wyrd.

Time for one of those standard examples – especially if you've been taught that old curse-belief of "you don't have much imagination"!

Imagine an orange.

An ordinary orange. What kind of orange is it? What does it look like – its shape, its size and so on?

Reach out and touch this imaginary orange. Give it a squeeze. How heavy is it? And dig your fingernails in: feel the 'give' and the sudden burst of scent as you cut the surface of the peel.

Peel it – but how do you peel this imaginary orange? Peel enough so that you can break off a segment – or would you prefer to slice it? In either case, place the segment or slice in your mouth: bite on it! Just how real is the taste of this imaginary orange? And yet it's all imaginary. . .

And let it all drift away, back into the imaginary space from which it came.

Review that experience for a moment. You will have had *some* kind of impression, if only from the recall of old memories – and those are 'visualisations' too. In what way did the orange

☞

'appear'? In what way do you 'see' and 'sense' this imaginary object? What is *your* way of visualising at the moment?

Everyone perceives *something* in this imaginary world: everyone has their own way of visualising things. It's true that for some people these images can be so definite and sense-like that they'd feel they can see it, could reach out and touch it; for most of us, though, it's much less spectacular – down to just a word-description such as 'an orange', for example – or anything between those two extremes. And yet we *know* that, whatever it is, for us it represents an orange – an image of the *idea* of 'an orange'. That image, in all its glorious ordinariness, is a visualisation: and that's what we can use to create a focus for our choices.

It's the very day-to-day ordinariness of visualisation that makes it difficult to recognise just how weird it really is. It doesn't come with flashing lights and bells and whistles – not often, at any rate – and yet there's something very weird going on. As with affirmations, we're 'claiming' a thread from among the infinite possibilities of wyrd. We choose the kind of image; the wyrd responds, but always with that so-typical twist, so that we never quite know what we're going to get.

Trust becomes a crucial part of the claiming – or reclaiming – of a thread of life: we let it go without abandoning it – non-attachment that's also non-detachment. We claim the thread, through visualisation and affirmation, and then let it go, trusting, in effect, that the wyrd will show us what it is that we've *actually* claimed – which may not be what we *thought* we claimed at all! We have to watch carefully those 'invisible images' that the wyrd shows us – especially as most of them will come out in some form of metaphor.

We've looked at this earlier, with the 'pink balloon' visualisation: but it's probably worth doing again with the wider awareness we've gained since then. So, as before, imagine, like a child: we make a wish, and then see what the fairies bring us! Place an image in your mind for the wyrd to play with – and let go.

Find a quiet space, away from the chaos of the fun-fair. Close your eyes; relax; look into the inner world for a while. And make a wish: build an image in your mind of something you'd really like to happen, something you would *choose* to have happen. (What *form* would the result of the wish take? – imagine that.) In your mind, write down the wish – or draw it, perhaps – on an imaginary piece of card.

And imagine a pink balloon, a light helium-filled balloon, tugging gently on its string. (Notice in what way this image of a 'pink balloon' comes to you: what does it look like? How do you 'see' it?)

Tie the wish-card to the string of the balloon, that wish you'd dearly like to happen. (How do you do this? How do you imagine yourself doing this?) And let go, let go; watch the balloon lift up into the sky, and drift away on the threads of wyrd. (What does the sky look like? – visualise it! And can you visualise those wyrd threads themselves – like gossamer spider's webs drifting on the breeze, perhaps?)

Don't just forget the balloon, though: remind yourself of it each day. Let the wyrd talk back to you: allow images to arise. Where is your wish-laden pink balloon? Where has it landed? Who's read your message? How is it being acted on?

You've let go: you're non-attached to the wish. You're also non-detached from it: it still has meaning, importance for you. Trust that somehow, in some way, there will be a response.

And watch how, *over time*, the wyrd responds to the wish. . .

Building images is only one part of visualisation: the other side is leaving space in the mind for the wyrd to pass images in return. This is perhaps the hardest part of visualisation: a lot of the time we're groping in the dark, trying to make sense of the vaguest impressions and suggestions. We need concentration, but here 'concentration' literally means 'centring' – resting quietly in our own centre – rather than screwing up in tension. As before, it's very much like looking for a dim star at night: we try best by trying not to try. . . It *does* take practice to be certain that what little we 'see' comes from somewhere deeper than our own wishful thinking – and that again means learning to trust ourselves as well as the wyrd.

WATCH THE DETAILS

This trust and self-trust is easiest to develop, perhaps, through watching the details of what happens, yet without interfering in what happens. Once we have some idea of the ways in which we 'see' the images we build in visualisations, we can begin to recognise how some parts of those images – especially in the smaller details – begin to change in ways that we don't expect: with time and with practice, it becomes a two-way process, an *interaction* with the web of wyrd. And that means that through visualisation we can learn to see new choices – though always accompanied by their inevitable twists, of course.

Visualisation is much like meditation: the simplest-seeming tasks turn out to be surprisingly difficult. Both involve a weird kind of mental juggling in which we need to keep out of the way and maintain an open and receptive mind, yet at the same time have to remember a sequence of instructions – especially in visualisation, where we need to know what images we're to watch out for at each stage. Often the simplest way round the problem is to do the visualisation as a 'guided meditation', where someone else reads the instructions to us – or we pre-record the instructions ourselves beforehand, and play back the tape at the appropriate time.

I've always found visualisations difficult without some kind of guide – I have a tendency to fall asleep before I've got to the intended imaginary place! But in both 'guided' and 'unguided' versions, the sequence is always much the same, and goes something like this:

Find a quiet place to relax. Close your eyes. (We would here have some sequence to 'talk you down' into a quieter, deeper, more relaxed state, of which the following is only one example.) ☞

Take a deep breath, and exhale slowly. Imagine yourself going down a deep stairway: go deeper, with each outbreath, counting downward from ten to one. Imagine you're going downward, deeper within, to your own private space: a safe space for you alone. What does this private space of yours look like? (Remember, don't *try*: just note what fleeting impressions drift by on the threads of wyrd, but don't try to hold onto any of them. Let the picture build *itself*. And no, it isn't as easy as it sounds, so don't worry about it! But you *will* find yourself 'seeing' something in your own way: fragments of images drifting together to form some overall picture.)

(From this 'safe space', to which you can return at any time, you can make excursions out into deeper and deeper layers of the imaginary worlds. Here's a simple example.) Imagine a door in this space of your own. (The wyrd sometimes needs a little help from us to keep 'on track'. Here, for example, *you* may have to do some work: if no door 'appears', make one up! Remember a door that you know: build an image of that in your mind. It's as simple as that. . .) Open the door, and step through into a landscape – a landscape of the mind. (A common recommendation is to remember a landscape you know and like: a beach, perhaps, or a mountain stream. Reconstruct this in your mind from your memories of that place.)

Sit down: make yourself comfortable in this quiet imaginary place. What can you see? (You probably won't 'see' much at first, but don't worry – just imagine it.) What can you hear? Smell? Taste? Sense? (Again, these are likely at first to be no more than a jumble of impressions – but if you can, *allow* them to build up an overall image, rather like one of those 'hidden pictures' with fragments revealed at random. The wyrd, being part of time itself, doesn't have quite our idea of time: fragments can arrive in a very weird order!)

Bring to the front of your mind some issue on which you'd like advice. What does this issue look like? – what images arise? Allow this place to show you, in response, something that will help you in this matter. Watch the images and fragments pass by: what do you see, hear, feel, sense? (Don't *try*, remember:

concentrate, but in the sense of 'centring'.) Spend some time here, quietly watching, and interacting with, the wyrd's response. (On the tape, allow at least two or three minutes blank time here.)

It's now time to return. Behind you is the door through which you came. (If you don't see it, re-create it in your mind: it's *your* world!) Return through the door to your private space. And begin to return. (Here we run the previous talk-down process in reverse, to return to 'ordinary' space. This part is important: don't leave part of yourself behind, lost in some imaginary world!) Notice your breathing: breathing in; breathing out. With each outbreath, imagine yourself returning upward to your own body, to here, to this world, this time. Open your eyes, look around you; and when you've returned fully, write down your impressions of your conversation with the wyrd.

For the first few visits into this inner world, the impressions seem ridiculously vague: for most of the time – much as we found in meditation – there's nothing more than an impressive amount of nothing. In fact the only thing we're certain to be aware of is our old friend the silliness-barrier... So don't let those simple-sounding descriptions in books on 'creative visualisation' get you down! This is *not* an easy process at any time, and especially not at the beginning. But it's a skill worth developing, because it does quite literally open doorways into new areas of the mind.

Slowly, with practice, fragments become more recognisable – or at least more definite – out of the midst of the chaos. And patterns begin to emerge – patterns that, in many cases, show the weirdness of their nature by recurring for different people, different cultures, different times. Jung's weird concept of a 'collective unconscious' begins to gain practical meaning for us here – though perhaps it's simpler just to call it 'wyrd', threading its way through every one of us. And remember too that there's nothing special in this: it's just wyrd, working in its weird but ordinary way, just as it always has done.

It's nothing special: but it can certainly be useful – very much so. And there's an infinity to explore in there: which may seem weird until we remember that, by the very nature of the wyrd, every point contains within itself the interweaving of everything, everywhere, everywhen – the inside is also the outside, and the boundaries between them blur. . .

REAL IMAGINATION

Because this 'imaginary world' is wyrd, it's sometimes hard to see the choices that we make in there – or the subtle twists that hide behind them. For example, there's often a sense that 'it's only imaginary – so it isn't real': which can be a dangerous mistake to make. We came across this issue earlier: things are never 'real *or* imaginary', but always 'real *and* imaginary'. Imaginary 'entities' are entirely real *in an imaginary sense*: as we saw earlier, it's up to us which ones we choose to 'real-ise' in the shared reality. But even if we don't bring them into the shared reality, they're still entirely real for us: and they can often have real and tangible effects. In that sense, we have to be careful what we choose to imagine. . .

Imaginary entities – 'thought-forms' – are *always* real. Think of that imaginary orange we looked at earlier: you could probably taste that, in fact you can probably taste it now – even though it never existed in a tangible sense. More than that, we could probably measure, physically, the effects of that imaginary orange: more saliva in your mouth, for example. And think of the effects that a good movie has on us: we laugh, we cry, we get angry or frightened, excited, exhilarated – but it's all 'only imaginary'. And remember too those imaginary fears from childhood that haunt us still – and that all too often drive those desperate games of power-under. It's all imaginary: the twist is that it's also all entirely real.

And none of it is under our control, especially in the darker spaces of our own 'shadow'. We all have things we'd prefer not to face: yet they're all there, lurking in the imaginary worlds, like some imaginary monster lurking under a childhood bed. A frightening thought. . .

It may not be under our control, but we *can* choose to bring it under our direction: this *is* the wyrd, which means that we do have choices. One way that we can do so is by remembering one of the central twists of wyrd: 'the inside is also the outside'. In visualisation, it often seems that the images we perceive come from outside of us, are things that just happen to pass by: but they're also always aspects of ourselves. Like the hall of mirrors, they're reflections of our own choices. So by watching the details, and by recognising that what we see *is* ourselves, we can use these strange images to see what we've actually chosen in our inner and outer life – and not merely what we think or hope we've chosen!

If the inside is the outside is the inside, then *everything* we see in the inner world – down to the smallest detail – is also an aspect of ourselves. This deliberate use of the inner world to reflect ourselves has been developed by Jungians such as Robert Johnson into a series of tried-and-tested tools known as 'active imagination'. We tend to draw the broader strokes with our conscious choices: the wyrd shows us our subtler choices in the subtler details. But being wyrd, there's always a twist: the message in those details is often concealed in an even more subtle metaphor.

So go back to that quiet, private inner space; go through the imaginary door into that private landscape. Everything here is you: every detail. Every grain of sand on the beach; every shape of every wave; the shapes of the dunes, the cliffs behind, the cries of the gulls – it's all you, interacting with the wyrd. The sound of the brook, the shapes of the trees and the mountain, the hum of the bees and the birds, the whisperings of the leaves in the wind – it's all you. What words can you hear, hidden in the wind and the cries? What do the shapes remind you of? What are you saying to you?

Sometimes people and things you know in the outer world appear, fleetingly, fragmentarily: but it's still always you, using that image of the outer world as a metaphor for some aspect of you. What does that tell you? Seeing these people in you, how does that help you see yourself in others?

Every person, every object in these images is actually ourselves.

That can be a little difficult to grasp, especially when they're obviously doing things that we're certain *we* don't do. But there's often a hidden metaphor: if a friend who's a crazy driver appears in an image, for example, the message is not about the friend, but about the way we *ourselves* are 'driving crazily' in some aspect of our own lives.

It's important not to project the reflection of our inner world, our inner fears, onto others. We all tend to do it, of course – as we've seen, this is what so often creates the drive for an illusory 'power' – but by recognising that it *is* our own reflection, we can minimise the confusion – and the damage.

We can also go into the inner world to ask for help from some deeper aspect of ourselves that knows our unconscious choices as well as our conscious ones. Along with those imaginary monsters, we also have imaginary allies, imaginary guides. Every spiritual tradition describes these differently – Christians would talk in terms of 'guardian angels', native Americans in terms of 'power animals' – but the sense of an inner ally is always the same. Help is always there: all we have to do is ask for it.

If you follow a spiritual tradition, you may well already know the 'inner guide' as described within that context. If not, all we have to do is watch the details in our journeys into the inner world: images that appear regularly are likely to represent help in some form.

There's always that weird twist: help sometimes arrives in strange forms! In my case, an image of a stag often appears: I've come to recognise him as some kind of guide who leads me to different spaces that I need to see. Others see recognisable 'people' – characters who occur so often in so many people's inner worlds that they have traditional names – or nothing more than some kind of symbol or impression. Our inner worlds may coincide at times, but every one of us is different.

Another approach is to go to that inner world, that private landscape, and formally ask for a help, a guide. Watch what images or impressions appear. Sometimes what purports to be

☞

'help' may actually be our own resistance in disguise – so it's traditionally regarded as wise to ask whatever imaginary entity arises for a token as proof of intent. What is this imaginary token that your guide gives you: a small glittering ball or a feather (two examples of my own), or a crucifix, perhaps? Remember this token – remember its *details* – and bring it back to the inner world on subsequent visits: with the help of your 'inner guide', it can act as a key to ever deeper and deeper realms within yourself.

We can't always rely on help in the 'outer' world: it's not that people won't help us, but that they sometimes can't. Often our problems are ours alone: no-one else can solve them for us. But the 'inner guide' is always there, for the simple reason that it's always part of ourselves. And yet it's also something wider, aware of infinity, since it's also a part of the wyrd – and when we're stuck, that wider awareness is what we need, in order to break free into being and becoming more truly ourselves.

INVENTING THE REAL WORLD

We can also use visualisation to relate to the *outer* world in a different way. For each of us, our ordinary work consists in part of bringing imaginary worlds into the shared reality: so being more conscious about what imaginary worlds we choose – we *commit* to – can make a lot of difference in our outer experience.

This is exactly the same as with affirmations: what we visualise matters as much as what we say. A phrase like "It's hopeless, it'll never work" becomes a self-confirming prophecy; we turn the process round with affirmations, and *imagine* a different experience – and then allow the wyrd to help us in bringing it into form in the reality we share with everyone else. We can do the same with visualisation: make a deliberate point of imagining an experience we would choose. But we have to remember to leave a space for the wyrd to fill in the details. . .

Although this sometimes sounds like airy-fairy nonsense – "it's only imaginary" – it does have practical, everyday applications. One well-known example is 'psyching-up' before a sports event.

Imagine you're a swimmer, just before a race. Imagine, then, that you're standing on the edge of the pool. Build an image of the crowd, cheering: what colours are different people wearing? Focus on the pool: what colour is the water? What patterns do the ripples make?

Re-focus on yourself: without moving, you can feel every muscle in your body, relaxed, confident, yet ready to move. The starter's gun goes: imagine a clean dive into the water. Build a clear image of each stroke through the water. Imagine the other swimmers, either side of you: slowly but surely, you're pulling ahead.

The first turn: a clean roll at the end of the pool – feel every fragmentary moment of it. Returning down the pool, you hear the crowd yelling louder, cheering you on; you hear them but you keep your focus on each stroke through the water, clean, powerful, efficient.

The end of the pool comes close; the other swimmers are close behind, so you feel every stroke, every move to a clear confident win. First home.

And imagine yourself on the rostrum, receiving your medal: which other swimmers are beside you? Who's presenting the medal? Who's beside them? What colours, people, images can you see in the cheering crowd?

An Olympic swimmer might go through this process many times before each race – creating a form for the imaginary world to take, to be brought into the shared reality.

We can do the same kind of process in business: it's used a lot in sales training, to help build confidence, for example. We can't visualise confidence itself, but we can visualise confident *action*: imagine every stage of the transaction, from first meeting to clinching the deal. Personally, though, I'd always be wary about using this in anything that thinks in terms of winners and losers – a wariness based not just on politics but from practical experience of the way the wyrd loops round on itself. Yet it's always our choice: so do as you will – but be very sure that you will it!

> We've already met one example of a 'win-win' visualisation in an area where resources are scarce: the parking meter game. Parking space is always short in this city – isn't that always true? – and finding a meter can be a frustrating business. But in a weird way, as we saw earlier, it often depends on how we look for one. If we don't look, and just spend our energy bitching about the shortage of space, we prove we're right – there's a ridiculous shortage of space. If we push, shove, fight, claw, control, manipulate our way to the only available parking space, there's a typical weird twist – such as finding that we've been wheel-clamped, and we now can't get *out* of the space! But if we 'claim' that thread of wyrd, we can *allow* ourselves to find a parking space – often exactly where we wanted it – and allow others to find their space too.
>
> Driving around, imagine a parking space. What does it look like? Where is it? (A warning, though: *don't* go deep into your imaginary world – you're also driving a very real car in this one, remember!) Describe this space in detail: but remember to allow the wyrd to change those details. And look: there's a car pulling out right now, just where you wanted to go. . .

We create the world we experience – or at the very least we can be active participants in its creation. With visualisation, we can re-create our past and, by using the wyrd to show us different aspects, different points of view on various incidents, re-under-stand ourselves. Let go, let go. . . And we can also use visualisation to reach *forward*, to build a clear image or aim of where or what we want ourselves to be, to become.

We can remember and re-create our past this way, to help us with issues in the present; we can also 'remember' our future. This probably sounds strange: but it shouldn't by now! In visualisa-tions, as with affirmations, we're claiming threads of wyrd, acknowledging our right to them as aspects of ourselves: in that sense we're always 're-membering' our future. But in another sense we could also literally be remembering our future: the wyrd is timeless, is the tool of the Sisters of Time, so within it what we think of as 'precognition' is just another way of knowing. . .

We never know what exact effect our choices have: but working this way we do at least have a choice, even though there's always that twist. We never know: all of the results could only be coincidence, it seems.

It's all imaginary, as we know: yet we can put it to use, in a way that's both real *and* imaginary. Yet it's also all coincidence: *everything* is 'only coincidence'. And once we understand the implications of that particular twist, we'll really begin to get somewhere in reclaiming our choices in this weird world of ours!

15

DIVINE COINCIDENCE

Coincidences – or lack of them – form the very stuff of wyrd. We've all had 'weird coincidences', and some of them undoubtedly have shaped or re-shaped our lives. Definitely weird!

Coincidences form the intersections, the choice-points in the web of wyrd. And they're everywhere: we could argue, from a technical point of view, that *everything* is coincidence, in the literal sense of 'things coinciding'. All we have is coincidence: it's our choice as to how we recognise it, and how we use it. Behind what we think of as order – that so-obvious concept of cause-and-effect – there's an eerie kind of chaos; yet once again, behind the chaos, there's an even eerier kind of order. Within the twists and turns there are subtle, hidden choices: but first we have to re-learn how to see them. . .

CAUSE AND COINCIDENCE

Stop for a moment. Look around, with an eye for the weirdness of reality. And recognise this: *everything* is coincidence. Everything we see, we hear, we sense, is an individual, unconnected event interweaving with others in space and time. What do we have? The short answer, of course, is chaos. That way madness lies. . .

To make sense of that chaos of coincidences, we *impose* a view of pattern and order upon it: but in reality that 'order' is no more than an illusion. The pattern isn't actually there: the connections we see – and especially the connections we choose *not* to see – are our choices. Like the image in a Rorschach ink-blot, it's both real *and* imaginary, a way of seeing, a way of making sense of the randomness.

Every concept of pattern, every description of 'how things really work', is a choice – and often an arbitrary one at that. The most common choice is the concept of cause-and-effect, which interprets coincidences in terms of patterns of perceived relationships repeating in time. This concept is so pervasive in our culture that it's often difficult to understand that what it shows us is not necessarily 'the truth'. The concept of cause-and-effect is never 'wrong' as such: but it's not always useful. It is indeed *a* way of interpreting coincidences; but it's not the only one, and it's certainly not always the best.

> Mulla Nasruddin was, as usual, arguing in the tea-house, confusing everyone with his weird way of looking at the world. "That's nonsense!", cried one of his opponents, "I believe in cause and effect". In reply, Nasruddin pointed out into the street, where some kind of formal procession was going past. "That man is being taken to be hanged, for murder", he said. "What is the cause of that? Is it because someone gave him the money to buy the knife? Because someone saw him do it? Or because no-one stopped him?"
>
> In a less dramatic sense, what is the cause of your reading this book? Is it because you saw a review of it? Or because a friend recommended it? Or because it said 'Hello' to you from a bookshelf, in the usual weird way? And if that was the cause, what was the cause of that? And the cause before that cause? Following the chain further and further back, what was the cause that started it all?

Our concept of cause is closely related to the idea of blame: we're trying to pin sole responsibility for some event on some previous event in time. But it's often too crude, too limited: *everything* is cause, everything and nothing is to blame. We can't prove anything in terms of cause, either: cause/effect chains always end up in some kind of circular definition, or with something that simply *is*, like gravity, or life – or wyrd. There's a tendency, though, to interpret everything in terms of causes – "Was there a cause, or was it only a coincidence?" – and dismiss 'mere coincidences' unless we *can* label something as 'the cause'. Different people choose different labels, and different levels of causality: skeptics stop short at science, while mystics and New Agers tend to think in terms of 'higher cause'. But both miss the point: a coincidence is a coincidence is a coincidence. What it *means* – and what use we can make of it – is up to us.

Asking "Was there a cause, or was it only a coincidence?" is rather like asking "Was it a Wednesday, or was it only July?": the question can never make sense. Cause and coincidence aren't opposites: cause is a tool for *interpreting* coincidences. Not 'cause *or* coincidence', then, but 'cause *and* coincidence'. And it's only one tool among many. It's a useful tool for working with groups of events that do seem to repeat in time: for that reason, it does work fairly well for most of our technology. But there's an old expression that "You can never step in the same river twice": nothing ever *does* repeat exactly, even in physics – let alone in technology, where the only ultimate truth is the weird chaos of Murphy's Law. Cause-and-effect is a myth, rather like control, and for much the same reasons: it isn't absolute, it doesn't cover everything, and it depends on a very crude concept of time. Reality is a little more weird than that. . .

One of my friends told me that she'd wanted very much to go to a particular workshop, but didn't know where the money was going to come from – it wasn't much, but on her tiny budget it was still significant. The day before the workshop, a cheque arrived in the mail: in the Normal Rules of wyrd, it was for exactly the same amount as the workshop. But the real surprise was where the cheque had come from: a long-forgotten insurance policy from twenty years ago, which she'd cancelled payments to, soon after starting it, on the grounds that it would never produce anything!

for exactly the amount needed at the time? Could we argue, for example, that the fact of the cheque's impending arrival had encouraged her to want to go to this workshop? Or that the she-of-now had asked herself-of-then to start and cancel the policy so that it would produce the right amount now? Think about it for a while: what other 'causes' can you come up with? And then recognise that we have no way whatsoever of knowing: all and none of them are true. . .

A coincidence is a coincidence is a coincidence: what it means depends entirely on how we interpret it, or what pattern we try to make it fit. Sometimes an interpretation is thrust upon us by the wyrd – we've all had experience of that! – but more often we have to choose a pattern, a context, a framework, a structure in which to interpret events. We don't so much discover reality as invent it: much of what we experience has arisen from how we've chosen to interpret events. By going back to that principle at the heart of our interaction with the wyrd – a coincidence is a coincidence, an event whose meaning *we* choose – we reclaim our power of choice. But if so, what reality do we choose? And how do we choose it?

EVERYDAY WEIRDNESS

Everything we experience depends on how we interpret the coincidences at its core. The wyrd is weird: the choices it offers us are often hidden in its twists. So if we interpret things only in expected ways, we're limiting our chances: things can only work for us in expected ways. Trying to restrict events to known causes is a way of trying to control the wyrd: but as we've seen before, 'it will respond to your need, but not to your command'. The way out is to be like those researchers into the mathematics of chaos: accept the wyrd for what it *is*. Develop 'an eye for pattern, especially pattern that appears on different scales at the same time'; develop a taste for randomness and complexity, for those weird 'jagged edges and sudden leaps'. *Enjoy* them: enjoy the weird jokes embedded within them.

We choose by being aware of what and how we choose to see, to sense, to know. So watch for different *kinds* of patterns: the wyrd contains a great deal more than simple cause and effect. For example, the psychologist Carl Jung long ago described 'an acausal connecting principle' that he called 'synchronicity', describing patterns of events linked by a common metaphor. (It's unfortunate that the term has drifted into use as a catch-all for 'meaningful coincidence', on the lines of "It wasn't a mere coincidence, it was a synchronicity": apart from being far too vague, it also misses the point that coincidence and meaning are quite separate – *we* ascribe meaning to events.)

> In one of Jung's most famous examples of a synchronicity, a woman patient was describing a dream in which she was given a golden scarab. At that moment a scarab beetle knocked against the window-pane, and then, uncharacteristically, flew into the darkened room: as Jung put it, "nothing like it ever happened to me before or since".
>
> It's the weird twist that gives it an identifiable meaning – even if the meaning is only some kind of weird joke. What examples of your own can you think of? And can you identify the metaphor that links the events in each case?

'Synchronicity' literally means 'at the same time': so the term can be a little misleading, because in some cases different times coincide in the same place. It's now understood that many so-called 'hauntings' fall into this category: they're a kind of image (known technically as a place-memory) that somehow becomes stored into a place, and is 're-played' under specific though still obscure conditions – the coincidence of two (or more) times in one place. As usual, they may be weird, but they're perfectly ordinary: simple place-memories – such as the general 'feel' of a place – can be found everywhere, and even complete visual images are far more common than we usually allow ourselves to recognise.

Another type of pattern is a 'clustering' of supposedly chance events. Seeing these is a matter of keeping an open mind – which is, however, never easy at the best of times. . .

Imagine: you've just bought a new car, a model you'd never seen before – but now there seem to be *dozens* of them. You read the name 'Lewin' on a headline in the paper; look up and see the same name on a store-front; then on a name-badge; on a book-jacket; even in a fragment of conversation from two passers-by – all in the space of a couple of minutes. These are typical clusterings, of a type known as Kammerer's 'seriality'. What examples have you experienced?

Another example, perhaps even weirder, forms what I call the 'left-and-right' series of puns. Exchanging an 'L' for an 'R', in a sequence of English words, changes the meaning from 'left-hand' lightness to 'right-hand' rightness: clown and crown, celebrate and cerebrate, flight and fright, play and pray. How many more of these pairs can you find? (A hint: there are dozens of them!)

With practice and awareness, the weirdness of so many everyday coincidences becomes more and more obvious. But it's important to keep a sense of balance: the ordinary is weird, the weird is ordinary, the Normal Rules of reality. There's no point in looking for a 'higher cause' or 'higher meaning': there usually isn't one. And there's no point in trying to calculate odds of the probability – or improbability – of a given event: every event is unique, and in its way is unrepeatable, so the concept of 'repeatable odds' is meaningless.

Another true-life story, told to me by a university student a few days ago. He'd mislaid his library book – or so he thought. He knew he'd had it with his papers an hour ago. . . He searched for it everywhere: all the lecture rooms, the library, the canteen – nothing. Gone. Weird.

A week later, he's discovered a second-hand book store on the far side of the city. Good, they've got a copy here – the same title. Might be able to replace the missing one with that. How much do they want for it? Picks it up. But it's not just another copy – it's the same book, library ticket and all. Normal Rules. . .

However improbable, each event just *is*. It means nothing by itself (yet also everything, anything): it's up to us to find the usefulness in it. But the 'weird feeling' attached to many of these events makes that hard at times! So the way out, once again, is to recognise that they're not extra-ordinary, not special – just plain, ordinary, everyday wyrd.

AS ABOVE, SO BELOW

Another aspect of the wyrd is the way that patterns seem to repeat themselves on every scale. This is hardly surprising: one of the basic concepts of wyrd is that every point somehow manages to contain every other point within itself. Everything is 'self-similar' – to use a term from chaos-mathematics – and everything is in some way a reflection of everything else.

To some extent that's because we make them so: to us, everything we see becomes linked to every memory of anything even vaguely similar. But there's also a natural reflection too: 'as above, so below' is one of the oldest-known patterns of wyrd. So it's worthwhile developing that 'eye for pattern, especially pattern that appears on different scales at the same time': there's information hidden there that we can't see any other way.

I wander down the street, seeing spirals everywhere: great swirls in the clouds, a snail-shell, the twist in a frond of fern, a dust-devil dancing down the street in the wake of a passing car – all self-similar, yet none of them the same. And I look at the shapes concealed in all sorts of places: a face formed by leaves in the trees, a frog and a bear drawn by cracks in the pavement, the great towering anvil of a thunder-head above. Yet all of them are transitory, subject to the whims of the Sisters of Time: the face appears only in a moment and from a certain angle, the shape of the cloud changes in minutes, while those in the pavement change over months. All these randomnesses gain these meanings only if I allow them to – if I invite them to do so – and even then often only have their meanings for me alone. Yet the meanings in these coincidences are *there*. . . subtle twists in the weavings of wyrd.

It's a childlike state: seeing everything in everything else. Wander around with a child's eyes – what do you see? (If you've forgotten your own 'inner child', borrow a child, and ask them what *they* see!) Watch for the choices, the metaphors, the jokes that are hidden in everything around us. . .

Everything echoes on every scale; like Benoit Mandelbrot's now-famous mathematical structure that's become a symbol of chaos, everything repeats without ever quite repeating. All forms of divination reflect this concept: a pattern of the whole can be seen in the pattern of anything reasonably random, from the fall of cards or rune-stones to the shapes of clouds, from clusters of tea-leaves in an empty cup to clusters of sounds whistling by on the wind. On the surface, it all seems so childish, silly: but divination isn't much interested in the surface appearances. Its concern is child*like*, the child's innocent awareness of a deeper, wider reality.

In watching coincidences, we *divine* their meaning: trying to understand the games of the gods, to see where they're leading us. This is true of all coincidences – even if our only concept of reality is that of cause-and-effect, and our gods are the so-called 'laws of science'. The aim of science, like that of traditional divination, is to predict future patterns of events: but it's questionable whether this can ever work in the way that most people expect. The wyrd is, after all, weird: there's always a twist. . . The best we can do is identify threads that are close to the surface – but even that can tell us a great deal more than we might otherwise know.

Face the silliness-barrier once more, and experiment with some form of divination. The actual form doesn't matter: the same weird threads run through everything. What matters far more is that we do something in a consistent, disciplined way.

So choose a form that seems to appeal, or that happens to be to hand: runes (the traditional tool of wyrd), tarot cards, the ☞

I Ching, whatever. (Choose something you can work with easily on a daily basis: this probably rules out astrology unless you already have plenty of experience, or access to a good computer program that can handle daily transits.) Each day, throw the I Ching to the winds of chance, choose cards from the hand of Fate, cast runes into the web of wyrd. And see what you get: see what coincidences arise.

To emphasise the consistency and commitment, make it into some kind of ritual. In my own case, each morning I shuffle a tarot deck three times, and pick out three cards for the day, to indicate the patterns that are on the surface, underlying, and in the background. I get what I get. . .

Experiment for a while: record each day what you get. How does what you get echo in the events of that day?

With awareness of the subtlety of wyrd and its many interweaving, interleaving patterns, we can usually identify the general flow of events. But we don't *predict*, at least not in the traditional absolute sense of prediction: divination never does more than indicate threads that form that flow. All we ever get is coincidence: new coincidences that may or may not lead us to a deeper meaning. In the end, it's always up to *us* to derive our own meanings from the patterns above and below, inside and outside of us.

PREDICTION AND PARADOX

Any attempt at prediction is beset with paradox. Time is a tool of Sisters of Wyrd: in science and in 'common sense' it may be linear, but in our own experience we feel it looping round and through and back in upon itself in a way that we can only describe as weird. Events repeat, without ever quite repeating; everything is similar, yet never the same.

The problem with using divination – or anything else, scientific or otherwise – for prediction is that we're always in danger of creating our own loops in time. If we believe the prediction without allowing for reality's weirdnesses, we create a self-confirming prophecy – or get upset when reality fails to deliver what we expect. Hence Murphy's Law; hence the dangers we've seen already in 'negative affirmations', careless phrasing and those cultural curses. It's important to shift the emphasis: since everything and nothing occurs everywhere and everywhen, divination gives us some aspect of totality on which to focus our attention. Out of the chaos of coincidences, it suggests events that might be interesting for us to reflect upon. Content, but not its context: that's up to us. In that sense it *does* predict – but only because we choose to let it do so.

If I think that my tarot cards *predict* the day ahead, I'm in trouble. One 'bad' card – 'Sorrow' or 'Failure', for example, let alone 'Death' – would have me running in panic all day; if I'd had a bad day with a hand of 'good' cards, I'd think the world was somehow being unfair. This is not exactly a sane way to run one's life. . .

Instead, shift the emphasis: the cards (or whatever it is that you're using) indicate threads of wyrd. Given that thread, watch how the outside world reflects the respective inner issues. If I pick out 'Failure', for example, I watch out for how *my* fear of failure affects what I do that day; if I pick out 'Happiness', I watch for how I allow, or block, or ignore, or try to control those so-transient little happinesses of the day.

With your daily divination, watch again how events of that type turn up in the day. Sometimes they'll thrust themselves upon you, sometimes you have to go looking for them, but they'll always be there – because that's what you choose to be there. Knowing that it's your choice, what can you learn from this? Each issue, each event in the outside world is a reflection of your own inner choices: what new realisations about *yourself* does this bring each day? Keep a diary of the 'daily divination' and any respective events: how does your response change over the weeks and months?

In this wider sense, even the idiocies of the newspaper horoscope can be useful: we never forget that it's all coincidence, but we can put that coincidence to practical *use*.

For the New Age movement, that linear model of time creates other subtle traps. One we've seen already, in the confused concept of past-lives; another, often more serious, comes from a too-literal interpretation of 'karma'. The original Indian concept is concerned with personal responsibility as linked to a world-view which includes reincarnation; the New Age, far too often, sees it simply as a new way of blaming others, a new way to *avoid* responsibility. "So you *chose* to be poor in this life-time: that's *your* problem, not mine". . .

We do have choices: but the results are far more subtle than that. We do have responsibility for what we choose: yet the results come back to us in a way that is far more weird than a simple crude concept of 'karma'. Since everything and everyone is interlinked, what we choose for others is also what we choose for ourselves. . . the outside is reflected in the inside, what is above is reflected in what is below. Within the chaos of coincidences, we do have choices: the key is to become aware of them.

There's an expression which goes "do what you love, and the money will follow". Life's not *quite* as simple as that: yet it does have a weird ring of truth. When we trust ourselves, and trust the wyrd to provide, it often does. Surprise, surprise. . .

Perhaps the most important issue here is to learn not to be surprised – or, more accurately, *afraid* of surprise. Instead, become clear on what you *need*: trust *yourself*, and allow the wyrd to give you feedback, reflection of your own understanding of yourself. Allow useful coincidences to happen in your life: but being surprised about them tends to drive them away! They're weird, of course, but they're also ordinary, both special and at the same time nothing special. "You have a right to be here, no less than the trees and stars": consider these useful weirdnesses a reflection of that right, perhaps?

So let go, let go. . . trust yourself, and trust your knowledge of the wider reality of wyrd. Watch, over time, the threads of coincidence: what do you learn? What happens?

Each event just *is*. It happens. Whether we happen to notice it is a different matter, however: yet unless we *do* notice it, we can't make use of it. But we can't force ourselves to notice the weirdness in events, and the choices hidden within them: we have to invite them, allow them to come to us. It's like the parking-meter game: if we do nothing, nothing happens; if we try, we push away the hoped-for coincidence (of ourselves and a parking space, in that example); yet somewhere, somewhere between those two extremes, is a balance-point. Maintaining that balance takes practice!

All science, all research, depends on awareness of 'chance' events – history is full of examples. But Fleming's discovery of the antibiotic properties of *penicillium*, for example, was no accident: he'd prepared himself to recognise the meaning of the weirdness implied by a saucer of milk that refused to go bad. He didn't know straight away what it meant: but he knew – allowed himself to know – that it was important.

In the same way, we can encourage ourselves to recognise the usefulness hidden in the events that the wyrd sends our way. The twist comes in seeing these events as *ordinary*: at that point we can also see the choices – and often the wry humour – within the weavings of the wyrd. To do that, though, we have to become comfortable with surprises, randomness, 'jagged edges and sudden leaps' – and that, too, is far from easy. But the awareness does come with practice: so let go, let go. . . dance with its weirdness. Allow the wyrd to be what it is: accept that it won't work to our command, but if we let it, it may work to our need!

16

DANCING WITH OUR SELVES

The coincidences we've looked at in the last chapter were all 'out there', in the world that seems to be outside of us. But the inside is also the outside: the boundary blurs, as the same threads of wyrd pass through both. . .

STANCE AND DANCE

It's often easiest to recognise this in terms of mood. We can feel our moods shifting as we pass through different spaces, different situations: the place, or the thought, or whatever, *coincides* with a different mood. It's a kind of dance of the emotions, one which never quite seems under our control. Each passing mood is like a different self, a different archetype – in fact expresses that archetype.

And each mood has a matching posture that coincides with it: each posture, each move, *represents* the different mood – the two are inextricably interlinked, interwoven on the same thread. As we change one, the other also changes. We know how our posture changes with changing moods – the slump of depression, for example – but the opposite is also true: that the posture itself can direct the mood.

Think of an Indian temple dancer. She moves, then stops, holding the posture: at each frozen moment she not merely appears to be, but *is* a different person – and yet is also the

☞

same person, the same dancer. It's not an act, something she does: it's a way of being, something she *is*. And yet she *wears* each of these passing selves, so to speak, rather than them wearing her. What 'selves' do *you* wear, as you move through the dance of life?

By becoming more aware of our own stance, we reclaim new choices about our mood: and we no longer feel so controlled by the world 'out there'. If we can't see how we change with each of these passing selves, it's hard to get any sense of our core self, the central, unchanging 'I' that watches all these changes. Without a knowledge of that which changes, and that which does not, it's easy to mistake these transient visitors with who we truly are: I'd say I 'am' angry, I 'am' depressed, I 'am' happy – rather than recognising that I *have* anger, depression, happiness, and letting each go as it passes on.

One way to distinguish is to dance with the different selves as they pass through – each thread of 'sub-self' standing, walking, moving, expressing who it is in a different posture, a different part of the dance. We dance this inner world awake. Each one of these selves is different; yet each one is invited in by a constant core, which can sometimes be glimpsed in the brief moments between them.

By deliberately wearing different postures, different movements, we can understand how our apparent – and felt – sense of 'I' changes with each one. We coincide with them, rather than 'are' them. With that understanding, we're no longer so much at their effect: we *know* it's a passing 'act'. And that knowledge gives us, more and more often, the chance to be who we truly are.

So reach out, and *feel* the effects of different postures, different movements. . . And *feel* how they move, they change, they come and go. . .

An example to start with: stand upright, legs slightly apart, arms at your sides. Breathe in, slowly, head tilting back, lifting your

☞

chest, with the focus about halfway between the nipple and the collar-bone on each side. Raise your arms slowly to about waist-height as you do so. Feel the sense of strength – elation, even – that comes with this slow inbreath.

Now breathe out, slowly, all the way: the arms fold inward, the shoulders and head slump forwards, knees become slightly bent. A sense not only of weakness, but also depression. What stages – different moods – do you pass through, between these two extremes?

Repeat this slowly, several times, feeling the constant shifts in *mood* as well as in stance, passing through many different shades with each inbreath and outbreath. How many different moods can you identify? With what postures do they coincide? What parts of the cycle do you try to hold on to, or move through as quickly as possible?

In that example above, there's a sense of strength and certainty that comes with the *stance* at the top of the in-breath. We'd all prefer that feeling of strength, of elation: so we'd often try to hold onto it at the top of the inbreath. What happens, though? In a moment it changes to something else: a caricature of strength, fragile, brittle – if anyone gave us a shove at this point, we'd fall over. . . It's not something that can be held: it exists *because* it's 'just passing through'.

But that sense of weakness, at the bottom of the outbreath – strangely enough, we *can* hold onto that. In a way, at any rate: the breathing becomes short, shallow, panicky, ineffectual, fearful. . . which is hardly useful. So the way we retain that real strength is not by holding the top of the breath, but knowing *when* we're about to reach the top of the breath, and putting our full commitment into the action only at that point – the rest of the time we *wait*, and maybe even rest. . . It's not what we do, but in the *timing* of what we do. And we have to accept that to get that strength we also have to accept, as part of the cycle, the stage of weakness – but without getting stuck in it!

Yoga postures, for example, stretch not just the body but the mind and the emotions as well. Yoga 'asanas' are static, which can make it easier to identify the matching mood. But most of the time we're moving – not static, but dynamic, as with the breathing example above – which calls for more awareness to watch the passing moods.

> As another example, try the parade-ground march of the soldier: head back, groin and chest pushed forward, feet pointing outward at 45°, arms swinging wide to match. There's a great feeling of importance, you occupy a lot of space – the *feeling*, the mood, is quite unmistakable. And yet, with your feet each pointing in a different direction to that of your travel, there's a subtle trade-off: you need someone to tell you where to go. . . It's a very hollow importance. . .
>
> Shift the march slightly, so that both feet are pointing forward, the arms swinging in line to match. The chest is still held up, though less rigidly; the groin automatically drops back. Immediately the mood becomes quieter: a sense of purpose, of definiteness. Switch back to the parade-ground march: your boots thud into the ground. Switch back to the forward walk: the feet land quietly, a move almost cat-like by comparison. What shift in mood – your *own* mood – can you feel as you shift between these two styles of walking?

It's easier to understand what's going on if you think of movements as being patterns woven in the fabric of time – and thus 'clusterings' of threads in the fabric of wyrd. The change of mood coincides with a change in the *pattern*, rather than of an individual thread, an individual sub-self. And these changes and shifts come not only with large changes in pattern, but with surprisingly subtle ones as well.

> Go back to the straight-ahead walk from the previous example. As you walk, let the shoulders slip slowly forward; with even the subtlest of changes, this quickly becomes a shift in mood, from the cat-like one to one on the edge of sadness. Quite soon, the feet begin to drag, and we move from the edge of sadness to the edge of depression – with hardly a change of posture at all.
>
> ☞

Stand up straight again. This time, hold a folder or large magazine – better yet, a clipboard – resting against your left side. Move into the cat-march again: notice how the board does not restrict you – if anything, it gives a sense of security. (Try it without the board, and hold your arm in the same position: it has almost exactly the same effect. It's the posture, not the prop, that makes the difference. . .)

Now shift the board so that you're holding it to your chest, with both arms in front of you: immediately the mood changes as the posture is forced, with the shift of the shoulders, into the sadness/edge-of-depression one. It's a posture we can also recognise as a defensive one: yet the subtle side-effect of the posture is depression and self-disempowerment, which in turn leads to the apparent need to be defensive. . . How would you balance the need – often a very real need – for defensiveness against the effect the posture has on your mood?

Each of these subtly-different postures has a matching 'sub-self' – though postures that are very close to each other can be very different in mood, while others apparently far apart coincide with strangely similar moods. If we don't recognise the effect that this has on our *own* mood – the mood that we ourselves choose at each moment – it's easy to get into a kind of battle within ourselves: our conscious choice ends up struggling against a mood which isn't 'ours' at all. The end-result can be far away from what we intended: a self-confirming spiral of depression, for example, or an indefinite anger at the world in general.

At this point it becomes easier to understand the movements of the secretary-character we saw from the café earlier. That sense of an 'imposed defensiveness' is a mode of being that many women can identify with all too easily: being leered at simply for being who you are would make anyone defensive. . . A defensive posture becomes habitual, and thus tends to be unconscious; her conscious choice of mood is probably quite different; the two choices clash, and pull her body in different directions. The result is a downward spiral into 'an indefinite anger at the world in general' – hence that heavy-footed stomp.

Try that posture and movement for yourself: choose a mood, then imagine, as you walk, someone mocking you for being who you are. (If this is all-too-familar, try doing it *consciously*.) How do you balance the need for defensiveness with your own chosen mood? What posture – and what mood – results from this *conscious* awareness of balancing these two choices?

The 'secretary' is a stereotype: but most stereotypes are the end-points of similar self-confirming spirals of posture and mood. Try some other stereotypes – the drunken businessmen in the café, the road-sweeper outside, or others such as the 'macho slob', the 'New Age wimp', the 'sex-kitten', the 'harassed house-wife' – especially those from the opposite gender. How much does wearing the posture of the stereotype bring on in you the same sort of moods they express? The stereotype is the end-point of an unconscious spiral of choices (or habitual non-choices): what are the *feelings* from which it starts? Being aware of that start-point, how would you reach a better balance of mood, posture and choice?

The secretary and the other stereotypes are caricatures: yet we can see them all around us. If we look, we can also see them in ourselves. . . It's not an act: it's more real than that. But if it slips into an unconscious habit, it can become a way of being – even though it doesn't match our true feelings at all. Here, we're choosing to wear the caricature as a costume, but we can also see how easy it is to let it wear *us*. . .

Yet if we try to control it, we move off into yet another kind of spiral: so the trick is to set a definite aim, but still let things be as they are. As we find our mood shifting, we watch the posture, watch the movement – but without trying to change it. And with practice we learn to recognise that if the mood changes as we change the pattern of moves, it's not 'I': it's just a passing 'sub-self', one that comes, and so will go when it goes. So we dance with it a while, accept it for what it is. And somewhere, somewhere between the dances, we find the core that is ourselves. . .

A DRAMATIC GESTURE

Another way we can notice these unconscious spirals of mood is to watch our gestures – especially our habits of gesture. Gesture is a language of the emotions, 'body-talk' in the way that words are mainly 'mind-talk'. When the two don't match, we can tell that something needs closer attention: but just by becoming more aware of this body-talk in a conscious way, we can learn more about what we are saying to *ourselves*. This is one of the key principles of techniques such as 'neuro-linguistic programming' – studying behaviour to study subjective reality. But we don't actually need a fancy name or fancy title before we can study it: all we need to do is watch.

The same threads pass through all of us, so it's often easier to start by looking at others. Some people use gesture very little, others a lot: "She'd be dumb if you tied her hands together", they said of one friend! And different cultures have very different habits of gesture: the flavour and even the language of many cultures is dictated by the expressiveness and expansiveness of their gestures – French, Italian, Greek and others. Or even the absence of gesture: so much of my native British culture is defined in terms of what people *don't* do and say. . .

Where it becomes most interesting is when people are talking on the telephone. The body-language – gestures and postures – can't be seen by the person they're addressed to: but the gestures are still there, in fact if anything are even more noticeable *because* they're not being responded to. So find some place to watch telephone users – an enquiry office, perhaps, or a café with a much-used 'phone. What do you see? What are people saying with their bodies? Can you guess, from their postures, what those people are hearing?

And when *you're* talking on the telephone, watch yourself in the same way. (Don't try to control or change the gestures: just watch.) What is your body saying? What muscles do you feel tense up or relax? What are your 'gut feelings' as you hear the other person speak?

☞

On occasion, you'll say or hear something and find your body respond in a quite different way – the voice sounds cheerful, for example, but the response is to slump in that 'sad/depressive' pose. What's going on? What different choices are clashing within you? Or what kind of 'trigger-phrase' have you heard, perhaps? Look within, deeper within. . . which response is *your* choice?

It's always easier to start by watching others: but we then need to look inward, at the way the same threads run through ourselves. The end-point of this kind of quest is to find out more about our *own* choices. The behaviourist approach has, perhaps rightly, gained a bad reputation from its routine abuse as yet another tool of the power-under game – its techniques are often incorporated into aggressive sales-training, for example, as a means to use other people's hidden choices to trap them into 'choosing' to buy. But that was never its intended function: the techniques were originally designed as tools for *self*-therapy, and are still most useful – and most effective – for that purpose.

In the same way that tiny changes in inflexion can change the entire meaning of spoken words – for example, the tiny lift at the end of a sentence that changes it to a question? – many of the crucial inflexions in body-talk are minute. It's not just changes in overall expression that we watch, but also shifts in the pattern of our breathing, tensing of different muscles, lip size variations and so on. Like posture, though, gestures and patterns that are very close to each other can match very different moods, while others apparently far apart coincide with those that are strangely similar. So the aim is not to pick out individual details, but to develop an intuitive awareness of the *overall* 'flavour' of what our own body is trying to tell us.

One useful trick is to use a mirror: it provides visual feedback of what we're feeling, and some of the subtleties – eye dilation, skin colour changes and the like – can only be seen in a mirror. We can then combine this with the work we've already done on ☞

affirmations, to provide a directly visible image of our own unconscious resistance to the changes we'd choose.

The catch is that we come face to face – literally – with our own resistance: the resistances that come up in writing affirmations are often a lot easier to handle. You'll also find yourself coming face to face with the silliness-barrier, too. . . So be warned: it's *not* a comfortable exercise! But it can show us things about ourselves that we couldn't see any other way: uncomfortable or not, it's worth doing.

All this consists of is to stand in front of a mirror – in the bathroom in the morning, perhaps – and repeat one of your affirmations until you feel comfortable with it. Watch your face: watch the different 'selves' passing through. Who are they? What are their opinions on that affirmation? What can they tell you, through this subtle body-talk, about the choice in your affirmation?

We can also use this awareness to provide a means to deal with one of the problems we looked at earlier: how to express feelings *about* someone's actions without dumping emotions *at* them. The outside is also the inside: often what we're actually upset about is our own perception of ourselves, being mirrored back by that person through the wyrd – so there's rarely much point in blowing up at them. Instead, we can direct the emotion at an *imaginary* representation, and then let go of our usual 'controlling': we then use this watching of our own body-talk to see what's actually going on within us at the unconscious level.

When we're dealing with really deep or old issues, even a visual representation of the person who's (nominally) offended us can be a bit too close – or, to put it another way, a bit too easy to avoid the fact that the problem is also in *us*. One common solution is a technique called 'the anger chair'. (This can sometimes reach some deep and painful spaces: it can usually be done on our own, but on occasion it may be wise to do this only with experienced help.)

Start by selecting some issue with some other person that ☞

181

you want to deal with – especially something about which you feel angry but feel unable to do anything about. Place two chairs, or two cushions, a comfortable distance apart. Sit down in one of them; relax, quietly, into a meditative state. Now imagine your 'opponent' sitting in the other chair. They're only imaginary: you can say exactly what you feel, and they won't interrupt you or answer back. So reach down, and look at your feelings about the issue. And tell them – this imaginary person – exactly what you feel. (You're facing not just an imaginary person but the 'silliness barrier' as well: don't worry about it, just let go, let go. . .) Stay seated in your chair, but say whatever you like: follow the *feeling* – shout, scream, cry if it feels appropriate. What words come out? What does your body say?

Continue until you feel it's time to stop – you'll find there's a point where the locked-up feelings are all gone, and it just stops. Suddenly, a quiet space – weird.

But we also have to link the wyrd, the inside and the outside. So the last part of the exercise – which is by far the hardest, but also absolutely essential – is to get up from your chair (or cushion) and sit on the one your imaginary opponent has been using. Look back at the now-imaginary 'you' in the other chair, and at your memories of you there: what do you see? What does *that* imaginary person's body-talk tell you? What do you hear and see from this point of view? Because during the whole of this exercise you've actually been talking to you. . . and that's why it's hard. . .

We're often unaware of our body-talk, of just how much our body is saying to us: yet it's always there. So it's the same as with any other habit: by becoming more aware of our unconscious choices, we reclaim the power of choice. It's not necessarily easy to reclaim that choice, or to decide what to do next once we've done so: but without doing it, we have no choice at all.

THE FLOW OF THE DANCE

Working with the threads of wyrd, weaving and interweaving within us and outside of us, is a kind of dance. We dance with its weirdnesses, its twists and our choices, and accept them for what they are: and in time we come to a strange new kind of freedom. We get to be who *we* are – or have always been. Though we never do quite know. . .

Dance is often a conscious way to express emotions, especially emotions that we can't – or daren't, sometimes – put into words. And it's also a way of freeing energy that's become stuck. Again, the best guides for this are children: think of the four-year-old skipping down the street, holding hands with its parents – or another child jumping up and down in anger and rage. By doing these kinds of movements consciously, we can reach the same threads in ourselves – but with a quite different awareness, and with a quite different effect.

When I've been 'had' by yet another salesman using my own fears as a weapon against me, it often seems there's nothing I can do. I'm furious: but there's nothing I can say to the guy that he could understand – and he'd just make me feel silly again. So one solution is to let my body do the talking – on my own, if appropriate – and dance the anger away.

Dancing away anger leads us into another one of these 'is-it-childlike-or-is-it-childish?' spaces. Our old friend the silliness-barrier has its usual opinion, of course, but the best answer is that it's up to us to make it child*like*, by appealing to the child within us. So set the stage with the right props: your favourite teddy-bear in the chair by the fire-side, perhaps. And let go: let go into an angry child's full-blooded tantrum – pound your legs, shout, scream! But do it *consciously*: keep the awareness, make it into a kind of dance. . .

Face the silliness-barrier, and let go. As with the 'anger chair', though, remember that this anger is not aimed *at* anyone – not even the salesman! The aim is to let the body say what it wants to say, and release the energy that's trapped in there: but do it in a way that harms no-one, else ultimately you'd only be harming everyone, including yourself. So keep a portion of your awareness

☞

---

to one side, watching: and with that awareness you'll *know* when to stop.

What do you feel? What comes out? What memories does it bring up – especially of times when you *weren't* allowed to express what you felt?

It's surprising just how much energy we each keep locked up in our own body. Release that, and we suddenly find we have a whole lot more energy than we thought we had – because it's no longer tied up in fighting *ourselves*. Most of us have long since lost the ability to relax beyond a superficial level – in fact, if we *do* relax, we tend to 'collapse in a puddle on the floor'. From habitual response to the fears that build up in the bitter games of power-over and power-under, almost every muscle has become tensed up, and has to be counterbalanced by another muscle pulling against it. We break through those blocks through sheer force, or will-power, at an enormous cost in energy: a far cry from the freedom of the dance.

Moving quickly conceals this near-battle of muscles, which is why our movements are jerky when we're tense: we most easily become aware of it through slow movement, such as in T'ai Ch'i.

As an illustration, curl (rather than clench) your fingers into a fist. Uncurl them *very* slowly – take at least a couple of minutes doing so, preferably longer, or you won't be able to see what's going on. At various points your fingers will 'stick' – at what positions in the movement do they do so? The usual way to release them from stuckness is to force them to move: but can you do so by relaxing instead? How do you do so? What other movements can you sense – tendons, muscles all the way back up the arm? And what moods do you pass through in this slow uncurling of the hands?

Paradoxically, slow movement can be one of the quickest ways of freeing this locked-up energy – mainly because it allows us to become more conscious of the subtle tautnesses in our movements. And often the tautnesses coincide with positions and postures that themselves coincide with moods that we try to hold on to – or moods that we prefer to avoid. The solution is to dance with them, dance through them *all* – and accept them for what they are. As we release our avoidance of certain postures and positions, we also release the fears that coincide with them: as we accept them, they instead become partners, like those 'visitors who drop by for tea', who come and go in the dance. It's a strange feeling, dancing with all these selves that pass by on the threads of wyrd. . .

Music helps this dance – there's no doubt about that. When we come face to face with the silliness-barrier, any excuse helps, and music is the traditional excuse for dancing. . .

From my own experience, the most useful music for this kind of dance is slow, fairly quiet, and with a definite structure and timing: a lot of classical music is too variable, for example, while rock music tends to be too mechanical for any of the subtler emotions. Some New Age music, especially the more structured kind, does well for this purpose – although most is just too vapid and gutless. My own favourite would be traditional Irish music, especially the uilleann pipes; another friend finds that 'jazz-fusion' works best for her; but for yourself, experiment!

The dance is harder than it looks: because when it's done right, the wyrd will tend to bring up within us issues that we're not keen to face. Many times that I've done this, I've found tears streaming down my face, with not the slightest idea why: clearly something was being let go, yet without 'my' involvement at all. So for this to work well, we need to let go into the flow of the music, allowing every movement, every mood be as it is, without controlling, without trying – and yet at the same time keep an open awareness and some kind of overall aim.

It's best to do this kind of dance on your own: you're not doing it 'for' anyone, it's more a gift to yourself. And with no-one else around, there's no-one watching, no-one to comment what you look like. No worries about whether it looks 'good' or 'bad': it is what it is. So maintain the focus on the threads *within*: just let go into the flow of the dance.

☞

Move with the music: the whole body. Don't so much 'do' as *be*. . . What moods and emotions do you pass through? Do you notice any patterns of movement that you fall into repetitively? Or others that you avoid? Let whatever happens happen; yet still retain a watch, from the core of yourself, looking out from within, or looking in from without. Be you, dancing with that infinite variety of 'selves' on the threads of wyrd. . .

Moving with the dance, we recognise those different moods: we allow them to be, and to be in us and within us, yet without being at their effect. Like the Indian temple dancer, we wear these moods, these selves: we have them but they don't 'have' us, we let go without letting go. As with any artform, the aim must always be to let go into the flow of the muse, without actually losing our sense of *self* in the process. It's a subtle balance – and one that is, once again, weird!

17

THE ART OF EMPOWERMENT

Letting go without letting go is perhaps the hardest part of reclaiming our power of choice: we have to find a way to 'go with the flow', with the twists and turns of the wyrd, yet at the same time keep a definite aim based on clear and (preferably) conscious choices. It does take practice. . . But as with the dances of the previous chapter, one of the easiest places to practice it is through an active expression of ourselves, in – or as – some kind of artform.

For most of us, the immediate response is "I can't do that". "I'm not an artist"; "I'm no good at that kind of thing" – phrases like this come to mind at once. But these are often 'curses' that we've been *taught* to believe: the complete phrase is often more accurately "People tell me that I'm no good at that sort of thing" – which is not necessarily true at all. In any form of art we come face to face not only with the silliness-barrier, but also with that cruel concept of perfection – which means that, whatever we do, it will never be good enough. To get out of this trap – one which often prevents us even from beginning – is to recognise that perfection is a *quest*, not an end-point in itself; and unless we do make a start, we'll never get anywhere.

Besides, the kind of art that's useful for this purpose is not 'for' anyone else at all: as with the dance, it's more a gift to *ourselves*. An expression of who we are – "I am what I am!" – and also a way of discovering who we are. So in a way it doesn't much matter what we do: what's more important is that we do it. And, for that, matter, *enjoy* doing it!

AS THE MUSE TAKES US

We tend to think of 'art' as something separate from our lives – something that belongs in museums or concert halls. But it's all around us, every day, everywhere: the muses, like the fabric of wyrd, interweave throughout our lives. What we tend to miss is just how much of this 'invisible art' is our choice, conscious or otherwise. And if the choice isn't a conscious one, it will, like those selves in the dance, affect our lives, even seem to control our lives – without our realising that it's not 'us' at all.

Music is perhaps the most obvious example of these hidden choices: we're so used to it that we often don't notice it's there. And yet it directly affects our mood: just as much as posture and gesture – if not more.

What's your favourite kind of music? Do you know why it's your favourite? What effects does it have on you? And how much does your taste in music vary according to your mood?

New Age music has been described as 'musical wallpaper', but at least it's fairly innocuous! Almost all films and television shows use music not just for its 'atmosphere' but for its emotional effect; supermarkets and stores play piped-music that is chosen with equal care, and for much the same reason. Make a point of noticing this hidden music: keep an ear open for it. Listen to the theme tunes for a few television shows, for example: what emotions are they trying to portray? What effect is that 'muzak' in the supermarket intended to have on you? And how well does it succeed in its aim – especially if you're not aware of it?

Listen in particular to the *background* music in drama: notice how it brings up emotions in you, encouraging you to empathise with the flow of the action in the story – excited one moment, tense another, triumphant at the next. But is this your choice? You may disagree politically with the action the film portrays, for example, yet the music leads you to its intended threads of mood. So, as with clash of moods brought on by 'imposed' postures, how do you become aware of the clash of threads within you? And what do you do about it?

The music we choose, and the music that's thrust upon us in various ways, all have their effects: by becoming aware of them, we regain some measure of direction over how they affect us. All that it involves is listening – yet it's listening *inwards*, to the 'inner music', as well as to what's more obviously 'outside' of us.

It's also useful to keep an ear on the music *we* create in our lives – the subtler music that comes from tone and pitch of voice, and the sounds we make as we move, we work, we play. Like gesture and posture, these all form subtle overlays to the overt words of language, flavouring our communication not just with others, but also with ourselves.

> Once again, it's easiest to recognise this by observing others – another visit to the café, then! Use as a guide the old proverb "Take care of the sounds, and the sense will take care of itself": ignore the words of the background chatter, and listen to the undertones, the subtle shifts in pitch and inflexion. What hidden language is carried by this music of the voice? What threads of the wyrd do they express?
>
> Accents are another overlay: you can hear them in the café, from all different parts of the country and beyond. But listen as *you* speak: what is your *own* accent? What do those 'subtle shifts in pitch and inflexion' say to you about *you*?

With practice, we can pick out a surprising amount of information from these subtle overtones. One colleague, a doctor in England, could often tell not only where someone had lived – usually to within twenty or thirty miles – but at what stages in their life they'd done so, and even what general area of work they did – just from the tone of voice. That took some skill, it's true, but it's quite easy to recognise a few traits: for example, the slight nasal pitch that's as characteristic of arts students as their inevitable stage of wearing black, black and black!

These tones of voice also act as a clear mirror of our own inner state. The hard part is that as we become more aware of this 'inner music', we get an overwhelming sense that it must sound awful – and there's a desperate urge to change it, to control it, to *make* ourselves sound better. It's not a good move. In fact this is much the same as at that point just after 'all the fun of the fair': and the need now, as then, is not to 'take control', but to wait, to let go, to let the voice change by itself. And as we do so, our connection with the wyrd changes too: as those overtones in inner music change, so does our choice of threads – our choice of mood, of state of mind.

Once we learn to let ourselves hear it, this inner music can give us direct feedback about how we're acting. All too often I catch myself speaking with a kind of high-pitched squeak that tells me I've drifted back into Panic Mode again; and if I hear myself braying like a donkey, I *know* I'm being arrogant, without needing anyone else to tell me! But how do we change this? As always, the trick is to let go without letting go: in other words we give some kind of aim and, especially, commitment, but otherwise allow things to be the way they are.

It also helps to practice not just listening to but *feeling* the inner music of our own voice. For example, take a deep breath, and go through a sequence of vowel sounds in turn, letting each one sound for the whole of the outbreath: 'o' (as in 'hot'), 'oar', 'oh', 'oo', 'arh', 'eye', 'air', 'ay', 'ee'. Do this at least twice in different pitches, high and low. Where do you *feel* the sound in your body? The higher notes you'll feel higher up, the low notes lower down: but where exactly? And what emotions, what moods, come through as the momentary 'dancing partners' of each sound?

The sounds we make are reflections of our breathing, which itself is a good mirror of our state of mind and being – as almost every religious tradition would tell us. It's a useful exercise to watch how we breathe, not just in meditation, but in ordinary everyday action – though perhaps we could instead view everyday action as 'breathing meditation'. Watching for the places we hold on, and others we avoid. . .

It's useful, too, to bring the inner music out into the outer world, expressing it in voice, in song, or with instruments of some kind. Let the inner child express the inner music: let go into a world of sound, yet remain aware of our choices within it. A drum, perhaps, to express our anger, or to drive away our fears; a penny-whistle with which to make music, to dance with our many 'selves'; or any other instrument you choose.

And notice the strange paradox: to let go and to reach something deeper than a childish noise, we in fact need a very real discipline – 'beyond the chaos lies an even eerier order'. You'll *know* when you reach that space: but in what way do you know? What feelings – or beyond-feelings – arise in that moment? Listen. . . listen to the music within. . .

Everything we do has its own music. We can never control it – or rather, we spoil it if we try; but by becoming aware of it, and working *with* it, we allow ourselves more and more to dance our lives in harmony with it – and with the weavings of the wyrd.

THE ART OF LISTENING

Music can also provide a bridge to bypass the old curse-belief of "I can't draw". A lot of what stops us from expressing ourselves visually is that old trap of perfection: if it's not a photographic likeness, it'll never be good enough. But what is a 'photographic likeness' of an emotion, a sound? There isn't one: which means that it's up to us. We can draw it as it seems to *us*: there's no 'right' or 'wrong', but simply something that *is*. Through this art of listening, we're free to create our *own* expression of each mood – and thus, in a way, of our own experience of each thread of wyrd.

The best music for this is something that has links to definite moods: try Holst's "The Planets", perhaps, or Vivaldi's "Four Seasons" – although it's also good to work with music you *don't* know well. To give you some kind of focus or 'handle' around which to construct an image, you may find it easier to set up

☞

something to draw: a vase of flowers, for example, or even your favourite teddy-bear! But it's not essential: the aim is more to build an image of the mood and the emotion rather than some supposedly 'accurate' representation.

Set out a box of wax crayons, and several medium- to large-size sheets of paper. (Use felt-tip pens if you prefer, or colour pencils: but not paint, because it would probably slow you down too much for this kind of work.) Tip the crayons out onto the table, without any particular order. Relax down into a quiet, almost meditative state. Now start the music playing. And move into that childlike state of 'letting go without letting go'. . . Don't think about what's happening, just flow with the mood of the music. Pick up and drop crayons at whim; draw whatever shape or texture seems appropriate; keep your focus on the music, and just let the image use you to build itself. (Even if you'd put out something to draw, you may find yourself drawing something quite different – more from the heart than the head. If so, accept it for what it is: a gift from you to you.) And at the end of each track, change to a new sheet of paper.

When the music comes to an end, take a look at what you've done. You now have several drawings which are your *own* interpretations of moods, threads in the fabric of wyrd: what do these tell you about those threads, and about you? And, for that matter, how easy was it to 'let go without letting go'? If you've done this with other people, what are the similarities, the differences between your images of each mood?

This kind of drawing is really a way of listening to *ourselves*, interacting with the world 'out there'. Once we've crossed that bridge, with the help of music or otherwise, we can see that we *can* trust ourselves to express what we feel – and that what we feel does mean something.

The core of any art is an intuitive understanding of that flow and interaction between ourselves and the wider world of the wyrd. There's always a boundary, but the boundary blurs – more and more so as our skill increases. A fair amount of that skill is physical, mechanical, manipulative: it only comes with practice, with discipline, with time. But unless we allow that intuitive flow to take place, none of this can happen – or rather, it might, but only in a way that we *see* is 'lifeless'. The drawing – or whatever – comes to life *because* of the life that we bring to it: what we draw is also in part a metaphor of our own inner life, our own inner awareness. It's a way of bringing that awareness to the surface. A true drawing of a landscape is also a true drawing of the inner landscape, the landscape of the heart, the mind, the soul. That's also what's frightening, at times: it's not always comfortable to see into our own soul. . . but even then, it's a further test of how easily we *can* accept who we are!

DRAWING OUR VISIONS

A drawing or painting can also be a direct visual representation of an affirmation – a way of bringing our visualisations into the outer world. Any kind of artform can bring to life our aim, our 'heart's desire', in a way that words alone just can't.

> Draw what you want; draw states of being that you want; draw postures, gestures, dances that indicate the choices that you want in your life.
>
> The same problems we found with visualisation occur here also. We can draw things, but not ideas; we can draw the results of a quality, but not the quality itself. By 'letting go without letting go' though, we can *express* these things as metaphor: what colour is freedom, for example? What shape is joy? What textures and patterns represent love, security, peace? Look closer at your drawings – or *listen* to your drawings, perhaps: these will all be in there somewhere – though often in disguised form – since they're always part of you. . .

Another way to build this kind of 'visual affirmation' is through collage: assembling your image from other people's images, somewhat reminiscent of the fragmentary way in which images in visualisations often come together. An important part of any affirmation is precision: we saw this earlier, looking at the subtle layers of meaning behind the words we use, and the same applies to affirmations in visual form. So what *exactly* does what you want look like? Watch out for it: look for it, but let it come to you, *allow* yourself to find an image that describes it.

Imagine, for example, that you want to work on a visualisation of 'a better place to live'. What would it look like? It's surprising how easy it is to recognise what we *don't* want, but how hard it is to be clear about what we do. . .

Look out for illustrations, drawings, photographs, of what seem to you to be 'a better place to live'. Cut them out of the magazine or whatever; stick them onto a large piece of paper or (preferably) card. And as you do so, notice – just as with affirmations – the resistances that come up: "I don't deserve that kind of place", "I'd never be able to afford that" and so on. (And as with affirmations, notice whose *voice* these resistances come up in.) Allow yourself to dream, but don't get caught up in the absurdities of the consumer-culture: fancy 'designer' spaces may look good at first, but there's rarely room for people – so what *feels* comfortable to you? Listen to the *feelings*, the messages from within. What do they tell you? How much does this 'picture of perfection' change from day to day?

Place the picture on your wall; use it as a visual reminder of what you want. And as with the pink-balloon exercise earlier, be 'non-attached yet non-detached': how is this visual 'pink balloon' being responded to in the wyrd? In what ways are you acting to bring it into reality?

A want is the outward expression of an inner need: and, as we saw earlier, our wants often express those needs in terms of metaphor. But we can't work directly with metaphor: we can't eat our words, the name of the thing is not the thing itself. In traditional magic, one solution was to reply to the metaphor with metaphor, in the form of a sigil or talisman – something that, through form and symbol, *represents* that which is desired. The simplest of these are the symbols that so many people wear: for Christians, a cross, or for Jews the Star of David, in both cases representing 'that which is greater'; a 'New Ager' might wear a crystal for much the same reason. Symbols representing 'household protection' can be found in almost every culture: the Orthodox icon, or the small recess in Japanese houses used as a Shinto shrine – or, for that matter, the crucifix dangling in almost every car in the Italian section of this city! A symbol isn't a thing in itself, it's a representation or metaphor for some idea or inner need.

What do various symbols mean to you? There are symbols all around: number, pattern, flags, even the ubiquitous company logos. Which ones catch your eye?

Our alphabets and scripts all started as symbols with ever deeper layers of meaning, of which the letters themselves are only the surface. In the Runic alphabet, used by the Nordic cultures who developed the concept of wyrd, each letter or carved mark represented a sound, an idea, a tree, a natural force or energy, an emotion, and much more besides: these were experienced as coinciding with the same threads of wyrd. Look for a while at your own and other culture's scripts – and for that matter your own handwriting: what threads of wyrd does each shape, each angle, each pen- or brush-stroke, seem to represent to you? Meditate on a small piece of writing for a while: what other layers of meaning suggest themselves to you?

A talisman is some kind of image that acts as a symbolic representation of 'our heart's desire'; a sigil (a 'seal') is usually more calligraphic, concentrating more on form and shape rather than a visual image – it's literally a seal that binds our commitment to that ideal. But the metaphor in both somehow reach deeper, beyond the surface level: as with the words we choose in affirmations, that become our bond, our commitment to ourselves, these symbols and images help us to draw out our vision – and to reclaim the choice and the poetry in our lives.

WORDS ON THE WIND

As with drawing, any mention of poetry tends to bring out an "I can't do that" response. My image of poetry was often either that

from school-days – impenetrable rhymes without apparent reason – or the equally impenetrable 'modern' styles. But it's much
more about listening to what's being said in the spaces *between*
words – the subtle messages of the silences, like the unspoken
messages spoken so loudly by two lovers' eyes. It's often in the
spaces that the interweavings of the wyrd in our lives become
obvious – or more recognisable, at any rate!

"i am the wyrd-one
    issues spiral through me
      on the threads of wyrd
    are unchanged
      by how much i am unchanged. . ."

In any form of poetry, the spaces matter as much as the words
themselves: as with the wyrd itself, much depends on the timing,
all building up to a greater whole.

We can use a kind of free-form poetry as another type of
affirmation – or rather, as a way of reaching a new understanding
of the issues behind an affirmation. So start by re-framing one
of your current issues: go over it as usual in your mind, perhaps
describing it in an affirmation, and watching the resistances arise
in their usual way. And let go: allow words to speak to you,
building themselves into form in much the same way that the
image in a visualisation assembles itself in apparently random
fragments. Listen to the words passing by on the wind; listen to
the message of the wind itself. Write whatever comes to mind. . .
allow whatever appears to be as it is – including the spaces.
Since this is an expression of *yourself* in relationship to your
chosen issue, what does it tell you about that issue – or yourself?

We'll get nowhere in poetry if we don't try; we'll also get nowhere
if we do! It's the usual problem of 'doing no-thing': so it's not
surprising – if typically weird – that phrases and structures appear
from nowhere after we think we've given up. That piece about "i
am the wyrd-one" came up in the usual half-awake state of a
too-early morning, after I'd been struggling for days to find some

understanding of why things around me weren't getting better: it gives a very simple answer as to why. . .

Again, as with any other artform, a few early-morning exercises won't make a true poet of anyone. But for us, here, that isn't the point: the aim of this kind of poetry is to act as a tool, to help us find out more about *ourselves* and our interactions with the wyrd and the world at large. Even so, it's useful to develop some degree of discipline, using a predetermined structure to give a framework for the words to fall into. For some people, this would be rhyme, or classical metre, or some other formal structure such as the nineteen-syllable Japanese *haiku*; for others the words may even come with music, forming themselves into a song, or a dance. It's up to us: it's always our choice – and a choice also to work with its twists.

But always the aim is to listen to the gaps between the words, the messages hidden in the silences and other spaces. In time we hear poetry in everything, we see dances and symbols in everything – even in the midst of the city. We see the weirdness in the surgings of the traffic, the weavings of pedestrians, the aerial dance of the birds, the crazy juxtapositions of street-signs; by opening our eyes, our ears, our hearts, to it, everything gains immeasurably in meaning.

We re-empower ourselves; it makes life worth living. And yet, in a way, we've done nothing: by letting go without letting go, it's all happened as if by itself. "If no thing is done, nothing is left undone", as the *Tao Te Ching* puts it: slowly, with a deepening awareness of ourselves, these old expressions – so meaningless in our earlier 'dark times' – begin to make practical sense.

18

WE'RE BUSY DOING NO-THING

The real trick with all of this is that there is no trick. There's nothing in particular to do. It's less about *doing*, than *being* – especially about letting things first be as they are, and then working from there with the weird twists and turns that arise out of our choices. And that's far harder than it sounds – not least because so many of our fears so subtly get in the way. But in time we do get there – simply by doing no-thing.

ALLOWING OURSELVES TO NOTICE

'Doing no-thing' consists of working with things as they are – acting in the moment, and only in the moment. But it's important to realise that the process of allowing things to happen is not one of passivity: instead, it's more like 'active non-action'. And there's a vast difference between doing nothing, and 'doing no-thing'. We don't just sit back and wait for things to happen – as we saw before, that's believing in the wrong kind of magic – but instead build a clear idea of the direction or aim that we want to go in; and then act, immediately, when the threads of reality point in that direction. To do that, though, we first have to learn how to notice when the threads *are* pointing that way.

> To illustrate this, it might be worthwhile to go back to that breathing exercise we did earlier, to use it as an analogy of 'active non-action'.
>
> ☞

Start off in the same way as before: stand upright, legs slightly apart, arms at your sides. And go through the same cycle as earlier: breathe in slowly, with the head tilted back, chest lifted slightly, and the arms raising as you breathe in; and then relax all the way down as you breathe out. Feel the stream of moods that pass by as you go through this cycle: from strength and elation, down to the depressive slump, and back to strength again, round and round in a matching cycle.

Go through this cycle a few times, to get the feel not just of the individual moments and moods, but the flow of the *overall* pattern.

We could act at any time in the cycle, but we can feel, quite clearly, that in many cases it would be ineffectual, or even counter-productive. In the whole of this cycle, there's really only one right moment to begin an action: and that's at the point just before the top of the cycle, *before* the top of the in-breath – so that the action has the full force of the out-breath behind it. Acting then seems effortless (try it!). But where is this point? How do you feel it? How do you sense its impending arrival – and gain a momentary warning of when to act?

Now apply this, by analogy, to how you act in the world at large. In what ways do you recognise the not-quite-cycles of our every-day wyrd? As you go through *these* cycles, notice how you get the feel not just of the individual moments and moods, but the flow of the *overall* pattern. Where is the point that's equivalent to 'just before the top of the cycle'? How do you allow yourself to become aware of this point? How do you sense its impending arrival – and gain a momentary warning of when to act?

With practice, we *do* get a sense of 'impending wyrd'. And through an increasing awareness of our connection with the wyrd, we learn to trust that through that connection we *will* know what to do and when to do it – and not waste energy in doing unnecessary work that only has to be undone or done again. In that sense, we allow the threads to tell us what to do: hence "if no-thing is done, nothing is left undone".

WHEN LESS IS MORE

'Doing no-thing' is not the easiest of concepts to grasp – still less to put into practice. The trick is that there is no trick; and although each moment of change is instantaneous, there are no instant solutions. Paradox within paradox, dilemma within dilemma. . . weird. . .

To work with the tortuous nature of wyrd, a quality we need to develop is patience! And yet patience itself presents us with another of these paradoxes: true patience is another form of 'doing no-thing'. It's not the same as waiting: it's a much more specific state than that. Mystical traditions describe this state as 'expectant gratitude', or 'inviting the guest'; commitment with openness, providing direction, yet allowing things to be as they are. Patience may be a virtue, as we were all told as children: but no-one told us quite how hard it can be!

What patience certainly is *not* is waiting on the edge of my seat in frustration, which was what I used to do too much of! Neither is it fatalistic resignation: there's no acceptance of the wyrd – or of choice – in that. So it's something closer to that subtle balance where 'non-attached' is at the same time 'non-detached', which we played with earlier with the pink-balloon exercise. We do have choices: we let them go, yet without letting go.

But often the hardest thing of all is *to let things be*. "Be here, now": that's what we usually need to practice on. If we're on our own – we're on our own. If we're with someone – we're with them. If things are going well, they're going well; if they're not, they're not. True patience is when we trust the wyrd enough that *it doesn't matter* what's happening or not happening; what matters is that it is what it is, and that we let it be as it is, enjoying it as it is in the moment. Then, strangely enough, it *can* change – because we've let there be space for it to do so. If it does change, what happens is not always what we'd expect: often what actually changes, for example, is our ability to find enjoyment in the way things already *are*.

How do you understand – or experience – 'patience'? How

easy – or hard – do you find its subtle balance of 'active non-action', of letting things be as they are, from moment to moment?

So often, we find that in acting we do not so much 'not enough', but too much. Doing less actually does more; acting *in the moment* is more productive than doing for the sake of doing.

Often all we have to do to change something is to notice *how it is* – we don't have to 'do' anything as such. We can see this easily, for example, when someone's angry: if we try to change the anger, to stop it, to reason it out, all too often it has the opposite effect: a comment is misunderstood, tempers flare, and suddenly *everyone* is angry. But if we quieten down within ourselves, and *let* them be angry, it all quite suddenly stops – there's often an embarrassed silence and a sense of bewilderment all round, in fact.

We don't have to do anything: instead, we let it be as it is, and 'do no-thing'. We don't *cause* the change as such: but the inside is somehow also the outside. As we quieten ourselves, creating space *within*, the world out there changes in parallel. It's a bizarre twist: one that's typical of wyrd, and one that reacts directly to our choices in the moment. And as we learn to recognise this, and see that reality *does* work in this weird way, we begin to be more able to trust the wyrd – and ourselves.

A lot of the pressure for change comes from that curse-belief of perfection: we want things to be *right*, and *now*. But things aren't perfect: they never are, they never will be. So the way we change ourselves, for example, is not by trying to *be* perfect, but simply by noticing that we aren't – and allow ourselves to be that way. Then in time, we *do* change – yet in a way that we often miss, as with that story earlier about "Wear thy sword while thou canst". Often the only person who's requiring us to 'be perfect' is ourselves – and we hurt ourselves, all the time, by trying so hard to be so. Or we're requiring everyone else to be perfect – and they aren't. The short answer is: it's an imperfect world! So we're best to let it be that way – in order to *let* it change in ways that we'd choose.

We don't change things by getting angry that they aren't perfect: we change them by noticing that they aren't, and allowing them, in the moment, to be that way. And then we can *let* things become as we would like them to be. The world is as it is because of our choices: it's useful to see what we've chosen. . . Change starts by starting from where things are: then they change *themselves* – without our 'doing' anything. But by rushing to change things, we slow change down; by demanding perfection, we lose it. Weird. . .

"But. . . what do I do now?" is my immediate question; to which the answer from within is "Nothing! *No-thing*. Be patient; listen; wait; listen. . ." In times like these, when impatience so easily gets the better of me, the habit of meditation, of finding the quiet space within, becomes more and more important. That helps me allow things to be as they are, and wait out the panic and the harder spaces. And in time, and over time, reaching patience *does* get easier, it *does* get better. It's not perfection: but then it never will be. But it *is* an improvement – a very real one. So I accept it, acknowledge myself for it; and move on.

What do you do in these circumstances? Does meditation, or some similar approach, help you here? In what ways do you notice a trend of improvement in your patience – and hence in your ability to ride out and wait out the ups and downs of our imperfect world?

Things change themselves, without our 'doing' anything; though equally without our doing nothing. We 'do no-thing' – which sometimes actually means doing a lot. But it's doing that is not so much planned or controlled as *directed*, from that quiet space within; there *is* an overall aim or direction, but each action happens, as it is, from moment to moment. Our actions seem to happen not so much because of us, as *through* us: it's certainly a weird feeling, but it works, and very well indeed when we let it.

In many ways 'doing no-thing' is a childlike spontaneity that's tempered by an adult's awareness of aim and purpose. Once again, this is something that we've lost from childhood: in some cases it would have been quite literally beaten out of us, because it's often not easy for others to tell the difference between 'doing no-thing' and doing nothing. The result is that most of us learn that 'doing something' has to be obvious: "can't you see I'm trying!", we might have said, face knotted into a frown, hunched up tight over some difficult school test. And that too becomes a habit – another habit that we somehow have to unlearn.

> "Don't just stand there, child – do something!" It's often difficult to prove that we *are* doing something, of a kind, when we're 'doing no-thing' – and if we're not doing something, then we must be doing nothing. That's logic, isn't it? Certainly school-level logic. . .
>
> So how do you let go of that illogical 'logic': how do you know when to do, and when not to do? How do you know when something's not working because you're not trying hard enough, and when it's not working because you're trying too hard? What are the *feelings*, and other messages from the wyrd and the world within, that tell you the difference?

This compulsive 'doing for the sake of doing' can be a problem. But in some ways doing nothing may be the greatest risk of all: we don't make new mistakes, but nothing changes either. We do have to act – but only when the time is right. And we have to trust ourselves, trust our awareness of the wyrd, to *know* when the time is right. Until then, though, the instruction might best be "don't just do something – stand there!"

Less is more: 'doing no-thing' is a very subtle balance. . .

TIME TO SLOW DOWN

The constant pressure on us all to 'do' – in order to prove that we are doing *something* – leads us eventually into a constant state of panic. If there isn't something to do, we'll invent one. . . faster, faster, faster! And since we never manage to catch up, that *proves* that we're no good, we're no good at anything. . .

This doesn't exactly help! In the normal weird way, often the best way to get more done, more quickly, is not only to 'do' less, but also to slow down. And *notice* what's going on. We actually get to see life that way – and get a chance to enjoy it, too.

In hurrying to catch up – the 'White Rabbit' mode of "I'm late, I'm late – gotta do it *now!*"– we tend to miss the detail; we also tend to expend a lot of energy needlessly. It looks impressive, but it doesn't get much done: as one friend put it, "You *can* chop onions with a battle-axe, but it's easier to do it with a kitchen-knife!" So slow down. . . slow down. . .

Slowing down has never been easy for me! My handwriting is a good indication: it's usually a mess, in fact it is only readable when I drop out of my normal near-panic state. When my hand-writing becomes unreadable again, it's time I slowed down. . .

All it really takes is just to stop for a moment; relax; be quiet. As we've seen, meditation is one tool that helps us do this: in meditation I slow down, 're-centre' myself – with the result that I usually get a lot more done after a session. But perhaps the most interesting experience has been with 'active imagination', a form of visualisation which consists of a written conversation with some imaginary entity within. Both sides of these conversations are ourselves, of course: but we get a chance to hear what some of those other 'selves' within us have to say about what's going on in our lives. The conversation consists of the same fast-changing impressions that flit past in any visualisation; the aim is to write them all down. The interesting point is that the best way to keep track of the changes is to *slow down*: they then slow down to match.

Try it: sit somewhere quiet with a pen and paper – or in front of a keyboard, if you prefer. And relax into that quiet meditative state, much the same as for a visualisation. This time the image you construct is of some imaginary entity – the usual choice is a character that's been appearing in your dreams. What you're doing here is in effect an active dream: so place that character in its previous dream-setting. Formally greet it – rather like greeting the 'inner guide' in a visualisation. And converse with it: see what it has to say, what comments it has to make on your ☞

WE'RE BUSY DOING NO-THING

life. Ask it questions about issues that are puzzling you now: what answers does it have to give?

Write down the conversation as it happens. If the impressions crowd together too fast to keep track of, it's because you're not slowing down enough! To illustrate this, here's a fragment from an actual conversation I had with an imaginary character I labelled 'J':

"I: I'm trying to keep pace with the thoughts, the words, the images.

"J: There's no rush. Have you noticed this time that they keep pace with you – there's no vast pile of impressions you can't keep track of? It's not been more ahead than the next sentence, the next question or answer. Like your response of "That's true", which is what comes next!

"I: That's true. . .

"J: So *don't rush*. Take your time. It isn't going to run away. . ."

It can take a little time to get started – especially to get past the silliness-barrier about 'talking to myself' – but once we do, active-imagination can be a very powerful tool. In a way it's similar to 'channelling' – the main difference being that we accept responsibility for everything that's said, since we *know* it's all part of ourselves. Try it; practice with it for a while. What do you learn?

In panic, or even the excited-little-child feeling of "I want to pack as much into this life as I can!", we tend to miss things. A lot: most of life, in fact, if we're honest. . . When we slow down and 'do no-thing', the answers we need arise. When we slow down, we get a chance to enjoy what we have, here, now; and everything necessary still gets done. Slow down. . . time to slow down. . .

DO IT CONSCIOUSLY

We also miss a great deal of life by not being aware of it – or rather, by having learned to be *un*aware of it. Most of 'doing no-thing' is really about awareness, which itself is a summation of everything we've done here so far: learning to watch for the senses-taker and the subtleties of power-over and power-under; learning to be aware of the blurred boundaries between 'inside' and 'outside', and the chaos of coincidences that forms the web of wyrd. Accepting things as they are, accepting that we'll only know later (if ever) the 'why' of the way they are; yet knowing that we *do* have choices in these tides of life. And learning too to take responsibility for our choices as well as reclaiming them – and working with the twists that always follow. Life is weird: there's always a choice, there's always a twist. . .

If we're not conscious of what's going on around us, we'll always seem to be at its effects; and if we're not conscious of our choices, we can hardly complain at the results!

Being conscious of what we do is not always comfortable: we can't hide from our illusions, or from the direct results of our choices. It's one reason why most of the time we *prefer* to be unconscious. . .!

So as one writer put it, "if you're going to raid the refrigerator, do it *consciously*". In which case, the sequence would probably go something like this:

"Now I am in the kitchen."
"Now I am walking towards the refrigerator."
"Now I am opening the refrigerator door."
"Now I am reaching out for the . . ."
"Now I am putting the . . . in my mouth."
"Now I am chewing the . . ."
"Now I am swallowing the . . ."
"Now I am feeling sick. . .!"

When we actually allow ourselves to become aware of what's going on, life becomes a kind of cosmic joke – a chaos of clowns, and we're part of it! In a way, it's only when we cease to be aware of the joke that it all becomes too serious for comfort. . . So practice being conscious of every move: walking becomes a meditation, signing cheques becomes an art-form, cooking becomes an act of love. Being aware – deliberately aware – of your moves and your choices, what's different about what you see? What difference does it make?

So 'doing no-thing' also involves becoming aware of these

choices, and the results along their respective threads on the wyrd. It's easy enough to say "be conscious of these choices": but the problem, of course, is that if we're not aware of them, we're usually not aware enough to realise that we're *not* aware of them. A kind of chicken-and-egg situation... We somehow have to loop 'being aware' back in on itself – in effect to use part of our usual unawareness to trip us into awareness.

Without a significant amount of practice, we'll spend most of our time unaware, or at best only vaguely aware of what's going on. (We often think it's only us that's at fault, but in fact this is true for *everyone*.) The way out of this loop is to place a clear intention to become more aware: and then do precisely 'no-thing' about it. We *allow* ourselves to wake up every now and then: when we're clear that we want to do this, the twists within the wyrd do this for us, and show us what to do.

There's a partner-exercise used in some workshops that we can adapt as an illustration of this. In the original version, you'd close your eyes, and your partner would steer you round the room (or whatever space you were in); and at some point would tilt your head in some direction and say "Click!" – like a camera. Your partner's trying to show you something, or at least presenting something they'd like you to be conscious of. So you'd open your eyes and grasp a brief, momentary impression: what do you see? What do you sense? Then you'd close your eyes, and move on.

Imagine a solo version of 'Click!' – with the wyrd as the partner guiding you. Carry on with your life exactly as normal; nothing different at all. But every now and then there's a sense of 'Click!' coming through on the web of the wyrd: so stop – pay attention. Look again at what you were looking at: what do you see right *now*? What do you sense? What is the wyrd trying to show you?

Remember that what you're being shown doesn't necessarily have to have a meaning: it *is*. Though there's often a wry joke in there somewhere, if you let yourself see it!

And then, after a moment, go back to what you were doing –

in fact for some people there's almost a sense of being 'let go of' by the wyrd. An odd kind of awakening. . .

Allow this to happen over a period of time: make a deliberate intention that it should happen often over a period of time. In what conditions do you find yourself 'being Clicked'? What patterns, over time, do you see, in what you're being shown?

The whole process is odd: we need to become more conscious, more aware of what's going on, and yet trying to 'be conscious' actually blocks that awareness. It's another kind of 'letting go without letting go', like that peculiar difficulty we had in looking for a dim star at night: we first need to become more conscious, and then let go even of that awareness, that *surface* layer of 'consciousness'. With practice, we move to a more conscious awareness; then with further practice, we move to a state that seems to be *beyond* that – but also beyond a distinction of conscious or unconscious, aware or unaware.

So at some point it looks, on the surface, exactly the same as before we started all of this: and yet something *has* changed. Despite the persistent incursions of those unwelcome 'inner visitors who come for tea', things *do* get easier: though there's no specific reason that we could pin down as the cause. Things do get easier: though often in very weird ways, ones that we'd not expected at all. And after a while, if we keep on practising 'doing no-thing', it becomes clear that something very strange – and yet very important – begins to happen to us. By making a point of becoming more conscious, yet not falling back into trying consciously to control what's happening, *something* within us begins to wake up. Something that finds it much easier than our normal sense of 'I' to work with the twists of the wyrd.

In a way it *is* the wyrd – but it's also us. And for a while, that's when things can get very weird indeed. . .

A personal example: I'd arranged to go on a long-weekend camping trip with a friend. We'd planned to go down the coast;

but at the last minute we changed our minds, and went inland instead. Odd: both of us had the same disturbing dream in our tents that night, the same fear echoed. . . Weird, perhaps, but by now we'd become used to that.

Heading back to the city, on a rough strip of road it seems for a moment like the steering has gone on the car: suddenly swaying from side to side, for no apparent cause. Definitely strange. . . but a few long seconds later it stops, so we stop worrying.

We're heading towards the city on the usual route; for no particular reason we change our minds, and decide to come in on the longer northern route. That's odd: I'd have thought we'd have been able to see the city lights from here. And the traffic lights are out too. Strange. Doesn't matter, though.

So we go home. Odd. . . everything here seems quiet, yet strangely breathless. . . phone doesn't work, either. . .

And it's not until an hour later that someone tells us what's happened. The date is October 17th, 1989; the city is San Francisco. The biggest earthquake here for decades. So that's what we'd felt on the road, then – well over a hundred miles away. But that's also what those dreams had been about; if we'd gone to the coast, as planned, we'd have been exactly at the epicentre when it struck; and with roads and bridges collapsed and debris everywhere else, the route home we'd casually chosen 'on the spur of the moment' had in fact been the only one possible. And yet we hadn't *consciously* known a thing.

'Precognitive recovery', one friend calls it – the art of *not* being in the wrong place at the wrong time. Weird. . . definitely weird. . .

A common mistake is to see this kind of weird experience as proof of something special, or of being someone with special 'powers'. It's not: in its way it's perfectly normal – especially once we let ourselves see that it *is* normal. We all do it, all of the time. All that's happened here is that we're now increasingly able to *see* that we do it – and begin to have some conscious choices, not so much in specific results as in the *direction* of the results. Yet to reach this point, we've had to become aware of the workings of wyrd in our lives – and then, with care, deliberately forgotten it all over again, in order to 'do no-thing' about it. That's often all it takes to 'do no-thing' – a kind of 'conscious forgetting'.

But to do these things, to make these connections, to know ahead the effects of so many of our choices in the way that we begin to do at this stage, it seems that we must know everything – or part of us must. Yet there's also a clear sense that it certainly isn't what I think of as 'I' that's doing it: I'm very ordinary, I *know* just how much I don't know! So what's going on in this weirdness? And if, as it feels, there seem to be many different threads of self weaving within and through me, who am I? Which 'I' is me?

19

WHICH 'I' IS ME?

Who are we? We never do quite know. I look at old photographs: I barely recognise myself in any of them. I catch a glimpse of myself in a mirror: who on earth is that stranger? I'm different with different people, in different places, at different times; my sense of self, and the self that other people see, are totally different – and changing all the time. And yet there is an 'I' that's always there, an 'I' that makes the choices – I *know* that. So who am I? Which 'I' is me?

WHAT – OR WHERE – IS 'I'?

We need to be a little careful here. By linking ourselves with the threads of wyrd, we connect to infinity – an experience that can often be frightening, since everything and nothing can be true at the same time. So we need to develop a sense of self, of personal space and personal boundaries, before going much deeper in our search for an understanding of 'I'.

At times in these changes there's a sense of craziness, which most of the time we're careful to avoid: yet sometimes we have no choice but to work with it. Reality *is* weird: there are some important issues that arise from that fact. And one of them is that a little craziness is *normal*. . . When things get a little crazy – such as in that bewildering sense of "Which 'I' is me?" – it does help to realise that there's nothing actually wrong with us. All that's happened is that we've allowed our connection with the wyrd to become conscious for a moment, so that we can learn something

211

new from a different point of view – and add it to the totality we each call 'I'.

The wyrd is the interweaving of everyone, everywhere, everywhen – which means that when we become aware of it, suddenly every possible point of view can be *here*, *now*. That's what makes it scary: for a brief moment, we see and believe from more than one point of view – and often incompatible ones at that. It's so scary that it might even seem insane. But it's not: it's just weird. . . wyrd. . . and perfectly sane and normal.

A quiet country walk. It's been a couple of miles since I last had a rest, so I stop, and sit for a while, looking out over the valley. And relax. And slow down. . . slow down. . . slow down. . . into a different sense of time. Without quite becoming aware of what's happening, I merge with the scene – not *in* it, but part *of* it. My sense of 'I' spreads out, wider, wider: I don't just hear the bees in the tree behind me, I *am* the bees, the tree. I'm not just sitting *on* a rock: I *am* the rock, an extension of the rock itself. I *am* the whole valley, ageless, timeless. . . I feel the grass and trees writhing on my surface, as years become seconds; seconds become years, as I become one with the lifespan of the may-fly and the moth. I become all of these things: everyone, every-where, everywhen. And my sense of 'I' dissolves.

Panic!

Where am I? What's going on? Am I going crazy?

I come back to myself – what I think of as 'myself' – with a crash: heart pounding, wild-eyed, frightened. That sense of totality, of boundarylessness, has vanished as completely as it came: hidden away, now, in the depths of 'conscious forgetting'. But it was weird while it lasted. . . and I'm not too sure I'd want it to happen again for a while, either. . .

Have you had experiences of that kind – of merging, dissolving into everyone, everywhere, everywhen? They're surprisingly com-mon: we do all have them, to a greater or lesser degree – when we *let* them happen. And there's nothing crazy about them – as long as we can retain a clear sense of 'I'. So re-link with that weird feeling of boundarylessness – and re-view it as being

☞

> *normal*. What difference does that make to your understanding
> of the experience?

That sense of 'I' is important: if we tried to be conscious of the wyrd all of the time – and especially if we tried to dissolve our sense of 'I' into it – we really *would* go crazy! As long as we *can* retain our sense of 'I' in our contact with the wyrd, we'll have no problems: the problem, though, is how to retain that sense of 'I'...

The usual idea of 'sane and sensible' is to be absolutely consistent, predictable, everything under control – always in character, we might say. But this leaves no room for change, for growth, even for experience. In fact, the only thing it leaves us is habit, which, as we've seen, is far from healthy for us – far from sane, in its literal sense of 'healthy'. We have to allow for change – which means we also have to allow for what seems, on the surface, to be a kind of insanity. It isn't: but it could look like it, and at times certainly feels like it... In that sense, much of our interaction with the wyrd could well be described as 'the subtle art of insanity'!

> This may seem new and strange, but in fact we dealt with this earlier, way back when we looked at the process of learning new skills. As you'll remember, there's a moment there of this same craziness: believing at the same time both "I can't do it" *and* "Oh – I can!". That's wyrd...
>
> We also met it, by analogy, in the hall of mirrors at the fun-fair – specifically, the big concave mirror. As we walk towards that mirror from a distance, everything reflected in it is upside-down and small; then at a certain point everything quite suddenly dissolves into a chaotic blur. There's no way we can make sense of it – insanity... But *keep moving*: after a brief moment the image resolves itself into something completely different – everything is now the right way up, magnified, clearer. A new point of view: but we could only get there by going *through* the moment of chaos. And also by not giving in to panic within that chaos, but retaining a clear sense of 'I'.

Perhaps 'insanity' is a bit too strong – but it certainly involves a letting go of control, to allow for a momentary descent into a chaos in which everything and nothing is true. If we hold rigidly to one point of view, we cannot change: yet sometimes the wyrd gives us no choice but to do so!

Beyond the chaos, the threads of wyrd do indeed have their own 'even eerier kind of order': but they can take us absolutely anywhere, so we need to know ourselves – a definite sense of 'I' – in order to have some place to return to. Amidst all the changes, this is a place that's always the same, and always ours: our 'centre'. We already have a description of it in an imaginary sense: it's that quiet inner private space – a beach, a mountain brook or whatever – to which we first go in a guided-meditation. That, in a very real sense, is 'home' – a home *within* ourselves.

What this centre *isn't* is what we usually expect it to be, which is a set description of our character. That changes: 'I' doesn't. Our characteristics are fluid: they'll seem fairly static at any one time, but over a lifetime there can be vast changes – and the whole point of personal growth is that we *should* change! So how do you change? What threads of your character have moved and changed in your life?

In terms of wyrd, a characteristic is a thread of wyrd, which passes through *everyone*: if we identify with the thread, the characteristic, we can easily be swept into someone else's sense of 'I', and lose our own. This perhaps shows why the answer to the question "Which thread am I?" is "all and none"! A better concept of 'I', in terms of wyrd, is that it's a point of *clustering* of the threads, a nexus in the web of wyrd – much as we saw in that analogy with the Chinese streamer, way back at the beginning of the book. But how do you choose which threads to hold at the surface of that nexus which forms your 'I'? How – if at all – do you recognise this 'home' within yourself?

In Jungian terms, 'I' is a unique combination of 'universal traits and possibilities' – in other words, of the threads of wyrd. All the threads pass through every point, every one of us: what we – or others – would call our character are the group of threads that, in

214

one way or another, we *choose* to have on the surface. In that sense, this surface 'I' is the sum of our conscious and unconscious choices of who we choose to be.

Yet 'I' is not that which changes: 'I' is that which chooses. It's the ability to choose which makes us special; our choices are unique. If we lose our sense of choice, we lose ourselves; lose our sense of self – our 'self-esteem' – and we lose our ability to choose. So it's unfortunate, but perhaps not surprising, that almost everything in the culture is intended to get us to do just that. . . and that's where so many of our problems lie, when we start to apply our inner knowledge of the wyrd to our dealings with the outer world.

CAUGHT IN THE WEB

'Enmeshment' is the formal term in psychology for that loss of sense of self: we get entangled with someone else's sense of 'I', and lose contact with our own. Enmeshment is when we have no sense of self to return to – a state of 'low self-esteem', where we defer our power of choice to others, and feel entirely at the doubtful mercy of the whims of fate.

It's important to realise that there are massive cultural pressures pushing us towards enmeshment, 'other-centredness', co-dependency – all of them based on unacknowledged fear, and an imagined need to disempower others. Everyone wants to remain in that childish state in which the world seems to be an extension of themselves; so everyone wants us to *be* an extension of their will – and deny ourselves the right of choice in *our* lives. We build layer upon layer of boundaries against these pressures, most of them – such as law, for example – concerned with how to operate in a world without trust. But as we start to dismantle our boundaries, as part of the process of reclaiming trust, we can put ourselves in real danger: if we forget to maintain our *own* sense of self, we can lose ourself entirely. A great deal of care is needed at this point. . .

215

The key part of that care, perhaps, is to maintain our own sense of a 'home' within ourselves, a place to return to from our wanderings in the wyrd. Returning to a centre – which is what 'meditation' literally means, and which is why meditation, visualisation and the like are so important in this process.

It's useful to make a habit of visualising this centre, this self, this 'home' – so that we can recall that image when we find ourselves enmeshed in the web. So relax into the usual meditative state, sitting quietly. And become aware of the surface of your body – the effective boundary between the 'inside' world and the 'outer', shared reality. Now imagine your body surrounded by a pale glow, a cocoon of light, expanding outward from that surface – a beacon for the self to return to. The cocoon is woven from threads of light, the threads of wyrd; but these also pass through everywhere, everywhen, everyone. How do you visualise these threads? Can you see where some of them lead?

Practise that visualisation in a quiet space a few times: then take it out into the world with you! Rebuild this image of a 'cocoon of light around my safe space' wherever you are: on a bus, at work, talking with friends, in the shops – and, especially, in situations where you feel 'not quite being myself', or where your sense of choice seems under threat. Holding this image, reclaim your centre – as best you can! – and watch where those threads lead. Where are they trying to drag you? Where do you tend to lose – or abandon – your sense of self to others' choices in the web of wyrd?

There are several levels at which we can lose our contact with self. One is the social level: it often seems much easier to just let go and get carried along with the tide – as in a football crowd, for example. In politics or in employment there's often a sense of frustration and disempowerment that arises from exactly this situation: we feel we're trapped, that we're forced to go along with this, whether we'd consciously choose to or not. But if we truly *do* choose to do something different, we have to go all the way with that choice: if we don't, and defer to the cultural norm by default, we've also in some ways given up our right to complain – choosing not to choose is still a *choice*.

To go against the norm may well seem suicidal: but if we look closely, there's *always* a choice, there's always a way through. And there's also always a twist: when we truly do follow the weavings of our wyrd – 'follow our bliss', to use Joseph Campbell's term – even the hardest-looking options do open out into gentler spaces. It's up to us: but we have to know – and trust – ourselves enough to recognise what truly *are* our choices: and put those choices into action in the everyday world.

It's easy, too, to abandon our own choices from a sense of 'anything for a quiet life' – especially in closer relationships, with family or friends, work-partners or life-partners. Boundaries are often statements of fear, especially a fear which that person does not want to face: backing away from that kind of boundary doesn't solve the problem, in fact the boundary often grows or becomes more vigorously defended. This is how co-dependency develops: each party agrees to 'protect' the other from their fears, in a way that actually helps no-one. What usually happens is that the problems get passed onto others: anyone who's willing to take responsibility will always get the worst of it. Cultural condition-ing illustrates this point: men learn early on that others (male or female) will instinctively go for weak spots, and take a lack of assertiveness as an invitation to aggression, while women are taught that their identity and purpose depends on making others happy – life becomes pleasant only if you're content to live for others. It doesn't work. . . we each have to reclaim our *own* choices to reclaim our own identity.

It's also easy to abandon self to the other in a relationship by *over*-commitment to that person – or to the relationship itself, especially if it's over-idealised. A relationship is a joint self, a sharing of 'I and We and I': but we also have to remember to maintain within it our *own* self, our own choices, our own 'I' – else if 'We' ceases to exist, so does 'I'. . .

A painful memory: a partnership has come to an end – and I'm lost. I've been totally committed to our 'We'; but my partner felt ☞

stifled, and backed out. 'We' has ceased to exist; so, it feels, have 'I'. Abandoned. . . I've no reason to live any more: I have to get my partner back, or I'll die. . .

But what's actually happened here is that I've long since abandoned *myself* in favour of an illusory 'We': and the wyrd has been kind enough to provide conditions to remind me of this fact. It may not be comfortable, but it's what I need to know. . .

How do you maintain 'I' in relationships? What are the *feelings* that warn you that you're in danger of abandoning your self? And how – at the end of a relationship – do you reclaim and rebuild 'I' now that 'We' has died?

The fear of abandonment becomes not merely a problem, but an apparent matter of life and death: so the pressure to *own* the partner in a relationship can become intense. As well as putting up boundaries to keep others out, we also put up boundaries to keep others *in*, because we rely on them to take responsibility for *our* sense of self. The power-under game develops out of this: if we're not willing to face what re-empowering ourselves would involve, we 'solve' the problem by disempowering others instead – "I'll make damn sure they *can't* abandon me. . .". It's only by taking the risk of non-attachment – especially in allowing others to be 'non-attached' to *us* – that we can reclaim our own sense of self.

And, at a deeper level, there's a subtle trap of becoming too attached to one thread, one characteristic. "I am strong, I insist on being independent", we might say: but sometimes we have to let go even of that. In the process of growth and change, we often find ourselves in situations that are a bit like one of those sliding-block puzzles: to make room for something, even if it's only passing through, we may have to dismantle some structure that we've become proud of. If we can't do it – if we're too attached to 'me-as-I-am' – we're stuck. And that too is a peculiar form of suicide: 'I' is not that which changes, but that which chooses, so a denial of the changing of self is also a denial of 'I'.

Quite often during these bewildering changes I've found myself in a strangely suicidal space: a sense of "I don't want to go on living like this any more". It's taken me some time to realise that it's actually a *normal* part of the process of change. In any change, part of my surface 'I' quite literally dies – the mistake is in remaining too attached to it, with a risk of letting it take the rest of me with it as it goes. . . . It's entirely true that 'I don't want to go on living *like this*', which is why the change is taking place – but it's important not to mistake the statement for "I don't want to go on living. . .". The 'letting-go' is supposed to apply to only one thread, not all of them!

If we're caught in this state of mind, what it's telling us is that there's a change taking place, but there's something specific we're not letting go: and that's what we need to look at and release. But at the time it's hard to look at anything, because the *feeling* is one of intense despair – and perhaps a fear of loss of sanity, because of that peculiar insanity of change. Like all these feelings, it does pass, usually in a couple of hours, though sometimes it can recur for a day or two: but in the meantime, it can be very frightening indeed – perhaps especially for others, if they don't know what's going on. And this is certainly one reason why it's important to have some kind of support network in place – and to know where to get hold of professional help if necessary – before descending into the depths of 'I'.

It's here that we need to remember what we've learnt about patience! It's useful to remember, too, that although the feeling is weird, it *is*, in its way, perfectly normal: and even though it can be frightening, it's important not to shut it out. (Shutting it out, by drink, drugs, denial or whatever, can often make things worse in the long run: as we've noticed, the wyrd has a habit of returning us to issues that we refuse to face. . .) In essence, it's a *metaphor* that some part of us is dying, to make way for a new thread of 'I' to come to the surface: it's important to accept it for what it is. Don't deny it: mourn the passing of that old aspect of you, and honour it accordingly – but above all, *don't* take its metaphor too literally!

Have you found yourself in these strange emotional spaces?

What was the change that was taking place? Sometimes surviving these emotional intensities takes a great deal of courage: where, within yourself, did you find it? And notice too that you did so. . .

The main defence against enmeshment is to work on our sense of self – returning to our 'centre', through meditation and the other tools that we've looked at so far. But we also need, once again, to accept that many people won't like us doing this: enmeshment is, to a large extent, the glue that holds the absurdities of our culture together – one result of which is that definite 'taboo against knowing who you are'.

Despite those pressures, it's always our choice: we reclaim our power of choice by reclaiming our boundaries – placing limits on how we choose to interact with others, and how they interact with us. Self-esteem *is* reclaiming responsibility for 'that which chooses'. The inside is also the outside: true self-empowerment is also, at the same time, empowering others to reclaim *their* choices, *their* responsibilities – or at least not preventing them from doing so. But only if they wish to: that's *their* choice, not ours. . . by the usual twist, 'helping' others who don't want our help is just another form of enmeshment!

A CHOICE OF BOUNDARIES

We need some means to define our sense of self – or at least to recognise when we *have* returned to it. If, in a childish way, our whole focus of attention is ourself, there's no problem: everything is 'I', everything is mine, everything is an extension of my will. As infants, we each of us believe that we own everything. But as we get older, we discover that we also share the space with other people, all of whom start off with exactly the same childish point of view – and that's where the problems begin. . . For everybody's sanity, we all need some clear understanding of the boundary between 'I' and 'not-I'.

So how *do* we define the boundaries of this 'I'? At first sight this seems simple enough: we could define it physically, for example, and say that I *am* my body. But what about emotions, feelings, fears? The more we look at this issue, the more the boundaries blur. . .

> Where does 'I' end and 'not-I' begin? I'd first think in terms of my body, the boundary being the surface of my skin: but what about the air that I breathe? Where does it become 'my' air, and cease to be part of others? – a point that becomes significant on encountering someone whose idea of pleasure is smoking a pipe that smells rather worse than stale socks. . .
>
> 'Me and mine', we think: our possessions are an extension of ourselves. We own them. Seems simple enough in terms of 'my body' (although in law, interestingly, we *don't* even own that – theoretically as a protection against 'bonded servitude' and slavery); but 'my house' or 'my car' are questionable in various senses, and we *really* hit problems with 'my cat' or 'my partner' – let alone 'my idea', 'my world', 'my hope', 'my fear'. There are boundaries, of a kind; but the inside is also the outside, and the boundaries blur.
>
> So where do *you* draw the line between 'I' and 'not-I'? How do you know when you've overstepped someone else's boundaries – or someone's overstepped one of your own?

One way to understand boundaries is in terms of ownership – but 'ownership' in the very specific sense used in psychology, that of owning responsibility. In this formal sense, "to establish boundaries is to know and respect what I want – and to take responsibility for same". If we want to reclaim the power of choice in our lives, to re-empower ourselves, it's up to us – and no-one else – to define, declare and maintain those boundaries. We're responsible for them: *we can't blame anyone else.*

In psychology, boundaries are crucial to the sense of self, in that they delimit the 'centre' for that self. Having no boundaries is equated with having no self: in terms of wyrd there's a specific sense in which this isn't so, but for practical purposes it's valid enough. It's certainly true that being 'other-centred' and deferring our *own* needs to those of others – as the culture constantly presses us to do – is a denial of self: suicide in a metaphoric, if not literal, sense.

It's useful to think of boundaries as defining 'defensible space' – a safe space in which to affirm ourselves, and a centre from which to expand outward. But it has to be something fluid, in order to allow for change and growth: ideally it's a kind of temporary structure of the self, assembled and dismantled in the moment – an intermediate step to a kind of dance.

Back to the café for another people-watching session! Watch how people sit in a crowded café: it's a very simple demonstration of the fluidity of boundaries – and how different they are for different people at different times.

The café starts off almost empty. A young man comes in, takes a four-person table; places his hat in one seat, his coat on another, his case on a third, spreads his papers over the table, leaving just enough room for his coffee cup, and finally sits down: 'my' space – personal space, defended space. Two girls sit down at the next table: they sit down facing each other, elbows on the table, chattering happily. A young couple are also facing each other, apart but with their arms reaching out across the space between them; the stiff distance between another couple to their left indicates that their relationship is professional rather than personal. And the elderly couple on the right sit side-by-side: a safe sharing of space, born of familiarity and time.

As the café fills out, watch where people go to take up empty seats. Another equally inseparable husband-and-wife are sitting opposite the elderly couple – it's clear they've been invited by the openness of the space left there, and are already in conversation with them. The two girls have company too, another youngish couple: but although they're sitting next to the two girls, there's no communication, almost as if there's a wall or boundary between them. The business couple have been joined by associates, and the conversation is now freer; but the lovers are still in a world of their own – as is the young man, who glares at

☞

---

anyone even hinting that they'd like to sit at 'his' table. Boundaries: they change, they don't change – it's up to us.

What is your sense of personal space – such as in this café, for example? How much does the boundary change when different people come close to it: for someone your own age? older? younger? the same gender? the other gender? for friends? acquaintances? enemies? What changes? What *feeling* accompanies the change in your preferred boundary – or when someone intrudes on your 'personal space'?

Sometimes, like the lovers in the café, we simply want to be alone; and usually the boundary is respected – quite automatically, in some weird way. Although 'no-thing' is done to defend the boundary, people simply don't cross over it. But if the boundary is like the young man's in the café, derived from fear or a need to control (which amounts to the same thing), it's challenged, repeatedly, again and again and again. In these cases, if we're honest about it, the boundary is not so much 'what we want', but a statement of lack of trust: a statement that we're *afraid* to be part of 'everything, everywhere, everywhen, everyone' – or for them to merge into us. The threads of wyrd pass through everywhere: any kind of boundary blocks their interweaving, breaks the flow of the dance. Ideally, we should be able to learn to trust warnings on the wyrd rather than the predefined rules of head and habit. The fears that dominate our culture, though, make a lack of trust almost inevitable, if not essential: in this culture an absence of some kind of definition of 'right' and 'wrong' certainly *would* seem like suicide. . .

With a growing understanding of the nature of wyrd, though, we can use the fact that our boundaries *are* challenged as a way of telling us that there's something we need to look at, some fear we need to face. But precisely because of those fears, there's a lot of dishonesty about boundaries – most of it unintentional, but dishonest nonetheless. The New Age and the new psychology place a lot of emphasis on boundaries – but often without much emphasis on the responsibilities that go with them. If anything, there's an implication that we're *not* responsible – especially not for anyone else – and there's a tendency to assume that everyone else is responsible for us or can be blamed for what happens to us: a kind of one-way boundary for which the formal term is 'denial'. Yet non-attachment is not detachment but *non*-detachment: everyone 'out there' is also a reflection of ourself on the wyrd, and everything we do loops back in some weird way. But it's something that we'd much prefer to ignore – and instead blame everyone else.

To be useful, the concept of boundaries depends on a rigorous self-honesty: without it, the concept too easily becomes a new way to blame other people for what are actually *our* fears. We may even find ourselves using boundaries as a *substitute* for our sense of self, rather than as a temporary prop: the fears are so all-pervasive that, as with 'power', we give them (or more accurately their negation) another name, and call them 'our rights'. And we all want those one-way boundaries – rights without the attendant responsibilities. We want the freedom to do what *we* want, but we're afraid to let others have the freedom to do what *they* want – which leads us straight back into the power-under game. It's hardly surprising, then, that so many of our interactions with others can be so chaotic. . .

Boundaries occur at every level of 'I': wherever there's a need to 'know and respect what I want, and be responsible for same', there's always some kind of boundary, a limit that we'd call 'fair'. A memory of a joint business-advice session I went to with a colleague: the end of the session, it's time to pay. "Oh, didn't I explain that the fee I quoted you is per-person, not just per-hour?" says the advisor. No, she hadn't, so she's expecting us to pay twice what we'd expected, and for a moment I feel angry. But then *we* hadn't checked this beforehand with her, either, so we're *all* responsible for the situation: none of us had been clear about our boundaries.

Being responsible for our boundaries means being clear about what we don't want as well as what we do – and allowing others

---

to do the same. If – to use a different example – we're trying to draw a prospective partner to us, and aren't clear about who is and isn't included, we can hardly complain if others respond as well! There's a tendency to be less than clear about this: an implicit demand that others be responsible for our boundaries where we're unwilling to be so – and blame *them* for what is often *our* inclarity. It's not exactly fair; it's not exactly honest. . .

Think of some occasion where you've got angry with someone who's overstepped your boundaries – of which the *feeling* will be that you're suddenly frightened, your trust overstretched. What *exactly* happened? You know what you think their misunderstanding was; but what was yours? It's rare for people to enter space without some kind of invitation – of which fear itself can be one. . .

The real problem is fear: when someone oversteps a boundary, it feels, in the moment, not only as if our rights are challenged, but our very existence as well. We'd immediately blame them: but that's not exactly fair on the other person – because the fear is ours, not theirs. And fear itself, by the usual weird twist, can actually be an invitation: remember, as we saw with affirmations, that "there's no image for 'not' in dreams" (or nightmares!). . . Fear tends to magnify the likelihood of that which is feared coming about: building walls against the fear doesn't solve the problem, but actually makes it worse. Boundaries are essentially walls against fear: they're useful as a short-term measure, but don't work as a long-term solution. Only by facing the fear itself do we resolve the issue – and find a real freedom beyond.

That can be hard to accept; but as we begin to understand the nature of wyrd and find the trust within ourselves, we discover that it turns out to be true. No matter how unfair it seems, our fears too are our responsibility: we resolve the effects of fear only by facing the fear itself.

The fact remains, though, that the fears are real and, in many cases, valid – and the cultural pressures that create them are enormous. In an ideal world, we might be fearless, able to live by trust alone, to do without boundaries, to flow with the dance of life. And in time, perhaps, we may be able to get close to it in our own lives: but here, now, in Reality Department, we're likely to be far from that ideal! The fears are real; we have to start from where we are, not from where we aren't. Losing our sense of self in the web of wyrd would indeed be suicide: so, for now, we *need* boundaries, to help us to maintain it. But as we grow, and change, and reclaim our ability to maintain that sense of self directly through meditation and the like, we need to have room in which to expand. That means that we also have to have some way of stretching those boundaries – which brings with it a whole new set of challenges!

20

STRETCHING THE BOUNDARIES

We *need* boundaries: we *need* 'to know and respect what we want and don't want – and to take responsibility for same'. Without that self-knowledge, and without a sense of choice, we tend to blow in the wind – we react rather than act. But as we continue our personal growth, our own boundaries become blocks and obstructions – in fact the primary barriers we come up against turn out to be our own boundaries. So we need a way of stretching the boundaries to allow us to grow – yet without stretching ourselves beyond breaking point. Somehow, we need to find some kind of balance – and a dynamic, changing balance at that. This *does* take some practice. . .

RECLAIMING THE BALANCE

If we're not to get entangled in the web of the wyrd, we *need* a definite sense of self. Since we're unlikely to have that – certainly to begin with! – we therefore need some kind of boundary or wall around our sense of 'I', within which to develop it. Boundaries define safe limits, to help us reclaim our choices: we reclaim our right to say No – or, for that matter, to say Yes. The problem is one of balance: boundaries prevent us from getting enmeshed in others' fears and wants, but a too-rigid defence of them prevents us from changing – or dealing with reality as it *is*.

As the interweaving of everywhere, everywhen, everyone, the wyrd has no boundaries: in that sense, all boundaries are artificial, a denial of trust and self-trust. So it's important to think of a boundary as no more than a *temporary* structure: not a fact, or a right, but simply a tool to help us maintain our sense of self in the face of fears. And there's always a twist, so at times the wyrd presents us with situations where we have to be flexible about even our most deeply-held beliefs. Trusting ourselves, trusting others, 'I' becomes a kind of dance. The more we develop a sense of trust – especially self-trust – the more we discover that all these threads do pass through *everyone*, including ourselves. Somewhere within us is every thread – including those characteristics we least like in ourselves, and also those we most admire in others. The discovery makes compassion for others *and* ourselves a little easier. . . and the self-honesty somehow also allows others to be more compassionate for *us*.

The wyrd is like a Möbius loop: the inside is also the outside, and although there *is* a boundary, the boundary blurs. For each of us, our 'I' is our own needs; but passing through it are threads that connect with everyone else's. By letting down our boundaries, we can discover what others need; by accepting what *we* want, acknowledging our choices and accepting that we *do* have boundaries, we can decide whether we're the ones to service their need. The answer may well be No; it may be Yes. We don't know: but by listening to our *own* sense of the wyrd, we can let it tell us with its 'words on the wind'. Raising or lowering our boundaries becomes a *choice*: and thus a real statement of who we are.

When, during that diet-for-increased-sensitivity experiment I described a while ago, I found myself taking on everyone else's feelings on a bus, it was a *choice* to put up my boundaries – walls around my 'I' – and withdraw. Although in one sense I'd become enmeshed, in another I never had – because I'd still retained the ability to choose. Discovering that I *do* have the choice to withdraw, I can then trust myself to be *able* to withdraw if I want to – and can then take the risk to go into that 'not-quite-enmeshed' space again. Going into those spaces is how I discover myself *in others*; it's how I learn what I choose –

☞

and don't choose – to be part of 'I'. Yet I still have to face, each time, the fear that I will lose my sense of 'I' by doing so. . .

What experiences have you had like this – where you could *feel* your interwovenness with others, yet still be free to return to 'I' as you wished? How did you recognise that you *were* free to return to your 'I'? And what did you learn in that balancing of 'I' and 'not-I'?

Enmeshment is a state of boundarylessness in which the ability to choose is lost – or is believed to be lost. But by lowering boundaries *as a choice* and with awareness, we become aware not only of our own needs, but everyone else's: we blur the boundary between 'inside' and 'outside', yet still retain a clear sense of 'I'. It's a balance: it takes practice, and a certain willingness to risk, but that's all. Eventually we come to see that the separateness of 'I' and 'not-I' is an illusion: the inside *is* the outside, others *are* part of us, and we *are* part of others. Everything we experience, everything we choose, has its echo along the threads of wyrd. "Issues spiral through me, on the threads of wyrd; are unchanged by how much *I* am unchanged".

The wyrd echoes our own state. When we're fearful, we're not only presented with experiences that 'prove' that the fear is valid, but we also increase the fearfulness everywhere. We never do 'conquer' fear: but if we can manage to accept it, get past it, we move into a quieter, freer space – and everywhere around us reflects the glow of that power-from-within. It's up to us what we choose: and it *is* a choice. . .

Every mother would be familiar with this choice and this echoing: children *are* part of the mother, and the mother part of the children, for a surprisingly long time. Most parents can interpret their children's needs long before they can be understood by others: they can *feel* the children's needs within themselves. And children echo the parents' state, particularly the mother's: when the mother feels overstressed, the children will often become *more* demanding, not less. Unfair as it seems, the most effective way to calm the children is to regain our *own* centre – preferably before the situation develops a downward spiral into chaos!

We could silence the children here through power-over or power-under: but it achieves the result by disempowering them rather than re-empowering us. Finding the power *from within* often seems the harder way at first: but it's the one that works in the long run. So when the world is echoing your overstressed state, how *do* you regain your 'centre'? How do you find the strength and the courage to find that power-from-within?

It does take courage to make that choice, to face our fears and lower our boundaries, and let the rest of the world in. Once we can see past the fear, we can see that the boundaries also keep the strength and power of 'everyone, everywhere, everywhen' *out* of our lives. Paradoxically, we *gain* strength by being open, rather than by being over-defended. If we expend all our energy on the *fear* of attack, we have none to spare when a rare but real one comes our way...

THE EXPORT OF BLAME

It's here that we come back to our earlier discussion of blame. With practice, we can eventually reach a recognition that 'everyone is to blame' – and thence, with further practice, that compassionate sense of 'no-one is to blame'. But it can take a great deal of effort, and a great deal of embarrassing self-scrutiny, to reach it: it's not comfortable at all. If everyone is to blame, then we're to blame too... for *everything*, for *anything*.

If we allow ourselves to see the totality of that, we can easily – as with direct awareness of the wyrd itself – become overwhelmed: and that's not merely uncomfortable, it's terrifying. Small wonder, then, that so much of our culture is concerned not merely with denying responsibility and avoiding blame, but passing it on – dumping it, exporting it – as hard as possible. No-one wants the blame for everything... and since everything is interwoven on the wyrd, at times accepting the blame for *anything* can be more than we can bear. . .

I'm standing in line in the café, waiting my turn to be served. Talking to his colleague, looking away from where he's going, a man comes towards me: a hot cup of coffee in hand. And catches his arm on mine, spilling his drink. "Now look what you've done!", he snarls at me, "Why the hell don't you look where you're going?" I cringe for a moment at this overwhelming wave of anger: somehow I must be to blame, somehow it must be my fault. . .

Hey! Wait a minute! This isn't right. . . How come it's *my* fault now? I wasn't even moving; and the guy certainly wasn't looking where he was going. All right, in principle I'm in some minor part responsible, simply by being there; but what he's doing, in order to avoid looking at his *own* responsibility in the incident, is exporting the blame – having spilt the coffee on me, he also wants to spill the blame. And the only thing that keeps me from falling for it – from accepting responsibility that isn't mine – is maintaining my boundaries, my sense of self. Faced with that snarling anger, that's not easy. . .

Recall some incidents where this exporting of blame has happened to you. What was the other person avoiding responsibility for? How did you recognise what was going on?

And also recall an incident where you did the same – blaming someone else for your own careless driving, for example. Do you know why you did so? What were the fears behind it?

There's a real but very subtle fear behind this exporting of blame: and it links directly with wyrd. The fear is that if we accept responsibility for any mistake, we're implicitly accepting the blame for *everything*. It's a kind of all-or-nothing attitude which can be surprisingly hard to shift – or even to accept in ourselves. So in turn, if we see someone who is accepting blame, either willingly or (especially through low self-esteem) unwillingly, the tendency is to dump *every* possible fragment of blame on them as fast as possible – whether it has anything to do with them or not – in order to avoid facing our *own* fear of being the scapegoat, the 'one who dies for the sins of the world'.

In order to avoid our own responsibility, we export the blame, and then rapidly put up one-way boundaries to prevent it coming back. It's far from honest: but we all do it. It's painful to watch it happen: especially when we realise that we ourselves are doing it. . . which is why we'll often expend a great deal of energy to avoid recognising that fact. And we do so in a weird process of 'projection': we 'project' our inside world onto others 'out there', and blame them for what are actually our *own* feelings, the aspects of ourselves that we're unwilling to face.

We can see this most easily when others do it. The man in the café, in the example above, is actually angry at his *own* clumsiness, but 'projects' it onto me, as something *I've* done. Having projected the blame, he can then feel justified in being angry at me, to seal the one-way boundary and complete the process of *exporting* blame.

There's usually a hidden fear – in that example, the old curse of perfection, perhaps – which projection and export can conceal. In the incidents you remembered in the previous box, where someone was exporting the blame onto you, what fears or responsibilities were they refusing to face? In what way were they not being honest with themselves – or you?

Exporting blame is an attempt to force others to face our fears on our behalf, so we don't have to face them ourselves. When you've done this to others, what fears were you attempting to avoid? What aspects of yourself were you unwilling to face?

We're none of us perfect – but we'd like to think we are! So anything that goes wrong *must* be someone else's fault. It's only a short step from there to the dualism that's common in many religions and worldviews: the world is divided into 'followers of the Light' (or whatever the chosen term happens to be), and 'agents of the Adversary', on whom all misfortune can be blamed. It's not honest, but it makes moral issues seem very simple: it's always someone else's fault, not ours. . .

Much of our culture consists of a complex web of export of blame: everyone oppresses everyone else! We experience it as individuals, as in the example above; but it also exists in a more subtle but pervasive form between groups – the age-old game of 'Us and Them', blaming others for our own sense of disempowerment. Half a century ago, it was considered 'obvious' that an 'international Jewish conspiracy' was to blame for the evils of the world. Or communists, or fascists, or anarchists, or 'blacks', the 'Yellow Peril' – anyone but 'Us'. Nowadays 'They' have new labels – 'multinationals', 'social security scroungers', 'bosses', 'bureaucrats', 'feminists', 'the patriarchy' – but the game is unchanged: the endless export of blame.

We all feel powerless at times: but we can only reclaim that power through re-empowering *ourselves*, which can be hard and painful work – so it always seems much easier to blame others instead. When you feel disempowered – at the mercy of the weird whims of fate – who do *you* tend to blame? Why? And since it tends to be automatic – literally a conditioned reflex – to blame some other 'Them', how do you become aware of doing so?

The usual aim of export is to create what is termed in psychology a 'double-bind' – "heads, I win; tails, you lose": and if we accept it, we're stuck with the exported blame. "Damned if you do, damned if you don't" – whatever we do, we're the scapegoat for what someone else is too frightened to face in themselves. Self-honesty is painful at times: we have to accept our imperfections. If we can't – or won't – do that, we 'solve' the problem by exporting it, disempowering others through power-over (anger, for example) or some form of power-under such as the manufacture of guilt. Export and projection combined can be lethal – the Spanish Inquisition being one classic example. "You must be tortured until you confess your sins; and then, for the sake of your immortal soul, we must kill you" – all of which is the projection of the Inquisitor's own 'sins', own fear, that he then attacks in the 'miserable sinner' before him. A cruel variant of 'double-entry life-keeping': trying to buy salvation in the next world, but landing someone else with the bill. . .

In a much milder form, the same process of export happens in 'channelling': rather than face the reality that the information comes from our *own* interaction with the wyrd, we pass the responsibility – or the blame – to some imaginary entity. The inner world is projected onto the outside – or anywhere but here, anywhere but me. Although originally applied to a different field, the psychologist Kenneth Batcheldor uses two useful terms to describe this process: 'witness inhibition' and 'ownership resistance' – which roughly mean "this isn't happening!" and "whatever it is, it isn't me!". . .

"I didn't break that plate", says a friend's small son, "It was my hand that did it! Abasson [an 'imaginary friend'] told my hand to do it!" He can't blame anyone else: but by exporting the responsibility to another facet of *himself*, he hopes to avoid the blame. . .

Most 'channelling' uses much the same kind of 'faceting', projecting an inescapable responsibility that's too hard to face onto some imaginary entity, much like the child's invisible friend. But we all do it to a lesser degree: how often do you try to explain away some 'uncharacteristic' action by saying "Oh! I wasn't quite myself there"? 'This isn't happening; and whatever it is, it isn't me'. . .

It always *is* us: every thread of the wyrd passes through us, so we're *always* to blame, whatever happens is *always* our responsibility. In part. . . often a very small part, but it's always there. . . It's up to us what we choose to do about it.

The key here is a sense of proportion: we *are* to blame for everything, or for that matter can claim the credit for everything: the question is one of degree. To know how far we are or aren't responsible, we have to know about ourselves – our many selves. The way out of those traps of export and projection is to be honest with ourselves and others, accepting who we are and they are – "I am what I am" – in each passing moment; and also to find the courage to face our own fears, and not take on those of other people's unless we *choose* to do so.

This takes a *lot* of practice: but the real world gives us plenty of that! So far, in reclaiming our own power through the wyrd, we've been working mostly on our own: yet when we start to meet with others again, maintaining our awareness of our *own* choices becomes even more important – as well as a great deal harder. Working with others, living in the chaos of the real world, we come face to face with our fears at every turn. . .

FACING FEAR

How *do* we face fear? The first stage is simply to recognise that we *are* frightened – and not pretend otherwise. Fears arise from uncertainty; the world is full of weird uncertainties. And precisely because the world *is* weird, we can't control those uncertainties – we can't control the wyrd. In the same way, we can't fight those fears – we'd only be fighting ourselves. So all we can do is to turn round and face them – face the way those threads appear within us.

But first we have to face the fears that arise from another of our old acquaintances: the silliness-barrier. A surprising number of the fears that drive us are remnants from childhood: they seem so silly, so childish, we'd prefer not to admit to having them. Surely we dealt with *those* years ago? But Ram Dass' advice applies here too: we never *do* get rid of fears. All that happens is that each time we face them, they get smaller: but they never do quite disappear. And if we're not willing to accept them for what they are, they can catch us unawares – leaping out of the weavings of the world in some weird, unexpected way.

> Like almost any child, I was afraid of the dark. I can't see anything! Bumping into things: small toys on the floor seem suddenly huge under my feet. And who knows what strange monsters might be lurking under the bed? Adults might think the fears are silly, but *I* know they're real. . . Childhood memories; childhood fears.
>
> With long practice, long experience, the fears do fade. I've

long since developed tools to cope in the dark – a juggling of sight and sounds and senses to accept the dark for what it is. With the ease of habit, it's no problem. Most of the time, that is: but the truth is that I *am* still afraid of the dark – only a little, but the fear's still there. It comes straight out at me when some strange sound calls out in the middle of the night. . . and then I have to face that fear all over again.

Were you afraid of the dark as a child? If so, how has it become easier now? Look at that process of facing fear, by which it became smaller and smaller over the months and years. And what kind of weird conditions bring up the same fear now? How do you – no longer a child – face that fear in the present day?

The usual way we're taught to 'deal with' fears is to ignore them – in effect, refuse to face them. It doesn't work: the fears come from the wyrd, and they demand to be noticed. One way to 'not-notice' fears is to attempt to dump them on someone else – hence that process of projection and export, and our culture's confused concept of power. That doesn't work either – or rather, it *seems* to work on an individual basis, but not on the culture as a whole. We see and sense the fear all around us: but in the usual weird way, we can most easily reduce it not by attacking it 'out there', but turning inward and taking responsibility for our *own* fears.

Many of our fears are manufactured by the culture we live in – people projecting their own fears onto us, rather than facing them themselves. Even those who want to help us do it: not trusting us to know danger, they actually prevent us from knowing it – or learning how to know. So often we were told "It's for your own good" – all those childhood 'don'ts', which develop so easily into the power-under game. "Don't go near dogs – they might bite!" "Keep away from the edge – you might fall!" "*Good* girls don't go out after dark" – with the implicit statement that if anything happens, it's our fault, and our fault *alone*. "And don't say I didn't warn you!" But the fear, by the usual weird twist, *increases* the likelihood of that which is feared coming about. . . Fear itself breeds fear – an imagined powerlessness becomes real. But is that what we'd truly choose?

Look for a while at a few of your fears. How many of them are actually yours – rather than those of your parents, relatives, teachers, friends? The fears are all real, of course, we *all* have them: but to what degree would you own them as yours? To what extent were those fears manufactured – especially fears of the past, the future, the unknown?

We face fears by accepting our own degree of responsibility for them. Meditation helps: in the midst of a morass of uncertainty, it provides us with our own centre of certainty, of self. Affirmations help: we reclaim our own sense of choice through an affirmation such as "I, ___, am responsible about my fear". Remembering to be present, to be *in* the present, helps: we don't get lost in panic, in memories of past fears or an imagined, non-existent future. A childlike spontaneity helps: acting in the moment, enjoying each moment. And accepting ourselves helps: developing self-love, self-trust, self-respect.

In self-love we remember to value ourselves: "I have a right to be here, no less than the trees and stars". And this too becomes an affirmation – as long as we remember that this right brings with it certain responsibilities that we cannot avoid.

In self-trust we remember to accept our own inner knowing. The affirmation here would be more like "I trust myself to be able to handle any situation". The more we learn self-trust, the more we become not merely able to handle situations, but *enjoy* them; every situation – including sickness, pain and, eventually, death – becomes something we can enjoy for what it is, for what it can teach us about ourselves.

And in self-respect we *act*, in the moment, on that inner knowing. We respect our own knowledge – including when *not* to stay in a situation. We respect our knowledge of what we want and what we don't want; and we respect our fears. Our knowing is blocked by self-doubt, and also by over-extending ourselves – there are many times when 'prudence is the better part of valour'!

That other quote from 'Desiderata' could well be our affirmation here: "Beyond a wholesome discipline, be *gentle* with yourself". The wyrd does require us to face our fears, in time: but it rarely demands that we face them all at once!

What *doesn't* help is reverting to power-over or power-under as a way to 'resolve' our fears. Neither does giving in to panic, running away or collapsing in a puddle on the floor: the wyrd requires us to deal with this fear – this aspect of ourselves – and if we don't do that, it will simply come and get us, again and again. We have to face the fear: the question is always one of *how* we do so. That at least is our choice. . .

> The usual choice is a non-choice – a habitual response. I'm somewhat timid by nature (or is it by nurture?): faced with that angry man in the café, my reflex response would be to apologise profusely, even perhaps to offer to buy a replacement – even though I'm barely, if at all, to blame. Someone else's reflex might be to get angry in return, to make sarcastic comments – power-under – or even to snap at some innocent bystander – "What are you looking at me like that for?" – in a response known technically as 'displacement'. If someone's just knocked a cup of hot coffee onto you and angrily told you that it's "all your fault", what would be *your* reflex response? And how would that differ from your *choice* of response – assuming you allowed yourself the time to discover it?

Collapsing in panic, in whatever form, simply hurts *us*; and any form of power-over or power-under, whether directed to the original 'attacker' or exported to someone else, only makes things worse. Blowing up at some passer-by, or kicking the cat, may seem to relieve the pressure: but in the long term, it always works its way back to us in some weird way. We resolve the fear by reclaiming our 'response-ability' for it: by remembering that our power comes not from outside – especially not from someone *else* outside – but from deep within ourselves. When we can hold our centre long enough to access it, in the midst of an 'attack', a very different kind of power comes into play, with results that are often weird – and wonderful indeed.

> Back at the café, a reflex response might be to yell back at this oaf – it's not my fault, so how dare he try to push me around like that? I'm a bit of a coward, though, so I make some cutting remark, hoping he'll feel guilty. But the result is not "Oh, I'm sorry. . ." from him – in fact he shouts back louder, angrier, violent now, until we're all but coming to blows. What's gone wrong?
>
> It's simple, but subtle: I've tried to put him down – disempower him – with the power-under game, instead of re-empowering myself, reclaiming my *own* power. To do that, I have to stop for a moment, and accept that I *am* afraid; then centre myself, find the quiet space within, and act in the moment with whatever response comes up from *there* – not from habit. There's a clear *feeling* of certainty when I let this happen: and the results can be quite startling, too. I don't actually *say* anything, or *do* anything, but the angry man just stops in mid-sentence, mumbles something, and walks off with a dazed expression on his face. No wonder he's confused: by my being willing to risk facing my fear of him, we've *both* come face to face with the wyrd. . .
>
> Power-over and power-under never work this way: only by finding power-from-within can we reach this fear-free space – especially if we're willing to risk power-with, seeing the man not as an 'enemy' but as a reflection of some aspect of ourselves. What's your own experience of situations like this? Can you see the habitual 'non-choices' you made, of reverting to panic, or to power-over or power-under? If the situation resolved itself, in what weird way did it do so? And what was the *feeling* within you when that happened? By facing the fear, what happened to your fear of that fear?

All that's involved in facing fear is to accept it, then turn round and face it. Acknowledge it for what it is: acknowledge that what's happening out there, what's happening 'to' us, is most likely an echo of the way we've allowed some fear to take control of us – a fear to which we've given away our power. We reclaim our power

239

by facing the fear, in whatever form it takes. And in principle, that's all there is to it.

It's easy to say this, of course: not so easy to do much about it, especially at first! For now, one of the key points is to remember to notice what *doesn't* happen, as well as what does: we face the fear, lower individual boundaries with care and awareness, and learn to trust *ourselves*, our own judgement in the moment, rather than trusting to the habits of the fear. A growing awareness that we *do* have awareness – that weird sense of 'precognitive recovery' – does help us build self-trust: and with it a trust that we *can* survive in a world with too many walls.

A WORLD WITHOUT WALLS

The wyrd itself has no boundaries: it threads through everywhere, everywhen, everyone. Yet for much of the time we *need* boundaries, to provide some semblance of consistency for our sanity, and to define limits for our sense of self.

We do need those walls – but it's important to remember that they shut us out from the dance of life if we hide too much behind them. Behind the boundaries, we find the strength to dismantle them, and rediscover a childlike trust: "the true sage is like a little child", as the Taoists would say. But that takes time, takes practice, takes trust. In the meantime, all we need to remember is that the boundaries are an *intermediate* step – if a clumsy one – in learning the greater steps of the dance.

We live in a world that's very full of walls: part of the reason for building them in the first place is that it hurts when we collide with those of other people! Boundarylessness, fearlessness, is a state of perfection, an ideal: which means, like any perfection, that it's a *quest* rather than an attainable goal. But it helps everyone if we can learn to trust, and let those boundaries go – as long as we *can* still retain our sense of self, and not require others to maintain it for us.

Working with the weirdness of Reality Department is never easy: the wyrd demands trust, and ever more trust. Yet a life that is predictable, 'safe', 'secure', in the usual rigid sense is also, in many ways, one from which aliveness has gone. Not merely boring, but dead: lifeless. But in a world in which there seems to be so little trust, trust can be the hardest thing to give – or to receive. It brings up our deepest fears – the ones from which we'd most prefer to hide. . .

So it's in relating with others in this chaotic world that we find out just how much we hide from others, and from ourselves; and it's also, through those relationships, that we can free ourselves at last from the fears that have driven us there.

21

SELF AND OTHERS

Our first level of relationship is with ourself – the world we see outside, the world of 'other', of 'not-I', is often a mirror of that relationship with ourself. And our self, our 'I', is our choices: our desires, needs, awareness, aims. We need to become more clear on these before looking at our relationships with others.

So we've looked at that weird confusion of "Which 'I' is me?"; we're learning more and more that we do have boundaries around our choices, but that these boundaries themselves are fluid and flexible in some weird way. What's next, then, in this weaving of our lives? And back comes the usual weird answer: 'no-thing'. Listen; wait; listen; says the wyrd. . .

THE SOUND OF SILENCE

Listen; wait; listen. If we were back where we were before we started our exploration of the wyrd, this would make no sense at all! But in time this listening is something that becomes part of our nature, is something we *are*, not *do*: not listening *to*, or listening *for*, but just listening. Listening: allowing the 'sound that is no-sound' to come to *us* – the hidden sound within the silence that Christians might describe as 'the still small voice of God', but is also ourselves talking with our selves on the threads of wyrd.

And 'waiting' is not simply waiting, passive, inert, energyless, but *patience*: an *active* 'doing no-thing' that consists of acting in the moment, and learning to know when that 'right' moment occurs. A sense of quietness, maintained by meditation in the midst of the chaos; the eye of the storm, the still-point at the centre of the hurricane. Listen; wait; listen. . .

Images, metaphors, come up in the quietness of that listening – sometimes with a slight pre-warning, a sense of 'impending wyrd', like the pre-echo we can sometimes hear on a record or a tape. And they can tell us a great deal about what's *really* happening in our lives – and our choices that have led us there.

Sitting thinking yet again why things don't seem to be working out, an image drifts its way into my awareness. It seems like I'm trying to open a door to a brightly-lit shop, but it won't open. I catch a glimpse of a sign that says 'Closed' – but I know damn well that the shop isn't closed: there are plenty of people in there, and – Hey! – they're picking up what *I* want, and walking off with it! This isn't *fair!* How come they're allowed to have it and I'm not? So I get angrier and angrier: I hammer on the glass of the imaginary door in fury, trying get attention, but all I get are occasional glances from people who clearly think I'm crazy, and don't want to know at all. Not *fair!* Why is it never *my* turn?

Until – still in this strange dream-like image – exhausted, weeping with frustration and rage and disappointment, I finally look down at the imaginary sign again. It does indeed say 'Closed': but that isn't all it says. 'Closed: please use other door'. And that door has been wide open the whole time. . . I was too busy being angry to look. . .

A lot of my life's been like that: a wry joke that hits me when I remember at last to look a little wider. It takes one of these metaphors to show me what's really going on: and those can only come through when I slow down enough to listen. Can you think of some examples of your own? And what doors into new parts of yourself did they open?

We close doors by trying to make things other than they are. I'd *like* things to be different, to match my current idea of 'fair': but they aren't. And until I look more closely – slow down enough to listen, wait, listen – closed is the way they'll stay. We can *choose* to change things; we change them by 'doing no-thing' about them. But we can't do anything useful until we *notice* which doors are open, and which ones aren't: and to do that we have to slow down, and listen to that 'sound of silence' from within ourselves.

Trust opens doors; fear and defensiveness close them. Our own boundaries – which are usually statements of fear, or lack of trust – close many doors, which is why learning to accept our fears and work *with* them is so important. We are who we are, exactly as we are in each moment: at each moment that's the starting point for our choices. But if I get lost in anger or frustration, for example, no-one else but me is blocking my path: if I'm too angry to listen, I won't be able to hear the choices I'm offered. And there's *always* a choice, a way out of every 'trap' – even though there's also always a twist. . .

The hard part is to trust that as long as we *do* maintain some kind of overall aim, whatever happens *is* part of our chosen path towards that aim – no matter what it looks like, and no matter how wrong it may seem in the moment.

Part of the weirdness of reality is this way in which things that seem wrong turn out to be 'a blessing in disguise' – ones which break us out of dead-ends that we've closed ourselves into. I think of the battles and the pain I went through to keep my old business going, and recognise now that its ending, in that form, was the best thing that could have happened: it gave me the freedom to choose again. In some weird way, I'd *chosen* to end it: I just couldn't see it – or wouldn't *let* myself see it – at the time. The pain, in fact, came from fighting *myself* – fighting against my *own* choices! The hard part for me now is to let go, to recognise and trust these deeper choices, in the moment: the more I do this, the more I put this into practice, the easier – or gentler, at least – my life becomes.

What's your experience of this? In what ways do you recognise some 'blessing in disguise' as being in part your *own* choice? There's a clear *feeling* that accompanies this 'knowing', when some event 'out there', regardless of appearances, *does* match our deeper aim: how do you recognise this feeling within you?

Gently holding that focus, that overview, that aim, is what guides our course through the wyrd. Sometimes there's a clear sense of connection with the wyrd: once we become aware of it, it may come and go, be near, and far and yet – as long as we *do* remain 'non-detached' – the connection never quite breaks. If our aim is clear, whatever happens *will* be part of our choices in moving toward that aim – no matter how weird that may seem in the moment. Even if what we're doing may seem totally counter to our intended aim, it's part *of* it if our aim is clear. If we let the mind, and our assumptions, get in the way, and say "Oh, this can't be right, this isn't what I expected", we lose focus, we lose aim – and then what we're doing *isn't* right! So the key here is to trust ourselves, trust our wider awareness, our greater connection with reality through the web of wyrd.

By listening to the 'sound that is no-sound', the metaphors and messages that come from within us, we slowly learn to trust that things *are* working out all right. But it *does* take practice. . . and sometimes trusting enough even to give ourselves that practice can be none too easy!

BEING SELFISH

We *do* have a right to be here, 'no less than the trees and stars': and part of that right – and responsibility – is to be ourselves, to notice what we do to ourselves and how much we stop ourselves from doing what we want. Despite those endless childhood admonitions that we mustn't be selfish, we *do* need to learn to be 'self-ish' again in this specific sense. In the power-under game we learn always to defer our needs to those of others: so for a brief while at least we need to concern ourselves with what *we* do, with what *we* need. At this moment, *nothing else matters*. It's much the same as affirmations: but now it's more an affirmation as a way of life. And as we discovered earlier, it's surprising what old issues and old curses come crawling out of hidden spaces within us. . . simply by hinting to ourselves that it's possible for us to do what *we* want to do!

For me, the immediate image that comes up about 'being selfish' is 'people won't like me any more'. But then what fears am I hiding from, to create that image? Listening to that 'sound of silence', back comes the answer: loneliness, not being wanted, fear of rejection. . . all the usual stuff!

Oh. So that's where this old obsession about 'trying to buy being liked' comes from: I've been too frightened to face those fears. And it slowly dawns on me that whenever I've tried to buy 'being liked', the person who's been *sold* – into a weird kind of self-created slavery – is me. I'd ranted and raged about what I'd seen as the unfair antics of a bunch of cowards in the world 'out there', but the real coward turns out to have been me. . . Needless to say, I'm not exactly pleased about this – which is why I'd hidden it from myself for so long – but I can at least see the irony in the situation. Some joke!

In what ways have you stopped *yourself* from 'being yourself' in the past? What were the hidden choices, the hidden fears? Through what weird twists and wry ironies do they become clearer now? And what kind of 'doing no-thing' do you find yourself doing now about these hidden patterns of self-sabotage?

One mistake I know I still make is taking everything too personally and too seriously (though others may find they're sabotaging themselves by not taking things seriously enough). We've been told that we must be 'selfless': everyone else always comes first. But this simply isn't true: even if it was appropriate – which often it isn't – we can't look after everyone else if our own needs are never met. And although we are, in some weird sense, responsible in part for everyone and everything else, it's only a very *small* part: our first responsibility is to ourselves. In any case, it's arrogant even to try to claim responsibility for everything – as well as impossible to do in practice.

In fact, the one person – the *only* person – I really need to be liked by is me; the one person I need to trust is me. And to find that trust I need to slow down and listen enough to notice, not what my *mind* tells me my life gives me, but what my life actually *does* give me – which may well be very different. Life *isn't* as hard as I think it is; and I make it much harder than it is. That's something else that, slowly, I learn to let go.

In the quiet of an active-imagination session, listening to the 'sound of silence' in another written conversation with those many aspects of 'I'. "Note how well you *are* kept", says one of these imaginary characters within; "note how much you *are* alive. And protected – though you have no idea how hard we've had to work to do so!"

"'We'?", I wonder. . .

"All of us!" comes the reply. "The rest of reality! What do think this wyrd is: you versus the rest? This is the Weaver that the traditions talk about: the Weaver is everyone, everywhere, everywhen. And we *do* look after you: protect you from your own choices, as much as we can. That we don't, and can't, gives you some idea of how much you try to hurt yourself. . . So let go, give yourself – and everyone else – a break: let things be as they are. And then you can *let* them be as you would like them to be. You have a good heart, but you do not know everything. . . You are yourself: that is enough. So *be* yourself: no-one but you is asking you to be more than this."

A sense of surprise, almost of shock. I didn't know I could *know* all that about myself: and yet here it is – a message from myself, in my own handwriting. Telling me that it *is* all right to be myself: "no-one but you is asking you to be more than this". A welter of confused emotions: then a sense of lightness as a mass of unnecessary 'shoulds' and 'oughts' and 'musts' and 'can'ts' drift away into the night. And I find I'm smiling a lot more these days. . .

Look around for a while: notice how much you *are* alive, and, for that matter, protected by the rest of reality from the results of your own less-than-careful choices. What do you see? What do you discover about yourself? And about your usual interactions with the world 'out there'?

Slowly learning that it *is* all right to like myself, I find to my surprise I'm liked more by others – a kind of living response to all those affirmations! And yet the only thing that's changed is

247

me: or rather my attitude to myself. As one friend put it, I'd spent most of my time wearing an imaginary version of one of those huge freeway signs that say 'Wrong Way: Go Back!' – and then complained that no-one seemed to want to know me. The simple answer was that I'd asked them not to. . . And when I finally let go, and let others into my life, weird and wonderful things *do* begin to happen. . .

After a lapse of many years, I've been reclaiming music: I'd been told so often that I was no good at it, but it's something I want to do for *myself*. Using the aloneness as time to practise again, my standard steadily improves: I know perfectly well that I'll never make my living by it, but all that matters is that *I* enjoy it!

Yet doing what I enjoy brings weird surprises. . . Down in the city: outside one of the colleges, three people my age having an impromptu session in the street – guitars and fiddle. They're playing an Irish tune I know; I have my whistle with me in my bag; laughing, and without stopping to think about whether I 'should' or not, I join in. And am welcomed. An hour of carefree fun, going back and forth through all kinds of different music; people stand around, listening, some even joining in. *Enjoying* life; enjoying the moment.

Time to go. Instruments back in cases. We're about to move off when a woman comes out from the college – a member of staff, apparently. "Wait a moment!", she says. "We've really enjoyed your playing, and you've helped bring people into our Open Day. We'd like to give you some money: it's one way of saying Thank You!" Reality Department, it seems, now even wants to *pay* me to do what I enjoy!

On the surface, others around us may seem to hinder us – calling us selfish, perhaps – when we begin to reclaim *our* choices; and yet there's usually a weird undercurrent of very real support from the wider world, as in that example above. In what ways does this happen to you?

Magic happens when we commit ourselves to *our* choices: we choose, and the world changes with us. Yet this is exactly what Crowley's definition of magic was about: creating change in conformity with our choices. "'Do what thou wilt' shall be the whole of the Law, ere it harm none": taking care "ere it harm none" is the only real restriction we need accept in the magical process of self-discovery.

We can do anything we like: anything at all. Somewhere in the weavings of the wyrd, there's always a way to do what we truly desire. As usual, though, there's a catch. . . we're always responsible for the effects of our choices, echoing and re-echoing throughout the wyrd: so we need to remember that warning about "do what you will – but be very sure that you will it!" In reclaiming our 'self-ishness' we need to be *very* aware of those subtle messages in the silences of the wyrd: the choice is always there for us, but there's always that twist. . .

BEING SELF-RELIANT

One of the stumbling-blocks in empowering ourselves to find the life we'd choose is that we give that power away so easily to others – most of whom don't want it anyway. Holding our focus in the midst of the chaos takes practice, takes discipline, and all the other things that we often try to get other people to do *for* us so we don't have to do them ourselves. We then assume we can only be given this power by other people – and yet at the same time we also want our independence. The result is a chaotic confusion that's often described as 'neediness': and we can only get out of it by deliberately relying more on ourselves.

If we're in that 'needy' state, we're in effect stuck with that "Wrong Way: Go Back!" sign – and until we do something about it, we can't make space for others to come to us. We do have very real needs: and as we work more on ourselves, a lot of old unresolved needs come up to the surface and scream for our attention. It's easy to feel lost, confused, panicked. So: one thing at a time; one step at a time. Before we can get help from others, we have to learn not to frighten them away first!

One of the main ways we frighten others away is by relying on them to fill what seem to be gaping holes in our lives. If I'm lonely, it's easy to assume that this need can only be filled by someone else – someone I both want and *don't* want, in the same moment, because the person I actually need to be with is *me*.

> "I can never 'get away from it all' on vacation", said a gloomy character in one of James Thurber's stories, "because wherever I go, *I* would always be there. . ." How much do you find yourself relying on being with others – or filling every scrap of time with noise, busy-ness, action – in order to avoid being with yourself?

As we've seen, many of our needs are expressed in metaphors such as "I'm hungry for company". One way to resolve these needs – and become more self-reliant, more able to rely on *ourselves*, in the process – is to apply the weird nature of metaphor to itself: we can often turn the metaphor around, and answer it with nothing more than another metaphor. As we've discovered, it's important that we *do* acknowledge our feelings, our needs, and act on them in some way: but they don't have to be translated into *literal* action – we can respond to them at almost any level.

> I'm 'hungry for company' – but there's no company to be had. So I acknowledge that I'm in need of attention (or whatever): and then *tell* that aspect of myself that I'm satisfying that need with whatever I *can* give it. I answer the metaphor with whatever is to hand: but I do it *consciously*, almost as a ritual, a formal response to the metaphor from within.
>
> "I acknowledge my desire for company", I might say to myself, "but since I don't have company at the moment, I answer it by giving myself the 'company' of the characters in this book I'm reading". Then I *do* have company: I don't ignore my desire for physical company, but I honour it by giving it what I can. And often these imaginary companions tell me things that I wouldn't have known any other way. Yet this doesn't always work – especially if I'm hiding in a book in order to avoid facing some issue of my own – so I have to *listen*, listen to those 'words on the winds of

the wyrd', to find out what response in each moment is appropriate. It *does* take practice. . .!

When we're feeling angry, or lonely, or frustrated, or so excited that things seem to be out of control, the usual 'solution' is to block the emotion: "I shouldn't feel like that!" Instead, allow the feeling to *be as it is*: and respond to it, consciously, with whatever you're doing. *Connect* them, link them in the weavings of the wyrd: make a formal statement, a ritual of it, much as you'd claim a thread in an affirmation. What difference does this make to your experience? What do you learn?

In this strange shifting of levels, we can answer an emotional need with an idea, resolve anger with music, fear with dance, or find new ideas from the depths of silence: and it can be – to say the least! – a weird experience. But this is the same process as we saw earlier about wearing masks: we bring the whole interaction with ourselves into the open by making it *conscious*, and it then quite happily resolves itself. We give *ourselves* the attention we need, without needing to rely on others.

And it's our *choice* to do so: that's what's empowering. There's always a choice, there's always a twist: using the metaphor is the twist, one which usually works best if there's some kind of wry humour attached to it. Find the metaphor, find the joke: create the wyrd twist out of our *own* choice. Then our needs strangely feel satisfied – even though by nothing more than a metaphor. It's weird, but it *does* work. . .

It also shows us that life doesn't *have* to be hard. We get what we get; we get whatever the wyrd gives us. And yet *always* in there is what we need in the moment. We don't have to wait indefinitely for others who may not, in any case, be able to give us what we need: we can resolve many of our needs directly in this weird form of metaphor. Often all we have to do about our neediness is *notice* – we don't have to 'do' anything about it. Or rather, we 'do no-thing' about it.

We'll often be told that to be 'needy' is to be imperfect: but we're none of us perfect – and we never will be. As we've seen, the way we change is not by trying to *be* perfect, but simply by noticing that we aren't. We don't change things – or ourselves – by getting angry about appearances: we change ourselves by noticing how things are *and letting them be that way*. By rushing, we slow everything down; by demanding perfection *now*, we lose it. It's a very neat trap. . .

Yet breaking free of dependency on others means that we can't blame them any more – and that, as we discover, brings all sorts of old issues out of hiding. . . More aspects of ourselves – our many selves – to explore!

A WEB OF CHOICES

From here we have to move on to *being* with others, reclaiming our power, our ability to be ourselves, in the weird twists and turns of the real world. In that world, we've learnt to be responsible for everyone *except* ourselves – and we expect everyone else to do that for us. They don't, or can't – as we've discovered the hard way. . . And as we begin to grasp that we don't have responsibility for others, and at the same time let go of the other-centredness that drives the power-under game, there's a tendency to slump as though our meaning for existence has gone. The chaotic squabbles about power-over and power-under sometimes seem to be the only purpose in life: and once they go – meaningless though they are – our reason for living can seem to go with them.

Yet we *do* have a purpose: to live for *ourselves*, to be responsible for ourselves. Since the wyrd connects us with everyone, everywhere, everywhen, that also means that we do also relate with everyone else: but we do so from where *we* are – from ourselves, from the quiet centre within ourselves. Our conditioned reflex in relating with others, though, is to assign that responsibility to almost anyone else – family, partners or whoever we can find. If we abandon that choice, we can't complain about the results. . . Being responsible for ourselves also means recognising that we *do* have a varying degree of responsibility for others, since everyone else *is* our 'selves', echoing across the threads of wyrd. But the aim is to end the dependency: we support each other, yet in a way that is both non-attached *and* non-detached. We care. That's what matters in the end.

The task doesn't so much have a form, as a *mode* – a way of *being* rather than doing. Listen; wait; listen. Listening is something we *are*, not *do*: not listening *to*, but listening. Quiet; an active quietness, 'doing no-thing'. We practice in the quiet space on our own (that's what the quiet space the wyrd kindly gives us, that we might mistakenly resent as loneliness, is *for*), but we then have to remember to hold it in the chaos of Reality Department. When we forget, we *allow* ourselves to remember – just as in meditation. And as with meditation, over time it *does* become easier. And easier. And with it life itself – our whole experience of life – becomes easier, gentler, too. "Beyond a wholesome discipline, be *gentle* with yourself": we need to understand that – and live that – before concerning ourselves too closely with the actions of others!

The wyrd is often described as a 'web', or a 'weaving': so one way to understand it – and ourselves – better is to visualise it as such.

Imagine 'I' as a centre: a single white dot in the darkness. Stay with the image for a moment.

Then slowly, steadily, imagine a myriad of fine threads passing through that centre – the threads of wyrd, spinning outward like the radial lines of a spider's web. They form a nexus, a clustering, at this central dot, your central focus of 'I'. But in the distance, faintly, you can see lines converging to form other clusterings, other centres that are different, and yet formed from exactly the same threads. 'I' and 'not-I'. . . the same, yet not the same. . .

Now imagine concentric arcs, like the cross-bars of a web, drawn between these lines at varying distances from your centre: your boundaries, the limits of your choices. The same kind of arcs cross the threads from other centres: a web of lines and cross-weavings, making up the fabric of the world.

☞

Carry this image with you for a while as you go about your everyday interactions with the rest of the world. Which threads pass directly between you? Which ones take a much longer, more roundabout route, passing through many others' centres first? Where do those concentric arcs – your boundaries – intersect with those of others? What happens as you move your awareness along the lines of the web – moving through what seems to be space 'owned' by others? And how do you recognise your *own* centre, in order to return to it?

Everyone has choices; the effects of everyone's choices – or non-choices – echo throughout the web of wyrd. To say that our experience is *only* our choice is far too simplistic: the New Age concept of 'it's all your choice' if you've been attacked in some way may be correct in principle, but only at an abstract level of perfection that we never actually reach. Before that, there *are* others, and they too *do* have choices. Their choices are part of the weaving too. It's exactly the same as that concept of 'no-one is to blame': it's only true because *everyone* is to blame. The only way in which our entire experience is *all* 'our choice' is when no-one else has choices – or when we merge with the wyrd sufficiently for us to experience everything as 'our' choice. And at that point there's no 'I' either. . .

So we could say – in New Age style – that it's our 'choice' to be a victim, for example: that we've brought the other person to us to be our tyrant. But another, more useful, way of looking at it is to use that weaving to *learn* – for the victim how not to be a victim, for the tyrant how not to be a tyrant. When at least *one* of the two makes that choice, the other often finds themselves either making a true *choice* (rather than an habitual response) – or at least is shown that it *is* a choice rather than something that 'just happens'.

When *either* holds their centre, *both* meet with the wyrd. But the moment we do it to disempower them – power-over or power-under – they'll revert to habit. By reclaiming our centre instead, reclaiming power-from-within, we also give them the power to choose. But that can be frightening for them as well as for us – habit always seems safer – so *they may not take that choice*, and revert to habit instead. If the habit is one of assaulting others, it's time for us simply to withdraw: we cannot *make* them choose otherwise, and there's no point in damaging ourselves trying to force them to do so. . .

Think of an example where tried to *make* someone 'choose' your choice. It doesn't work. . . What actually happened? How did you – or do you now – recognise that it doesn't work?

Now go back and, in your imagination, *allow* them their choice. Trust that if it does 'go wrong' you *will* still be able to withdraw: note your feelings on this, note the sense of 'impending wyrd' that tells you what choices *you* have. What happens?

Having tried it in imagination, allow yourself to notice how it also happens in the everyday world: allow yourself to let others choose, whilst still retaining your *own* choices. What difference does this make?

We cannot *make* others choose what we'd choose them to do – that's power-under again. If we try to do that, we're not taking responsibility for our *own* power – we're trying to control theirs. In effect, we're trying to invert the concept of boundaries: in order to avoid our own responsibility for ourselves and our choices, we're trying to take control of its outside forms. So we try to take responsibility for others, telling them what they 'ought' to do, and then demand that everyone else 'must' do *this* or *that* for us in return. And we complain like crazy that it isn't fair when they don't. We can't actually rely on others to look after us: eventually we discover the hard way that we have to do that for ourselves. . .

Once we become aware, though, of just how many of our actions backfire on us, it's easy to get in a kind of frozen state: *nothing* works, whatever I do is wrong. But even doing nothing is wrong: 'doing no-thing' is what we have to do. And we do have to act some time: we do have to put those choices into action. Supposedly, every action brings about an equal and opposite reaction; but every inaction also brings about an equal and apposite re-enaction – the lessons we refuse to face simply loop back again in some weird way. The solution is to listen, and to trust ourselves and our awareness of the wyrd – and with that weird knowledge, what we do *does* work.

22

RELATING

Every choice, every decision, is about relationship – both with ourselves and with everyone and everything that we consider 'not-I'. From a known centre, a known 'I', we can expand our relating outward, from self, through links that we discover with partners and family and friends, to a wider family or community that eventually includes the world as a whole – every part of it. We *are* them – interwoven with them on the wyrd. By letting down our boundaries, yet still retaining that sense of 'I', we can discover what those 'others' need; and by understanding how their needs interweave with our own, we can gain a better understanding of what our *own* real needs are. In relating, in inter-relating, we reflect each other: a weird hall of mirrors...

Understanding that this *is* the wyrd that we live in, one habit we need to develop in all our relating is compassion: "to recognise oneself in others..." Others have choices too: but often it's up to *us* to break the old cycles that cost everyone their power, their aliveness. Reclaiming our true power, that power-from-within, necessarily involves others in the weavings of the wyrd; and in empowering others, we also empower ourselves. That's what relationship is *for* – though in the chaos of Reality Department, it's not always easy to recognise this!

SOULMATES AND CELLMATES

Life would be so much easier if our relationships *worked*! That beautiful romantic dream: the perfect soulmate, a partner with

257

whom we feel energised, dynamic, warm, powerful, loved, wanted, who complements us exactly, who makes us feel whole, who's always there when we need them, who understands our every need, every desire. But Reality Department, as we discover all too soon, often has rather different ideas about relationship. . .

Nasruddin was slumped in a corner of the tea-house, the very picture of dejection. "What's the matter, old friend?" asks the proprietor. "I've been searching all my life for the perfect woman", came the gloomy answer, "and I finally found her yesterday." "But you should be delighted! Why on earth are you looking so miserable?" "She told me *she's* searching for the perfect man – and she's still looking. . ."

Part of the time, every relationship *is* perfect – or *feels* perfect, at any rate. But *why* can't it stay that way? It *should*, surely? Loving and being loved *ought* to be easy. It isn't *fair*. . . And therein lies a clue: those magic words like 'should' and 'ought' come from the power-under game, which we already know Reality Department takes no notice of at all. In which case there's some weird aspect of relating that we need to look at more closely. . .

If we were perfect, our relationships *might* match that romantic ideal: in most cases they don't, for the very simple reason that we aren't perfect. *Nobody* is – ever. More than that, there's often a sense of being tested, by Reality Department if not by our partner – hence "the course of true love seldom runs smooth. . .". Every partnership contains for us at least one lesson: and the aim, as always, is to recognise this and work *with* it rather than fight against it. That way the lessons *do* lessen, and the partnership *does* become easy, enjoyable, enlightening – everything the romantics claim for partnership, in fact.

The trap is that it's all too easy to use relationships as a way of *avoiding* those issues, those life-lessons: and the wyrd is kind enough to remind us of this fact. . . That appealing image of a 'soulmate forever', for instance, is all too often a way of hiding from fear of abandonment: and as we've discovered, the usual result of that kind of fear is that, courtesy of the wyrd, we find ourselves being brought face-to-face with it the hard way – again and again and again. . . A wiser – and, in the long term, less painful – approach is to strip away the New Age gloss, and look more closely at what the wyrd is trying to tell us about our relating.

> "Addictions are habits with teeth", as one writer put it: and relationships are where our addictions tend to show up the most. A relationship becomes 'co-dependent', for example, when one or both rely solely on their partner, rather than themselves, to deal with personal issues. So which issues do you try to get your partner to shield you from – fears you don't want to face, or responsibilities you'd prefer to avoid? And in what ways do they echo back on the wyrd, however hard you *both* try to sweep them under the carpet?

One thing is clear: we rarely get the partner we'd expect. At times it's almost as though we're thrown together with our partners, often under circumstances we'd certainly describe as 'weird'. So it's useful to think of a partner not as a 'soulmate', but more as a 'cellmate': someone who's presented to us as a *learning*-partner by the wyrd – and by our *own* choices echoing through it. Someone who'll reflect our issues in some weird way – and may not necessarily be any help at all in resolving them!

> "I suppose I'm angry at *life*, Chris", said a woman friend the other day. "I didn't want *him* to be my 'soulmate'. But there's a kind of inevitability about it: I feel that Fate is playing some kind of game with me. And I don't like it at all. . . he pushes my buttons the whole damn time. What did I do to deserve this?"
>
> Is this familar? If you're with a partner now – or reflecting on previous partners – for what issues of yours do they 'push your buttons'? Note how easy it is to blame them – pushing buttons is 'something they do *to* me'. . . How easy is it to get caught up in the whole tangled web of projection and export of blame?
>
> Now turn this round: consider that you've brought this partner ☞

to you, as *your* choice echoed through the wyrd, to deal with these specific issues. Not so much a soulmate as a cellmate: the whole point is to provide an environment in which to *learn*. Not 'something they do to me', but a mirror reflecting your own unclarity – and often challenging you to be clear about your boundaries, your *own* choices. Re-viewing it this way, what issues do they *actually* represent for you – rather than the ones you thought they do? What difference does this make to how you could respond to them?

With a partner, I am that person, and I am not that person – all in the same moment. There are many boundaries between us: and yet the boundaries blur and fade. So we have to be careful to maintain *our* boundaries, *our* choices – and not to lose ourselves in that powerful yet often disempowering urge to merge with 'the other'. It can take a lot of practice to get it right. . .

So much of my energy in relationships went into trying to find out what my partner wanted me to *do*, or what I was supposed to change – looking for 'the rules' that would make the relationship work. The reality is that the only rule is that there aren't any rules. . . but it's still frightening when I feel that my boundaries – when I even identify them as such – have been overstepped, or when I'm accused of overstepping my partner's. It can feel a bit like being slammed in the face with a huge sign saying 'Wrong Way – Go Back!': so it's taken a *lot* of practice to recognise that I'm not actually under attack – and slow down my reflex reaction until I can *feel* what an appropriate response would be.

How you learn to recognise when your partner oversteps your boundaries? How do you maintain your *own* choices? And how do you minimise the emotional loading with which you react, so that others can learn the *feel*, rather than the 'rules', of those boundaries?

With our partners, we get to discover more of who we are – and how different we are from others. Our sexuality, for example, is an important aspect of our humanness: it provides a unique way of seeing just how what we see in other people turns out to mirror aspects of ourselves. And it's also one of our few direct experiences of the strange nature of wyrd: in that moment of one-ness with our partner, of absolute union, we're also our separate selves – 'I and We and I'. "Vive la difference", we might say!

Another aspect of sex is the very different experiences of the world we have by virtue of our gender – both by nature and by nurture. Since we're all both male and female to some extent, working with a partner, or even a different kind of visualisation, can open a new perspective on hidden aspects of ourselves – as well as making it easier to understand why others act the way they do.

Some of the differences between us do seem to develop out of natural biases: and it's worth while experimenting with wearing these 'unnatural' perspectives – rather like wearing different postures as different selves – to feel how 'the other half' of *ourselves* lives.

There's what we used to call 'the male mistake' in the clients of my old business: a tendency to be over-active, to 'go for it' without thinking of the ramifications; 'the female mistake', by contrast, was to be over-passive, a tendency to say "I can't do it, I'm only a woman". It seems easier for men to be single-minded, focussed on single details without much of an overview; women tend to see ever-increasing implications, in a way that often makes it far harder to make decisions. The male attitude, faced with a door opening into some unknown space, would tend to be "there's the door, let's go through it" – and assume that there'll be no problems on the other side of the door; while the woman's attitude would often be more like "if I'm meant to go through the door, it'll be open in some way. . .", feeling out her own connection with infinity. How 'unnatural' would the other gender's point of view seem to be to you? Try it for a while: what does this different world-view *feel* like to you?

We often forget just how pervasive our conditioning is – the cultural curses handed out to each of us by virtue of our gender. As a result, a phrase such as "I am strong" can have very different

261

meanings for women and men. . . Again, the idea of 'blame' just isn't useful: things are the way they are because they got that way. What *is* useful is to realise that much of what our partner does, that pushes our buttons so, isn't because they're being awkward, but because they've been told so often that it's 'right' to act that way – even when they know consciously that it isn't. These conditioned reflexes are habits, just like any other: and most of us need help in dealing with them, rather than being blamed for being who we are. . .

It's hard to grasp just how ingrained and unnatural this 'natural' conditioning is until we swap the rôles over, and see just how bizarre they are. And until we *do* see this, and respect the conditioning that our partner is trying to resolve, we're unlikely to get anywhere. One counsellor friend in Sydney, working with mixed groups, uses this as an example:

For a woman (he says) who wants to be an ally of men, imagine what it would be like to be conditioned from earliest infancy to accept that you would be required to kill or be killed by another woman, simply in the name of your womanhood. Think about that for a moment. . . what do you *feel*? What would it be like to be with other women if they had that conditioning too? How safe would you feel with other women? What would your feeling be about yourself with this conditioning? And what would it be like with the other sex if they were conditioned to accept always nurturing and comforting others?

For a man who wants to be an ally of women, imagine what it would be like to be conditioned from earliest infancy to accept that your rôle as a man is to nurture and support all in your immediate surroundings at all times – regardless of whether you're tired, or don't want to, or whatever. What would it be like to be with other men if they had that conditioning too? How safe would you feel with other men? What would your feeling about yourself be with this conditioning? What would it be like with the other sex if they were conditioned into violence and isolation, or found temporary relief from loneliness or stress through sex?

☞

And what would you do if you were only to care and comfort, out in the world as you know it now?

Going deeply into that inversion of rôles can be 'a bit like swallowing broken glass', as one participant put it. . . But try it. Does it help you to understand what your partner is trying to deal with?

Our partners are our choices as 'allies' for dealing with some of our deepest issues: it's hardly surprising that things sometimes go awry! The wyrd is the wyrd: what we won't face weaves back to us through the loops of time, the same issue wearing different faces, different places. . . And yet by working *with* the weirdness of what happens between us, we find there's a twist in the choices: the boundaries can blur until we find we *do* also have a union, and 'cellmates' can indeed become 'soulmates' at last. That's what makes the relating worth while! But it's up to us: we always have choices that twist and turn within the wyrd. . .

HAPPY FAMILIES?

Our original 'cellmates' are our family – which is why so many of our old family issues come up again with our partners. And we could argue that, in this wider sense of wyrd, we chose our family too: in some weird way, we each chose each other. So perhaps the first place to apply this compassion and this awareness of our own history of choices is with our childhood family.

Everybody's family 'should' have been perfect: reality says that it wasn't. No matter how much we might have wanted it to be so, no matter how much it 'ought to have been', it couldn't: perfection is an ideal, and nobody's perfect. Once again, 'should' and 'ought' and 'must' are words from the power-under game: they don't apply to the real world. . . So we all have troubles left over from our childhood. Blaming others; blaming ourselves. People who didn't make the right choices, and hurt each other in various ways: sometimes physically, sometimes more subtly but often more deeply, leaving bitter, painful memories. It's all there: waiting for us the moment we stop to look – which is one reason why we usually prefer not to look!

But as with fears, the pain simply grows larger if we don't turn round and face what those memories mean. What they're trying to tell us, when they keep coming back, is that there are lessons that we haven't yet learnt – lessons that may well go back many generations. Those troubles come from inherited habits: non-choices, choices avoided from fear. We inherit unlearnt lessons from our family; the ones we fail to deal with we pass on to our children – "the sins of the fathers are fetched even unto the seventh generation. . ." It's up to us – if we can – to break the cycle. And being aware of choice, that we *do* have a choice, we can choose to do so – to notice the moment within the loop of wyrd that allows us to break free. But it does bring up all the old fears, the old anger, the old blame. . .

An old friend of the family. Talking about old times. "You know", she says, laughing, "the clearest memory I have of you as children is driving back from primary school and your mother saying 'Anne, stop hitting Chris or you can get out and walk'!" The friend thinks it's a joke; having been literally on the receiving end so many times, I don't think so at all. I'm angry: they never believed me. . . they kept on telling me it'd never happened. . .

And then suddenly realisation hits: it wasn't some kind of cruel conspiracy, it was just that no-one knew what else to do. Everyone doing the best they could, with something that had been going on for generations. No choice: everyone just stuck in habit. Loops of wyrd, that repeat until the lesson's learnt. Well, I've learnt it now. So let go, let go. . . And quite suddenly, it's gone: years of painful memories lift, and fly free. Gone. And in their place, a wry smile, a deep sadness: a quiet compassionate space. I'd held on to all those memories to justify a childish desire for revenge – but there was never the slightest point in doing so. The pain just sits there until someone learns how to stop: and it may as well be me. Things were the way they were

---

because they got that way: 'nobody's perffect' – least of all me. . .!

What old childhood issues still hurt for you? Look back again and review them from that awareness that 'things happen because they happen to happen'. Sure, they might not have happened if everybody had been perfect, as they 'should have been': but they weren't. 'Nobody's perffect': we all have choices, but most of the time we all avoid them. The choice you have now is to accept that it was what it was; or continue the old, festering inner torture. So let go, let go. . . What difference does this make? Where can you *feel* that memory, and your feelings about it, in your body? And what do you feel as it moves, begins to go after all these years?

Forgive, we're told. Forgive and forget. Not as easy as it sounds. . . we can't *make* ourselves forget something, in fact the only thing that happens that way is that we suppress the memory, pretend it never happened. And if we do that, the wyrd will keep coming back with reminders, helpful as ever. . . Often a better solution is to deliberately set out to *not* forget, to *not* forgive: bring it all out into the open – though preferably in some safe environment, away from the people we'd blame. And then, 'doing no-thing', the old memory forgets *itself* – and at last leaves us in peace. No-one's to blame, because *everyone's* to blame; nobody's perfect, so things are the way they are because they got that way. And there's really 'no-thing' to do: let it be as it was, as it is. . . because, in the wyrd, all we really have is ourselves, and *now*.

"You *shouldn't* feel that way", they said. Well, I did: looking deeper, it's obvious that I still do. Feelings are feelings: we can't control them – much like the wyrd, they simply *are*. But we *can* direct our responses to them: we don't have to translate them into the matching action. So, rather than lashing out at others, I 'forgive and forget', in a conscious, almost ritualistic way, by re-awakening the memory, then drumming my anger, dancing my sorrow, or whatever else feels right in the moment. By allowing

☞

265

the feeling to *be* – acknowledging it, accepting it – it drifts away of its own accord. And the energy that's been locked up in fighting myself, holding the old anger down, is released at last – re-empowering myself *without* putting others down.

The habit is always to continue the old feuds, blaming others for the feelings we were told we 'shouldn't' have had. But allow the feelings, the memories, to *be*: accept them in a *conscious* way. Others' actions are so often a reflection of our *own* choices: so allow that compassion – 'to recognise oneself in others' – to come through, forgiving others, forgiving *yourself*. What happens?

Once we *do* allow those old feelings to come through, they make room for a lot of other old feelings too: all the good memories that we'd locked down at the same time. It brings our memories of childhood and beyond back into balance: there *were* good times, along with the not-so-good ones – all the intricate interweavings of the threads of wyrd.

And it also helps to bring those hurts into perspective. I remember that we used to have great childish battles about who would have which knife, which plate, who would sit where: it all seemed so important at the time. It doesn't now! Yet a lot of the childhood hurts are much the same: the pain was real, but because we were told we 'shouldn't' have felt it, it's sat there festering ever since. And we've learnt to feel wrong to feel it at all. So most of the problem comes from our old friend the silliness-barrier: once we can get past feeling wrong for feeling wrong, a lot of old issues just drift away.

One technique that I've found helpful is a variant of the 'anger chair'. Set out two chairs or cushions as before; sit in one of them. This time, rather than some person you're angry with, imagine that it's you as you are *now* that is sitting in the other chair – a 'you' who'll listen intently and supportively to what you're saying. So go back in your mind, past the silliness-barrier, to some of those old childhood "it's not *fair*!" experiences:

266

remember them, recreate them, tell the imaginary 'other you' about them. Allow whatever feelings that come up to *be*: there's *no* feeling that's wrong in itself. So let go. . . let go. . . until, as before, at some time the flow of memories simply stops. What happens – simply by being listened to by someone who cares?

Now turn it round: sit in the other chair, looking back at that now-imaginary 'child-you'. What does that child look like? Reach into yourself with compassion: that child is asking you for support, acknowledgement, so what can you give – how can you help *you*?

Although it may seem easiest to continue blaming others – 're-sentment is a demand that the other should feel guilty' – it doesn't get us anywhere: all it does is keep the pointless power-under game going. And if we've carried the blame for others, it's important to build a sense of perspective: there's a lot of difference between 'toxic shame' – which again is simply part of the power-under game – and a healthy shame which comes from accepting that we *did* make mistakes. We made mistakes: so what? It's part of being human. . . a little compassion for our family and ourselves can help a lot. If we realise that something still needs fixing, we fix it: but we don't need to wallow in faked-up guilt in order to avoid fixing our mistakes!

It's also worthwhile remembering that a lot of what happened to us in our family environment stemmed from our own choices – or avoidance of choices. And the wyrd, as always, responds as requested. . . A surprising amount of what we did as children would have been tactics to gain attention – often 'that special attention which is the prerogative of the miserable'. We don't need to maintain those tactics now. . . it may have seemed to get us what we wanted in the past, but making misery a way of life only hurts *us* in the end.

Our 'cellmates' were there to help us become who we are: and they did their best to help us. They did so in whatever way they could, either consciously or not – it's all been part of the weaving that's made us who we are. So *whatever* they did was part of that help – regardless of what it might have seemed like, either then or now. If it *is* all our choice, then even the 'bad' times, such as bullying, were *our* chosen method for teaching us skills that we couldn't get any other way: it may not have been comfortable, but there's no doubt that it worked! Sometimes, though, it takes a weird point of view to recognise that we *have* learnt valuable skills from the bad times. . .

I've spent so much energy recovering from having played the rôle of scapegoat that it took me a long time to realise I'd *chosen* to play it – partly because I refused to face the fears enough to pull clear of it, and partly from a mistaken notion that I was helping by doing so. . . I can't honestly blame anyone else. But instead I can see what I've *learnt* from it: real skills like the ability to sense certain types of trouble long before they develop into tangible form. I use those skills every day in my work: and yet I have to admit that I'd never have developed them without that unfortunate form of encouragement. . .

Look back at some of those old familial hurts, and review them instead as *learning* experiences. What skills did you learn – including the ability to avoid that kind of problem now? Under the circumstances, could you really have learnt these skills any other way? And can you shift the point of view so that, rather than blaming, you can *thank* your 'cellmates' for their help with these lessons? What happens to your feeling about *yourself* by doing so?

By looking at family issues, we learn how we've become who we are. In a way the argument about nature-versus-nurture is irrelevant: we are who we are, we are what our wyrd has made us. We're none of us perfect: we inherited some of our past problems, we ourselves created others for the members of our family, and we'll pass on some more to succeeding generations – that's the reality of life with 'cellmates'. But if that comment about 'the sins of the fathers' is correct, then if we manage to resolve more than a seventh of what we've been given, we're doing well. . .

'Je ne regrette rien': there's no point in regretting the past, because it was whatever it was. It might have been different, might have been gentler: but *everyone* makes mistakes. We learnt a great deal then: the remaining lessons keep returning to us on the wyrd, and the only way to lessen them is complete our learning of them now!

FRIENDS AND OTHER ALLIES

From our family we get to discover how we've become who we are; with our partners we get to discover more of who we are; and with our friends we get to *practice* who we truly are. Friends are allies *we* choose – or at least choose more consciously – to help us to resolve our issues. Partners too *can* be allies, but it takes a great deal of trust – with friends the emotional stakes are not quite so high. . .

We do make mistakes. In fact we *have* to be able to make mistakes – otherwise there's no way we can learn anything new. It's here, in learning to work *with* our wyrd, that we find who our real allies are. . . because when we do so, we're constantly learning, constantly changing – changes that are unpredictable and frightening for others as well as for ourselves. True friends will stay with us, accept that our anger, or whatever, is a passing thing; others won't, which often gives us the impression that there's something badly wrong with *us*. If we then try to control our changes to keep everyone happy, we'll *all* end up in chaos. . .

> Talking with an old friend, trying to understand why I feel so upset about yet another apparent social disaster. "What's the problem?" she says. "You've taken responsibility for their fears – and repressed your own. Do you wonder that you're so angry inside? You've rarely allowed your true self to speak – let it speak! You'll make mistakes – *accept* that. You'll survive them. But unless you take risks, you *cannot* learn. It's like your juggling, Chris: you will drop a ball from time to time, especially while you're learning. Just make sure that you're in a place where you're less likely to break things when you do so. . ."
>
> ☞

It's never comfortable to find ourselves in a situation where a friendship is at risk: but when we 'go with the flow' of our wyrd, *anything* can happen. We'll make mistakes: yet if we listen within, we can *feel* when it's safe to do so. How do you recognise this feeling? Which friends can you safely practise this with? And how do you *know* what and when it's safe with others to let go into the flow of the wyrd?

As before, the key is to maintain our awareness of our aim, our focus – and allow *whatever* happens to be part of that. It's not always easy. . . We're so conditioned to pleasing others *before* ourselves that it's sometimes difficult to grasp that pleasing ourselves – in the deepest sense – is also *necessarily* pleasing others. Compassion has its positive side: to recognise oneself in others involves recognising joy, happiness, exuberance as much as anything else!

But the usual accusation is "you're being selfish!" – which is hardly surprising, given that what we're doing is reclaiming our sense of self. Getting lost in childish selfishness is always a risk in this process, though – which is why we need allies to keep us on track. . . And if we listen, there's also that strange sense of 'impending wyrd' that can tell us so much about what's going on under the surface. But it's up to us – it's *always* up to us – to keep checking-in: both with our friends, and with the wyrd itself.

My friend Eddie said many years ago: "If I tell you to push off, Chris, I mean it! But I mean it *now*: not tomorrow, or forever. There's always another day. . ." He was very clear where his boundaries were – and also clear that they changed from day to day, hour to hour. By being clear, he made it easy for me to find out what *I* wanted – and to check in with him as to whether he could help. "If in doubt, *ask*", was more of his advice: yet slowly I've found that I don't even need to ask any more – I *know*, myself, through the weavings of the wyrd.

Inclarity and blame are two of the main weapons of the power-under game: friends who are clear and non-blaming are

> our key allies in breaking free. Which friends of yours help you in this? How do you 'check in' with them? What subtle fears do you face by doing so? And what is the *feeling* – the 'impending wyrd' – by which you can know in advance what the outcome will be?

To build up our awareness of the wyrd, and of *our* connection with it, it's worthwhile making an agreement with certain friends to let go of the normal rules of what's 'sensible', and interact with them entirely in the moment, according to the *feelings* that drift in from the wyrd. We can only do this at first with friends we trust – ones who won't dismiss us as 'weird'! Yet when we do this, weird connections do happen: coincidences become part of the Normal Rules of life. . .

> I try to phone a friend: after three different wrong numbers I give up – and the next day I discover that although he'd been in, he'd wanted to be alone. Then for no reason, and with no excuse, I call round to see another friend – and find others there who've also been 'called' to help in an unexpected crisis. Normal Rules. . .
>
> Connections: we become allies for each other, in a weird weaving of interconnections. What experiences do you have like this? What does it take for you to trust the whims, the feelings, that make up these not-quite-connections? How do you 'check in' with the wyrd – and yourself?

The reason for practising this with friends is that they're known, safe allies with whom we can make the mistakes that are a necessary part of learning. A true friend is a distortion-free mirror, reflecting what we project onto the wyrd. Slowly, though, and as our awareness of the wyrd increases – along with our ability to work *with* it – we discover that ultimately everything, everyone, everywhere, is an ally. . . no matter what they may seem on the surface. When we trust ourselves, help and advice is *always* available – although it can take some very weird forms! And that trust is what we now need to practice, as we expand our understanding of wyrd in the everyday work of our everyday world.

23

WORKING IN A
WEIRD WORLD

The concept of wyrd, in itself, is simple enough; and with a little practice it's easy enough to include its weavings into our experience when we're on our own. When we try to retain that awareness in the world 'out there', though, things may not seem quite so simple!

Through the web of the wyrd, we have a direct link to everything, everywhere, everywhen, everyone – which can, as we now know, be immensely useful. But it's also something that most people, most of the time, are extremely keen to avoid, for the simple reason that it can be frightening. We get to see Reality Department, not as our illusions would prefer it to be, but as it *is*, in all its chaotic glory... In the weirdness of each moment, it may not seem comfortable, or certain, or safe. But even though there's always that twist of uncertainty, there's always a choice: there's *always* a way through, if we can allow ourselves to find it. Yet to do so, to work *with* the wyrd, demands from us trust, and ever more trust: a trust that leads us, eventually, to a very different experience of the real, everyday, 'out there' world.

A WORLD OF CONNECTIONS

The outside is also the inside: that's one of the basic principles of wyrd. So we'll often find that our interactions with others in the community will echo and reflect our own inner state in some weird way or other. There are real boundaries between 'I' and 'not-I' – that's obvious enough – and yet the boundaries can blur in any way, at any moment. Watching what happens outside can tell us a great deal about our own beliefs and expectations. . .

In time it becomes obvious that much of what we see 'out there' is a reflection of our own fears, echoing through the web of wyrd. Less obviously, it's also an echoing of what we *don't* have problems with: less obvious, in that the reflection is mostly in terms of what *doesn't* happen to us rather than what does – such as in that weird process of precognitive-recovery. But at the first level, when we first start to apply our awareness of wyrd in the wider world, we're likely to be in much the same state as after returning from the trip to the imaginary fun-fair: namely, it's a great deal easier to see what's going on – and how it follows from our choices and non-choices – than to do much, if anything, about it. . .

That's *not* comfortable. . . But as before, the key is to let things be: 'doing no-thing', just watch, both the 'inside' and the 'outside' – and see what happens.

The wyrd – obliging as ever – can always provide us with 'proof' that our fears are correct. . . but is that what we really want? We *do* always have a choice – even if there's always a twist!

The wyrd echoes boundaries by creating a greater want for those boundaries. So our experience of the world can be a direct reflection of our fears: the more we give in to those fears, or refuse to face them, the more we meet them on the street. Look around at the obsessive concern with 'security' in our culture: fences, locks, alarms, dogs, guards, guns – what are we *really* protecting? Does this kind of 'security' actually create a sense of security – or just a deeper sense of insecurity? Is the best defence no defence at all?

The need for outward security may simply reflect an inner insecurity, perhaps. What are your thoughts, feelings, experiences of this? In what ways do the thoughts, feelings, experiences differ from each other? And how does your experience of the world 'out there' change in those times when you've reached an *inner* security, an inner sense of peace?

We all have choices: the whole point of working with the wyrd is to reclaim our sense of choice. Those stereotyped responses, such as the violence we may fear, usually come in only when we *abandon* our choices, leaving our experience to the doubtful care of the senses-taker. We'll know about it soon enough: there's always some weird loop to remind us of abandoned choices, bringing us face-to-face with the result. All we have to do, though, is *notice*. . . no matter how much we'd prefer not to!

That sequence of 'listen; wait; listen' also changes after a while to something more like 'listen; *act*; listen'. Another form of 'doing no-thing': trusting our *own* knowing, our own sense of connection with the wyrd, and putting it into action in the moment, in each and every moment. It does take practice. . .

This sense of 'listen; wait; listen' has taken me quite some time to develop: but my attempts to 'control' things are rarer these days. And I also trust more that I *do* know when to act in the moment – though I still need more practice at listening to know when to *stop* once I've started! But while I can maintain the discipline of 'doing no-thing' fairly well when I'm on my own, it still tends to fall apart as soon as I'm with others, out in the real world. So many distractions, so many things *here, now.* I just forget. . . Once again, though, I 'do no-thing' about this as well: rather than getting upset about it, I *allow* the discipline to fall apart – and let the wyrd work in its own way to remind me of my aim. It does work – in its own weird way.

That 'solo Click' exercise we looked at earlier would be useful here: carry it out into the everyday world, let the sense of being 'Clicked' by the wyrd remind you of your aim. What do you find yourself being 'shown'? What does that tell you about your connection with the world? – with the wyrd? – with yourself?

The world 'out there' is a reflection of our own state: "issues spiral through me on threads of wyrd – are unchanged by how much I am unchanged". As we change, our experience of the world changes: and whether or not it 'really does' change, in an objective, measurable way, is not all that relevant, because what matters is that for us it *does* change. Once we learn to notice it, we see – and experience – that the world does also echo what's clear in our inner state: there are definite responses to those threads we've claimed in the affirmations and other techniques that we've used.

> As we work to reclaim our choices and our sense of self, there *are* real changes – though sometimes they're hard to recognise. What changes have happened for you – especially improvements in your ability to handle old loops, old habits – since you started working with the wyrd? What *doesn't* happen any more? – or happens much less than it used to? And as you have changed, what changes do you feel in the way others work with *you*?

And it certainly works best when we share it with others – when we empower ourselves *and* others at the same time. Yet at times that's strangely difficult, because many people will find it hard even to believe that we'd *want* to share. It's a chaotic world out there: 'insane' might well be an understatement. . .

From the work we've done so far with wyrd, we can see that there's total confusion about almost everything: habits, choices, wants and needs, rights, responsibilities, fears, concepts of self, of blame, control and, especially, power. But there's no point in complaining about it: that's how it *is*. In a sense, we've chosen, if only by default, to have it be that way; so it's part of our wyrd that we now have to learn – or re-learn – how to deal with it.

A WORLD OF CONFUSIONS

Once again, at the first level it's often far easier to see what's going on than to do anything about it. . . and that *hurts*. It'd be much simpler to turn a blind eye to it all, pretend it doesn't exist, move to some other planet. . . Reality Department, however, reminds us that we're *here, now*: which means that it *is* our problem. But to what *extent* it's our problem is still our choice – although there's still always that twist. . .

In one sense this mess is all our choice; in another sense it definitely isn't. Very little of it is the result of anyone's *conscious* choices: rather, it's the result of a chaos of *non*-choices. And we'll get 'an equal and apposite re-enaction' until we choose otherwise. But until we know what the choice *is*, it's extremely hard to choose: and since most of the culture (and, it sometimes seems, the wyrd) seems to be designed to prevent us from knowing what the choice is – or even that we have a choice – at times finding *any* choice becomes in itself a quest!

It always seems much easier to hide in habit. I go to the supermarket, and am immediately confronted with a *chaos* of choices. All those boxes and packages designed to grab my attention succeed in doing just that: I get 'visual indigestion' in no time at all. Instant solution: pick up only what I know, and run. . .! So how do I learn to choose for *myself*? In this kind of chaos, how do I *choose* at all?

How do *you* choose? Try something different next time you go shopping: make a point of leaving your habits behind. If you usually make a list, don't: instead, spend some time beforehand reclaiming – through meditation or whatever – an awareness of your aim. (If this sounds excessive, remember that it's an experiment to illustrate a point, not necessarily a way of life. . .!) And go out to the shops. How easy is it to lose that awareness, that sense of *choice*, in the chaos of life: the moment you move outside the door? further down the street? or as soon as you enter the shop?

Reclaim your awareness in the shop. Notice how many things are designed to prevent you from doing this: the clatter, the clutter, the music, the layout, the sense of being part of someone else's process. How much effort does it take to reclaim your sense of choice?

Go down the aisles, in a systematic fashion. Imagine that the shelves are filled, not with packages, but with people. Listen to the imaginary clamour of all those packages requesting, calling, cajoling, screaming for your attention: with what voices do they speak? Maintain your awareness of your aim: respond to things which match your aim in the moment, and politely refuse the rest – exactly as if out in a crowded street. What difference does this

☞

> make to what goes into your basket? Why? What 'voices' do you respond to differently when your aim is clear?
>
> Maintaining our sense of self under this kind of pressure is hard work: even a simple shopping trip can be exhausting when our barriers are down. Which is why most of us, most of the time, hide away from life in the illusory effortlessness of habit. . .

Re-empowering ourselves, reclaiming our sense of self, centres round reclaiming our sense of choice. But much of the culture we live in is centred round the *avoidance* of choice: always trying to make it 'somebody else's problem'. And we then complain that this 'somebody else' seems to have all the power: but if we choose to give away our power this way, we really can't complain. . .

Most people are very afraid of change, too, because it forces choices. When things change, the 'safe' non-choice of habit simply doesn't work any more: and that can feel very unsafe. As we go through the changes that the wyrd thrusts upon us, true friends will stay with us; but many others won't. They'll either run, or try to make us stay 'in character', or even turn round and attack us – because they're frightened. Few people will admit it: but that's the way it *is*.

So we discover very quickly that most 'friendships' in our culture are more co-dependent than supportive; and courtesy of that inversion of boundaries – from which everyone expects everyone else to look after them – most people know only how to take support, and honestly don't *know* how to give or receive it. Everyone is needy at times: in this chaos of a culture, where the power-under game is almost 'the only game in town', most people are needy most of the time. . . including ourselves, if we're honest about it. And that's the way things *are*. Complaining about it won't change this: but working *with* the wyrd, rather than against it, will – as will continuing to work on ourselves and our choices.

> "I am what I am" applies to *everyone*. Which means that, just like us, others 'out there' *are* likely to be afraid at times; they
>
> ☞

are likely to be irrational, without warning; they *are* likely to be dishonest with themselves, and with others. We *all* do it: 'nobody's perffect'.

If you've been doing the practical work described in these boxes, you *are* likely to be gaining a clearer – though never perfect! – understanding of yourself and your interaction with the wyrd. But most people 'out there' haven't done this – or anything like it. This doesn't make you better (or worse) than them, but it does mean that they're less likely to be aware. . . And since breaking the cycles of habit requires at least *one* person in any situation to be aware of their choices, that means – however unfair, however uncomfortable – that the responsibility's often on you. How do you deal with this? What happens when you're suddenly reminded – by the wyrd or whatever – that you *do* have a true choice in how to handle some habitual re-enaction?

In dreams, every person, every incident, is a metaphor for some aspect of ourself. Much the same is true 'out there': what we see is as much an echo of 'shadow' aspects of ourselves as anything else. So what are these 'cellmates' telling you about *yourself*, when you find yourself going through yet another 'apposite re-enaction'?

Reclaiming our sense of choice involves breaking free from habit, and re-learning to trust – re-learning who, what, and when to trust. Considering that the standard view of 'working in the real world' seems to be about learning to lie and to *dis*trust, this is not always easy. . .

Re-empowering ourselves also means that we somehow have to break free of the confused assumption that power is a 'zero-sum': there's only a fixed amount of power, I'm told, hence the only way I'll get more is by making sure that someone else gets less – to feel powerful, I first have to make someone else feel *less* powerful. In reality, this is nonsense – a smile, for example, costs nothing, and is usually empowering to all concerned – but the idea is so pervasive that it sometimes requires a weird point of view to see that it *is* nonsense.

Since there's that confusion that 'where there's fear, there's power', we'll also see this in the artificial manufacture of fear in advertising and the like – "are you *really* protecting your children's health?", "is your home *really* secure?". And we'll see everywhere the export of fear as well as blame: the whole aim of 'deterrence' is to make someone else afraid, rather than take the risk of trusting the wyrd. Their choice, in effect, is to try to force us to take responsibility for *their* fears: notice how often that forcefulness backfires. . .

When someone else tells you that "women shouldn't walk alone at night", what do you *feel*? When a junkyard dog leaps at the fence and snarls at you as you walk past, how do you react? What do you think about the people who trained that dog to export their fears and distrust to you? And in what ways do *you* manufacture and export fear to others?

Power is not a zero-sum: as we empower ourselves, claiming that power from within *ourselves* rather than from others, we find that we *can* take the risk to empower others to discover their choices too. We learn to trust ourselves by trusting others: we don't really have a choice in this, since those others *are* also aspects of ourselves, interwoven with us on the web of wyrd. And we learn to trust others by trusting ourselves: acknowledging our inner awareness – that sense of 'impending wyrd' – that tells us when it's safe to trust, and when not to. We'll make mistakes, of course: but when it happens, it's worth noting how much *doesn't* happen, as well as what does. "Note how much you're alive, how much you *are* protected", says the wyrd. . .

A WORLD AT WORK

Given the chaos, the confusion, the fear, what's the point in being here? It's difficult at times to hold on to a sense of meaning, of purpose – especially at work. The same empty actions, repeated day after day. . . a sense of fatalistic gloom. . .

But that's where we started this exploration of wyrd: and we now recognise that we *do* always have choices, even though they're often hidden in some very weird twists. We'll find, for example, that it's not only (or even) money that matters, but the general sense of meaning and value that we get from our work: the key is in the *context* of work rather than solely in its content. In other words, it's not what we do, but *the way that we do it* in which we're most likely to find a real sense of meaning. It's not up to somebody else: it's up to *us*.

There's probably nothing as dispiriting and meaningless as that experience we call 'clock-watching': "Only another six hours to go; thank God it's Friday. . ." And yet if we can *find* meaning in what we're doing, the time just vanishes in some weird way. What's your experience of this? Under what circumstances does time seem to drag? Or flash by 'in no time'?

We don't so much invent meaning as discover it from within ourselves. "True talent", said one writer, "is usually one which, when we use it, tends to make us lose all track of time" – reaching deep within ourselves, we connect with the weird timeless world of the 'Sisters of Time'. What does this sense of timelessness *feel* like when it appears within you?

One of the more cruel cultural curses is the myth that work *should* be boring: work as a kind of penance for some imagined misdeed. "You think the world owes you a living, huh?" snaps a supervisor. In fact, the answer's Yes: otherwise I wouldn't be here – I do have 'a right to be here, no less than the trees and stars'. But that's only true because I owe the world a living too. . . We each have our place, our purpose, in the workings of the world – in the *total* world, that is, not just the strange insanity of the ownership economy.

Again, it helps sometimes to look at the world through weirder eyes, to see just how strange the 'normal' world turns out to be.

Imagine: a strange imaginary world. Within it, you're woken out of a dream by an indefinite shrill sound: it's still dark, but you find yourself getting up, as if driven by some kind of

☞

---

compulsion. After a brief libation under a shower, you dress in an uncomfortable kind of ritual clothing – including, for men, something like a noose around the neck – then rapidly stuff your face with some substance that looks and tastes like shredded cardboard, before rushing out to sit in a tin box with wheels, which goes nowhere slowly for an endless time. Everywhere around you are other people in these strange tin boxes, expressionless, silent, sad – is this some kind of funeral procession?

Eventually, the tin box stops: you leave it, and go to some faceless building set amidst serried ranks of these tin boxes. Then you find yourself sitting in crowded isolation: there are people all around, some of whom talk at you, but there's no real sense of connection. And there's an indefinite, all-pervading sense of urgency, but no real sense of *meaning*: just these bits of paper with markings on them, some of which you know you've made, but don't really make sense. Every now and then a bell rings, and you find yourself talking with a disembodied voice that drifts, muffled, out of something that looks like a coloured piece of bone. All of this seems terribly important, but there's no way of telling *why* – it just *is*.

On some kind of hidden signal, everything stops: the building suddenly empties of people. You find yourself back in the tin box once more, moving slowly: people around you, again isolated in their slow-moving boxes, their faces still expressionless, still sad, but clearly tired as well. This part of the dream drags on – empty nothingness, a blur of half-understood impressions – until you find yourself standing in front of a door, a twisted piece of metal in your hand. There's some kind of ritual connection between them: they meet, the door opens. Inside, a glowing box sends flickers of blue-tinged light around the gloom; there's a jabber of incomprehensible sounds and snatches of music, all with an overlay of that same strange sense of empty urgency. Somehow captured beyond any sense of will, you stare at the flickering light for hours, until your eyes close in exhaustion.

You're woken out of this dream-state by an indefinite shrill sound; it's still dark, but you get up, driven by some compulsion. . .

Nightmare. . .

Everyday reality?

We each choose our own wyrd. . .

But whether or not this world of ours is seriously insane, we happen to live in it: so what form would a 'right livelihood' within it take? That's up to us – we each choose our own wyrd. Despite what we'll be told, we *always* have a choice about what we do – though the choice is often hidden deep within the twists of fate. To find the choice that actually does feel right for us will often demand a great deal of trust, in ourselves and in the workings of the wyrd: one twist is that some of the choices feel more than a little frightening at first!

To trust is frightening: we're not in control, we can't be certain that life will treat us fairly, we're at risk of being hurt. But in the real world, there's no such thing as 'fair': we each of us deserve everything and nothing; we owe everything and nothing, and are owed everything and nothing. To break free of the myth of 'double-entry life-keeping', we need to *trust* that we'll get what we need – and notice that we *do* get what we need, even if it's not always what we'd want. Reality Department doesn't keep a simple set of accounts: it works in a weirder way than that. . . In the long term, frightening though it may seem, the costs of trusting are less than the costs of not trusting: by trusting, we *do* get what we need. And if we only allow things to work in expected ways, we're limiting our chances. . .

We have a right to be here; in principle, at least, we have a right (as another writer put it) "to work, to be maintained while working, and to share the product with all who need it". But it's up to us to assert that right. . . Whoever we are, we have certain talents, certain skills: the point – which seems to be our *reason* to be here – is to put them to *use*.

What talents do you have? What do you *enjoy*? In what ways do you feel empowered, while sharing that empowerment with others? That's where your real work lies. . .

To get there does, however, take a different kind of work – finding the power-from-within to identify our own *knowing* from within. A process of self-questioning, exploring what we *feel* as well as what we think about ourself, our choices, our interactions with others. Richard Nelson Bolles, in his well-known annual "What Color Is Your Parachute?", suggests using these questions as a starting-point for that self-exploration:

What *tasks* do you enjoy?

In what *settings* – both physical and otherwise – do you enjoy doing these kinds of tasks?

What *tools or means* do you enjoy using for these tasks? What kind of people, information, things do you enjoy working with?

What kind of *outcomes* are important to you? in the short term? long term? for yourself and your immediate associates? for the world as a whole?

What kind of *rewards* would you need? (Or, to put it more in the terms we've been using here, what responses from the wyrd would you need, to show you that your work has true meaning in the widest sense of self?)

Our talents are the threads of wyrd that we've claimed as being our choice for tools to work within the wyrd: having chosen them, it's up to us to find out how best to use them. There's always a choice, there's always a twist: we each choose our own wyrd. . .!

Viewed in this way, our work thus becomes an affirmation of *who we are*: the real reward is that we get to discover who we are, and who we've become. 'Right livelihood' brings with it a sense of *aliveness*, a sense of being at peace with ourself and with the rest of reality. When we allow ourselves to connect with it, there's even a sense of being *called*: by letting go, and trusting, we find ourselves doing what the world most needs to have done, at the same time as doing what *we* most need to do. It's there that we find meaning and purpose, at 'the place where our deep gladness and the world's deep hunger meet'.

This is very different from the usual image of work, which is that it's something that we *have* to do to survive, or to justify to others that we have a right to exist. There's often a sense of being trapped, powerless, with no choice at all. And the fear that drives this feeling is very real: one of the fundamental beliefs in our culture is that unless we *can* convert our actions into a marketable form, we *don't* have that right to exist. Even though this is actually a manufactured myth, part of the power-under game, it can be hard to break free of the fear when we're *in* it. . .

Part of this trap comes from what I call the Priest's Dilemma: "I have a vocation, a calling, to commit myself to the service of others. But how am I to live? For if I ask them for support, requiring them to serve me, I'd believe I'm not truly in their service; yet if I do not, I have no means to survive, and I cannot serve them. . ." A cruel dilemma: one that strikes hard at anyone who commits themself to *caring* – which is one reason why cash and caring rarely coincide. . .

One standard 'solution' is to place yourself *between* people and their needs, as an indispensable 'between-taker': the legal profession, for example, stands between people and 'justice' – often ensuring their indispensability by ensuring, unconsciously, that justice never happens. . . And the other classic 'solution', commonly known in New Age terms as 'poverty consciousness', guarantees nothing except lack of support and an increasing sense of futility – which rather defeats the object of the exercise. Neither of these 'solutions' really work. . .

So how do *you* resolve the Priests' Dilemma in your life and work? How do *you* 'assert, by your talent, the right to work, to be maintained while doing it, and to share the product with all who need it'? Somewhere, there's always a choice, always a way of doing so: but often it's hidden deep within the twists of the wyrd. . .

Once again, the key to resolving this trap is in 'doing no-thing'. Not doing nothing, however: "In the field of observation, chance favours only the prepared mind", as Louis Pasteur once commented. Seeing the threads, seeing the lessons concealed within those threads, we can 'dis-cover' opportunities everywhere. It's the same as that weird experience of precognitive-recovery, but this time in the opposite sense: allowing ourselves to recognise when we're in the *right* place at the *right* time! And the *feeling* when this is about to happen is clear: it's the same as that strange sensation of 'impending wyrd'. It does take practice to learn to recognise it, though: 'listen; wait; listen. . . listen; *act*; listen. . .'

Much of the trap comes from accepting other people's one-way boundaries: "it's your *duty* to do this", "you *must* do this". It's true that we do owe the world a living: in that sense it *is* our duty to do some kind of work. And sometimes those external demands can help us maintain our sense of aim and purpose when our own self-discipline falters. But how do you balance these needs of duty and discipline? How do you maintain your own boundaries, and respect those of others, while still retaining your ability to flow and move with the weavings of the wyrd?

And another key is in respecting our own needs: doing what *we* most want to do. "Follow your bliss" – it applies as much to our work as to anything else.

"Do what you love, and the money will follow": it's good advice, but without awareness of the wyrd it can conceal a dreadful disappointment. Once we trust that we *can* survive by doing what we love – once we accept that we *do* have a right to be here, 'no less than the trees and stars' – we'll discover ways of expressing that in our everyday work. But the rest of ourself comes along as well: all our resistances, all the issues we'd rather not face. They're part of us: we never do escape our wyrd. . .

Following our bliss is a commitment to *ourself*: and just as with affirmations, once we truly commit, all our resistances come straight back up. We suddenly find that what we'd always enjoyed is boring, hard work; somehow it isn't fun any more. And somehow, too, the joy can disappear when we have to create an audience for what we do, or in the process of converting our vocation into a marketable skill. What's gone wrong?

> The short answer is: nothing. By the usual backwards twists of the wyrd, this is actually an improvement. . . Our resistances to doing what *we* want are echoing back through the wyrd: exactly the same as before, but they've now taken a different form. The reality is that the *form* of our work really doesn't matter all that much: it's not what we do, but the way we do it, that matters. It *is* easier, though, to find that meaning in something that we enjoy to start with!
>
> What's your experience of this? What do you *feel* when the joy seems to fade? What kind of quiet self-discipline do you need, in order to keep going in the 'empty' times? And how do you find the trust that allows the joy to return in its own weird way?

"Chop wood; carry water. Enlightenment! Chop wood; carry water. . ." *All* work is like that. The 'enlightenment' comes in caring, both about ourselves and the end-results of what we do, and in compassion, that weird sense of recognising oneself in others.

And if we look only at what doesn't work in work, we'll tend to miss what does. . . The wyrd is the interpenetration of every-where, everything, everyone: all work may contain meaninglessness, but it also contains joy, meaning, laughter. Yet it can only be there if we *allow* it to be: so it's up to us to find it, to discover it, both in our work, and in ourselves.

We can use the same awareness, too, to relate to the wider environment – learning to see, to listen, to sense and to savour the infinite variety of the world. It *is* a beautiful world out there. . .

24

IT ISN'T EASY BEING GREEN?

Pollution. Salination. Deforestation. Desertification. Environmental disasters by the score: an increasing sense of gloom and doom. As the puppet character Kermit the Frog would say, "It isn't easy being green. . ."

Wait a moment. We've seen *this* kind of fatalism before, too. What it tells us is entirely true, at one level; but it's not *all* of the story. Once again, so much depends on our point of view. And how we *experience* reality, as we've seen, certainly does depend to a great extent on our point of view.

By understanding the nature of wyrd, we realise that we can *choose* our point of view about the environment, about the world 'out there': and though there's always a choice, there's also always a twist. The outside is a reflection of the inside: the chaos 'out there' is also a reflection of ourselves. And what we see reflects in part what we choose to see, in part also what our wyrd chooses for us to see – often what we most try to avoid. So it's up to us – and it *is* still a beautiful world out there. . .

A SENSE OF VALUE

Everything has its value: which is *not* the same as 'everything has its price'. The confusion between price and value is much the same as that between wants and needs: what we call 'price' is, in much the same way, an outward expression of an inner value. And as with wants and needs, it works well enough as long as the price relates to something tangible; it's when we try to put a price on

288

something intangible – an emotion, an idea, a sense of meaning – that we get into trouble.

> What price would you put on a smile? An idea? A joke? Yet what is the *value*, to you, of a smile, an idea, a joke?
>
> For that matter, how much does happiness cost? Where can we buy a sense of security? We might discover happiness in paying for an evening out with a friend; we might imagine we're a little more secure for having bought a bigger lock for the door: but is that really the same as buying happiness, or security, or whatever?
>
> Do happiness or security *have* a price as such? Or would you describe them as 'priceless'? And if they're priceless, do they still have a value to you? The bland statement that 'everything has its price' is perhaps not as simple as it seems. . .

I remember having a long conversation with a man who insisted that money was the only way in which we could measure value. He'd spent his working life valuing things, 'making money' for the company he worked for. He'd just retired, he said; he talked long about the motorcycle he'd just bought, how much he enjoyed riding it, how sad he was that his wife wouldn't ride it with him. But if its value could only be measured in monetary terms, he'd have been better off not to have bought it, and certainly never to use it, since its value in a monetary sense was reduced every time he rode it! Yet he found it almost impossible to understand that the real – in many ways the only – value of the motorcycle was in the *enjoyment* that he gained in using it. . .

It also had a value in terms of metaphor, in terms of what it *meant* to him: even when it was parked in the garage, it was a *symbol* of that enjoyment. And although much of 'valuing' consists of applying a price to a symbolic value – a sense of the future expectation of its value – the price itself is a kind of symbol: a metaphor for a metaphor.

What are you worth? What do others think you're worth? What do you *value* about yourself? What do others value about you? And are these all the same?

What do you value? Choose an example of something that you value. How do you know you value it? What does 'value' *feel* like? How do you distinguish between what you feel its value is, and what you think its value is – or is there no difference?

Could you put a price on that value? And would the same relationship of price and value be 'self-evident' to everyone else?

Our sense of 'value' is often a chaotic blurring of feelings, beliefs and much else besides – a blurring of metaphor and fact. Within this confusion, it's perhaps not surprising that price so often works against a sense of *felt* value: as we've seen, cash and caring – a valuing of both 'I' and 'not-I' – rarely coincide. . .

It's difficult to put a price on beauty; it's difficult to put a price on joy. Under the influence of the senses-taker of habit, it often seems simplest to say that they don't exist: price alone is all that seems to matter, especially if we've learned not to feel our connection with others through the wyrd. Given this confusion, and the cultural confusion about power, we can also begin to understand why vandalism is so common on so many levels, and why some people seem to be so obsessed about destroying what others value: in a typical weird twist, they experience it as 'being powerful' precisely *because* it disempowers others. Creating change in any form gives a sense of choice, a sense of self – and destruction, however pointless, is a quick and easy way of creating change. . .

There's a subtle trap for us in this, though. When we value things, it's easy to become attached – too attached. If we're too attached to something as it is, we can't allow for change: and change is an inevitable part of the wyrd.

Walking through the park, it's all too obvious that there's been a dance at the youth club last night: there's litter everywhere, and the glass door of the telephone booth has been smashed again. . . What do you *feel* when something you valued has been

☞

destroyed – especially if it's happened through vandalism or some other pointless power-game?

Much of that sense of disempowerment and loss comes from attachment to the way things were – and now no longer are. How do you let go of that attachment, while still valuing that which was destroyed? For that matter, how do you preserve something that you value, without inviting its destruction by becoming too attached? An interesting dilemma. . .

It's easy to become angry when something beautiful, something we value, is destroyed, especially by someone who doesn't care; but it's important to be able to shift that anger more to a sense of sadness – and let it go. We can usually tell when we get too attached to something, because, by the usual twists of the wyrd, it seems instead to *invite* an enforced 'detachment', whether we like it or not. . .

Yet non-attachment is also non-detachment: there are also times when we do have to stand by what we value. In this sense, 'the personal is also the political': we 'have a right to be here, no less than the trees and stars', but we also owe the rest of reality a living at the same time. Being 'green' is often a test of our commitment to be who *we* are, to stand by our valuing of ourselves, as much as standing by our values about the world 'out there'.

Reclaiming a sense of value allows us to reclaim a sense of connection with everyone, everything, and everywhere – we start to *experience* ourselves as an included part of a totality. Valuing ourselves, we value 'the other'; valuing 'the other', we get more of a chance to value ourselves. There is a boundary between 'I' and 'not-I'; but the more we experience and value our connection, through the wyrd, the more the boundary blurs. . .

A SENSE OF PLACE

We can perhaps experience this most easily through building up a sense of place. Learning to listen to those 'words on the wind' that describe the intricate interweavings in a place: listen; wait; listen. . . Reaching deeper within *ourselves*, we find that the wyrd can show us very different ways to see, to sense and to savour the infinite variety of the world; and by connecting with a wider sense of self through the threads of the wyrd, we discover the magic in the spirit of each place.

'Spirit of place' is perhaps best understood as a clustering of the threads of wyrd, characteristics that make up a character that's little different, in its way, from the character of a person. In ancient Europe and elsewhere, the spirit of each place was often personified as a local 'spirit', an entity: in terms of wyrd, this makes perfect sense, but it can take a weird point of view to see it as such!

But try it. In the midst of the city, try looking at the landscape beneath the surface skin of buildings and roads – what do you see? What images come to mind? What shapes do the hills, curves, valleys suggest: animals, people, whatever? What aspects of *yourself* do these shapes represent – echoed in the shaping of the place?

Out in the park, lie down in the grass, and look at the landscape from different points of view. Moving through the grass at the height of an ant, or the height of a cat, what different worlds do you see? Or from the constantly changing point of view of a bird? And yet all these different worlds interweave in the same space: in what ways do they merge into a whole, that forms the character of the place? Wearing those different points of view, what do you learn about yourself – and your usual assumptions about the place?

A place also provides a continuity in *time*: through the threads of the Sisters of Time, we can reach another kind of understanding of ourselves and our place in time by reaching down through the layers of time at a place. As with the notion of 'spirit of place', the weird concept of ancestor-worship actually begins to make sense within this kind of context – recognising ourselves as part of a community in *time* as well as in space.

In a country town in England, I walk into a big airy old building. There's a large square sign with an 'S' painted on it, pointing down into a space that was used as an air-raid shelter, half a century ago. But the wall the sign's mounted on is that of the Norman castle, almost a thousand years old; and the shelter space, above which the castle was built, is the barely-altered structure of a Roman temple, a thousand years older still. And elsewhere is a subtler but still tangible memory of past life, and past death: the layer of ash and charcoal, many inches thick, everywhere beneath the town, is a forceful reminder that the story of Queen Boudicca's revolt against the Roman occupation is no idle myth. Continuity in time. . . memories live on in their different ways within each place.

Look around in the area that you live, and the countryside around. What overlays of life, of generations, do you see there? The shopfronts may change with the passing fads of fashion, but the buildings above stay much the same for decades, even centuries: so what changes can you see written there? Standing in the streets, move backwards in time with all your senses, ten, twenty, fifty, a hundred, a thousand years: what sights, sounds, smells are different from now?

In what ways would you wish this to change, or to stay the same? Which threads of the wyrd would you claim for this place? There's always a choice; but remember that there's also always a twist. . .

In some ways everything we do, everything anyone has ever done, becomes another overlay in the fabric, the weaving, of this place. In that sense actions, emotions, feelings, ideas are like affirmations recorded in a place – *by* the place – bringing different threads to the surface, to be repeated to ourselves and every passer-by. And as with affirmations, everything we do *matters*: "do what you will", says the wyrd, "but be very sure that you will it. . .".

Arriving back at some place, what memories does it recall? In what ways does going back to a place help in recalling things that you'd forgotten? Or do you sometimes get the feeling that your wyrd has led you back 'by accident' to some place, to recall memories that you'd *hoped* you'd forgotten?

And memories not just of your own: sometimes there's also the weird feeling of retrieving someone *else*'s memories or feelings from a place – a 'place-memory', like paint splashed in layers of emotional colour. Have you had experiences of this? What is the *feeling* that comes with it?

Some places are more prone to this than others: why? Work your way past the senses-taker, the habit of ignoring: keep your awareness wide for a while. What differences can you *feel* between different places? What overall flavour do they each have – and in what ways, and at what times, does it change?

Given the different feel of each place, which places are 'yours' – the ones that feel most appropriate for you? Why? What's special about them for you? What are the different layers of feelings and impressions that go with the place? And in what ways do these threads of the place echo within you – and you with the place?

Every thread of the wyrd passes through us; every thread passes through every place. If we try to pretend that certain threads don't exist – which is essentially what our fear-driven civilisation tries to do – we're likely to find ourselves feeling empty, as though some aspect of ourselves is missing: and then go looking elsewhere for it. We might look for the good life in the country; or search for a sense of wildness and freedom in the mountains or the bushlands. Looking outside for something that's missing *inside*, we take the emptiness of the city with us: and then wonder why we can't find what we seek. "I can never 'get away from it all' on vacation", said that Thurber character, "because wherever I go, *I* am always there. . .".

More than that, we change the places we go to, spreading the illusions of the city wherever we go – until, eventually, they're painted over everywhere, everything. Rather than looking outside for solutions, it might be wiser to look *within* – and bring 'the good life', the wildness, the freedom, back into the cities of our lives.

So much of civilisation is concerned with the export of fear, the export of responsibility and blame – not just to other people, but to other places. When you go out to the country, in what ways do you take the city with you, in your actions, your attitudes? Do you expect the countryside to solve your problems for you?

In some weird way it *does* solve problems: a walk in the woods, past the quiet rippling of a stream, can be strangely refreshing and healing, helping us to reclaim our sense of self. But if the place is over-used – as so many sacred sites are – the place itself becomes destroyed: eventually, people 'love it to death'. Yet the same threads pass through you as through that place – so try going *inside*, in meditation, in visualisation, to a quiet stream in the world *within*. What do you find? And in what ways do you bring what you find there back into the shared reality of the everyday world?

There's a lot of talk about the need to heal the planet: but in many ways what we really need to heal is ourselves. The outside is a reflection of the inside; what's happening 'out there' is an echo of what we choose, if only by default, to do to ourselves. It's not always a pretty sight. . . but by understanding more how we're interwoven through the wyrd with each place, with the rest of reality, we create the space for a very real kind of healing. It's up to us: we *always* have a choice – though we always have to be careful of that twist!

A SENSE OF HEALING

We do have a right to be here, no less than the trees and stars; but also no *more* than the trees and stars. Rights only exist side-by-side with matching responsibilities: but responsibility is exactly what everyone seems to be avoiding, because no-one wants to take the blame for the mess we see around us. 'No-one is to blame' is too easily translated as 'no-one is responsible'. . . Yet responsibility is not the same as blame: it's 'response-ability' – an ability to *respond*, in the moment. Responsibility, understood in that way, is another form of reclaiming our self, our choices: another form of 'doing no-thing'.

As we've seen, 'doing no-thing' is not the same as doing nothing. Nothing is going to happen at all unless we do *something*. But we don't have to do it all: just something. And usually, something that *feels* right in the moment – the usual words on the wind, a message weaving by on the threads of wyrd.

Most of what's involved in healing the planet is quite astoundingly trivial: making a point of tidying up as we go, building and maintaining a new habit to 'walk lightly upon the earth', and so on. Like the wyrd, there's nothing particularly glamorous or special about it: but it *is* something we need to remember, something we need to be aware of. As usual, though, the wyrd will find some way to test us in our choices: so every now and then we might find ourselves faced with a real challenge – something we don't want to do at all. And that's when we need to look closer at our 'impending wyrd', and be honest about what we choose...

We don't have to do it all: sometimes other people find easy that which we find hard, and we can do things *they* find hard. I've always been terrified of authority figures: I'm amazed that others have no difficulty in talking with police, or can stand in a protest line against evident public disapproval – even when it's obvious that this does need to be done by *someone*. Others are content – feel fulfilled, satisfied, valued – with meticulous detail-work like filling envelopes, or sorting papers: work that would drive me mad in minutes. But I find it easy to write, to express ideas in words – something that other people, to my great surprise, often find extremely hard. Each to their own: we each have a part of this weird puzzle of life. What part is yours? What talents do *you* have? What keys to the wyrd do you alone hold?

Yet we each tend to meet up with everything in a greater or lesser way – including, or perhaps especially, that which represents our fears. In living what I claim I'm committed to, I do get challenged, especially by people who don't *want* choice or responsibility: "I'm only following orders, I'm only doing my job",

☞

> they'd say – angrily. The real challenge for me, right there, is to find a solution that disempowers neither of us, and preferably empowers all of us – including the rest of the world. And that's rarely easy. . . When you come – literally – face to face with what you most fear, how do *you* retain your sense of choice – and come up with a solution that works? What does that situation *feel* like? And by what feeling do you *know* that you've made the right choice?

There's another subtle trap here: it's easy to use 'taking responsibility for the planet' as a way of *avoiding* being honest and taking responsibility for ourselves. It's not some unknown, anonymous 'Them' wreaking havoc in the world, but *us*: we're part of it, if only by default. We heal the planet by healing *ourselves* – not by telling someone else what to do. We're interwoven with everything, everywhere, everyone through the weavings of the wyrd: by following the *feeling* of what seems right, in the moment, we 'dis-cover' what to do in each moment. Healing, literally, is 'wholing', making whole – and "there's a whole in my bucket, dear Liza, dear Liza. . ."

To make practical sense of this, we also need to break free of that trap of 'double-entry life-keeping'; we need to break free of thinking in terms of reward or punishment. But every now and then we do get strange comments from the wyrd. . .

> Once again, crossing the park, there's yet *another* empty bottle to pick up and put in the bin at the far end of the path. It's no trouble: why on earth don't these damned kids do it themselves? So, in the dull light of evening, I pick up the brown-paper bag. The bottle's not even empty – what a waste! Wait a minute, though: it's *full*. Not even opened. A first-class bottle of wine. It seems to be the wyrd's idea of a joke. . . or a comment on my habit of tidying up.
>
> But not a reward. I still pick up loose bits of rubbish – it's not *for* anything, it's not in expectation of another miraculous gift of a bottle, but simply that it seems to be the least I can do. It's

not something that I *have* to do, or that someone tells me to do: it's just that it seems to be my 'response-ability'. What's yours? What do you find yourself doing, in this respect? And what strange comments do you receive, weaving their way through the wyrd?

The saddest problems, and the strangest dilemmas, come from the core of the ownership-economy. Within it, making a mess – especially on a large scale – seems to be the mark of high prestige and power; tidying it up is always 'somebody else's problem'. . . But however low-prestige, someone is usually paid to pick up some of the litter, especially in a public park: so if I pick up a bottle or a bag, am I threatening their job – their livelihood – by doing so? Such is the absurdity we've woven ourselves into. . .

There's no simple answer. . . we have to learn to trust, and to *know*, when what we're doing is right. And that trust itself is perhaps the most important part of healing: weaving *ourselves* into the whole of the wyrd.

A SENSE OF TRUST

The process of allowing things to happen is not one of passivity. Instead, it's 'active non-action': we learn to trust that through our connection with wyrd we'll *know* what to do, and when to do it – and don't waste energy in doing unnecessary work that only has to be done again. In trusting ourselves, in trusting our connection with the wyrd, we allow the threads to tell us what to do: 'if no-thing is done, nothing is left undone'.

The hard part is trust itself. To let go into trust, without any 'control' at all, brings up every fear, and often a sense of panic. "Don't I have *any* guarantees?" I find myself saying. . .

I've been visiting an old friend, talking *at* her again, bewailing the iniquities of my fate, the way everything seems to go wrong, that no-one's being fair and trusting me, and so on. And finally she cuts in:

☞

"Chris! Slow down! Shut up, you idiot! Can't you see how you talk yourself down? You're being asked to *trust*: yourself especially. You can't expect to trust others, or be trusted by others, if you don't trust yourself. You *are* learning to listen; you *are* learning to trust. But right now you're in the middle of it: I know it's not easy for you to let go, but learning to trust involves *trusting*. . ."

"Don't I have *any* guarantees?

"No", she says. "That's the whole point about trust. There *aren't* any guarantees: just trust."

"But what happens when it breaks down?"

"It breaks down. Then you start again. And again. . ."

"That doesn't sound very gentle. . .", I say, doubtfully.

"It's a lot more gentle than throwing yourself at walls. . . The more you trust – *listen*, to *know* when to trust – the less it breaks down. It's not 'guaranteed safety', Chris, but then nothing in life ever is. . ."

Practise the 'un-safety' of trusting in a safe environment, she says; listen to *know* when it's safe to let go. So make that part of your overall aim: to allow yourself safe environments – or *safer*, at least – in which to practise trust. Then take this sense of trust in your *own* knowing out into the wider world. What changes when you trust?

Letting go into trust also involves letting go of the usual view of our interactions with Reality Department: not so much in terms of reward or punishment, but more as a series of lessons from the wyrd. And each lesson exists only *at* the choice-point: not before and, usually, not after – at least, not in the same way. As we learn the lessons – what they tell us about ourselves and our choices – they lessen: life *does* get easier as we learn to trust.

Nothing is a mistake: it's a lesson. And with that change of view, we move *forward*; we let the past go. With sadness, perhaps, but not regret. Life *is*: that's all.

"But I don't want to repeat those mistakes!", I say, almost in panic.

☞

"A mistake is simply a 'mis-take', Chris", she says, gently; "something you need to re-do in a different way in order to get right. A little reflection may help to minimise mistakes, but you still need to learn the *lesson* in each. You don't get a chance to do so until the choice-point – no matter how much planning you do, it's only *at* the choice-point that the choice becomes clear. And if you're trying to plan for everything, you won't *see* the choice-point – you'll be seeing your expectations. Just allow the lesson to return; allow yourself to *see* the lesson. And resolve it *then*, in the moment – you *cannot* do it now, because you don't happen to be there. You're here, now: *be* here, now. Not in the past, or in the future. The issue will return on the threads, in the usual way: simply let it do so. Then it *isn't* a mistake: it's a lesson. Do you see the difference?"

Slowly, I do. Do you? In what ways can you re-view mistakes as *lessons*? Breaking free of the notion of blame, what do you learn about yourself and your choices?

In what ways can you re-view 'mis-takes' of others – such as vandalism, or environmental 'disasters' – as *lessons*? What do *you* learn from them – about yourself, and about the aspects of *yourself* as echoed by those 'others'?

"A little reflection may help to minimise those mistakes, but you still need to learn the lesson in each. . ." When the choice-point comes round again – which it always will – in what ways does your response to it change? How do you allow yourself – trust yourself – to *know* what to do?

Since life *is*, any action – or inaction – just *is*: it leads to a different choice, a different lesson, weaving its way along the threads of the wyrd. Our aim provides us with an overall sense of direction; our choices tell us which thread to follow in each moment. If we get it 'wrong', well, the wyrd will find a way to tell us. . . and we have to be able to trust *ourselves*, as well as the wyrd, to know what to do in each moment about that.

It's important to keep the focus narrow, on the individual choice-point *here*, *now*; but also to keep our awareness wide at the same time, to maintain that sense of aim, or purpose – and of

a greater sense of self. It *is* always our choice to see what we see. . .
it *is* always our choice to do what we do.

> Leaving my friend's house, I look around in the streets of this quiet inner suburb. The greyness, the bleakness of the city is always there: but so too is the green, the bright colours of flowers and fruit and foliage, if only I'd care to see them. Trees and tilework; the chatter of birds mixed in with the rumble of aircraft overhead. It's a strange world we've chosen, between us; but it *is* still a beautiful one. . .
>
> Denying the existence of the greyness is a mistake, because it denies us any tools to deal with it; but to see *only* the greyness, the bleakness, is a mistake too. How do *you* reach a balance in what you choose to see – and how to deal with it?

'Being green' isn't always *easy*; but it's not particularly hard, either. Like everything else, it all depends on our point of view – and 'doing no-thing' about what we see. What do we *choose* for ourselves, and for what we share with others? – that's the real question. There's always a choice, but there's always a twist in the weavings of the wyrd. . .

25

A WYRD WAY OF LIFE

Slowly, subtly, the changes happen, like the changes in the seasons of the year. I still have no idea why I'm here: but now it doesn't seem to matter quite so much. I'm still on my own: but that's how it is, in this moment, at this time, and I find I *enjoy* it as such. "There's a whole in my bucket, dear Liza, dear Liza. . ."

Down by the river, I exchange smiles with a couple walking hand-in-hand down the path, as a cyclist whistles past. Sharing the quiet joys of a bright spring day: a real sense of power, of enjoyment – a very different kind of power, one that exists *because* it's shared, one that opens up a new sense of self, a new sense of choice. And although those plastic bags can still be seen entangled in the trees, new leaves have appeared, as if by magic, concealing most of them; and there's a blanket of springtime flowers on the river-bank, to remind me that nature *does* heal itself, without needing our active intervention to make it do so. Life *is*; and for now, right now, that seems to be enough.

Slowly, subtly, changes do happen. Somehow, in some weird way, life *does* get easier, gentler – yet I've done 'no-thing' to make it so. Slowly – though never steadily! – I notice that I *do* get what I need in life. Not necessarily always what I want, of course: yet over time, it becomes as interesting when I *don't* get what I want, as when I do.

I still have choices: in fact I sense that what happens to me is far more my choice that it's ever seemed before. It's not in my control: but then it never was. But I choose a direction: and something happens. There's always a choice, there's always a twist: so each happening is no longer either a success or a failure, but something that tells me more about who I am, more about my *choice* of who I am – and about my strange yet strengthening connection with the web of wyrd. Weird. . .

We each choose our own wyrd: and regarding our lives as 'the way of wyrd' allows us to be more deeply connected to it, yet paradoxically far less vulnerable to its ebbs and flows. The changes we discover from making that change – working *with* life's weirdnesses – are very real: and yet most of them come from 'no-thing' more than a change in our point of view. And we discover, too, that as we change, the world changes with us: our own better experience leads to a better world for all. Given the choice – and since we *do* always have the choice – is that not what we'd prefer to choose?

FURTHER READING

You may find some of the following books helpful for further exploration of the ideas in this book. Some may be out of print, but will be available through libraries or second-hand book dealers.

WYRD

Bryan Bates, *The Way of Wyrd*, Beaver Books, 1986.
Brian Branston, *The Lost Gods of England*, Thames & Hudson, 1957.
Brian Branston, *Gods of the North*, Thames & Hudson, 1955/1980.

SELF-EXPLORATION

Richard Nelson Bolles, *What Color Is Your Parachute?*, Ten Speed Press (annual).
John Bradshaw, *Healing the Shame That Binds You*, Bantam Books, 1991.
Betty Edwards, *Drawing on the Right Side of the Brain*, Fontana/Collins, 1979.
Shakti Gawain, *Living in the Light*, Whatever (CA) 1986/Eden Grove 1988.
Robert Johnson, *Inner Work*, Harper & Row, 1986.
Jessica Macbeth, *Moon Over Water*, Gateway Books (Bath), 1990.

PHILOSOPHICAL PERSPECTIVES

James Burke, *The Day The Universe Changed*, British Broadcasting Corporation, 1985.
Bruce Chatwin, *The Songlines*, Jonathan Cape, 1987.
James Gleick, *Chaos: making a new science*, Penguin, 1987.
F. David Peat, *Synchronicity: the bridge between matter and mind*, Bantam, 1987.
Robert Pirsig, *Zen and the Art of Motorcycle Maintenance*, Bodley Head, 1974.
Alan Watts, *The Book on the Taboo Against Knowing Who You Are*, Jonathan Cape, 1969.

FICTION

Marion Campbell, *The Dark Twin*, Turnstone Books, 1973.

Alan Garner, *The Owl Service*, Collins, 1967.

Ursula le Guin, *The Earthsea Trilogy* (A Wizard of Earthsea, The Tombs of Atuan, and The Farthest Shore), Penguin Books, 1979.

Ursula le Guin, *The Dispossessed*, Harper & Row, 1974.

Keith Roberts, *Pavane*, Gollancz, 1966.